MILITARY HISTORY FROM PRIMARY SOURCES

THE ANGLO-SAXON CHRONICLE

Illustrated and Annotated

Edited and introduced by
Bob Carruthers

Pen & Sword
MILITARY

First published in Great Britain in digital format in 2011 by Coda Books Ltd
First published in this format in 2013 and reprinted in 2014 by
Pen & Sword Military
An imprint of
Pen & Sword Books Ltd
47 Church Street
Barnsley
South Yorkshire, S70 2AS

ISBN 978 1 78159 148 2

This edition originally published as 'The Anglo-Saxon Chronicle' and published by
Everyman Press, London 1912. With a translation by Rev James Ingram (London, 1823).
With additional readings from the translation of Dr J A Giles (London, 1847).

Printed and bound in England by
CPI Group (UK) Ltd, Croydon, CR0 4YY

Pen & Sword Books Ltd incorporates the Imprints of Aviation, Atlas,
Family History, Fiction, Maritime, Military, Discovery, Politics, History,
Archaeology, Select, Wharncliffe Local History, Wharncliffe True Crime,
Military Classics, Wharncliffe Transport, Leo Cooper, The Praetorian Press,
Remember When, Seaforth Publishing and Frontline Publishing.

For a complete list of Pen & Sword titles please contact
PEN & SWORD BOOKS LIMITED
47 Church Street, Barnsley, South Yorkshire, S70 2AS, England
E-mail: enquiries@pen-and-sword.co.uk
Website: www.pen-and-sword.co.uk

Contents

Introduction

By Bob Carruthers

The Anglo-Saxon Chronicle is one of the most important sets of historical documents concerning the history of the British Isles. Without these vital documents we would have virtually no knowledge of some of the key events in the history of these islands during the dark ages.

Without the Chronicle and Bede's Historia Ecclesiastica Gentis Anglorum (the Ecclesiastical History of the English People), it would be impossible to write the history of the English from the Romans to the Norman Conquest. It is clear that records and annals of some kind began to be kept in England at the time of the earliest spread of Christianity, but no such records survive in their original form. Instead they were incorporated in later works, and it is thought likely that the Chronicle contains many of these. The history it tells is not only that witnessed by its compilers, but also that recorded by earlier annalists, whose work is in many cases preserved nowhere else.

Its importance is not limited to the historical information it provides, however. It is just as important a source for the early development of the English language. The Peterborough Chronicle changes from the standard Old English (Anglo-Saxon) literary language to early Middle English after 1131, providing some of the earliest Middle English text known.

The Chronicle is not without literary interest either. Inserted at various points since the 10th century are Old English poems in celebration of royal figures and their achievements: "The Battle of Brunanburh" (937), on King Æthelstan's victory over the combined forces of Vikings, Scots and the Strathclyde Britons, and five shorter poems, "Capture of the Five Boroughs" (942), "The Coronation of King Edgar" (973), "The Death of King

A Medieval depiction of the Venerable Bede from the Nuremberg Chronicle, 1493.

Edgar" (975), "The Death of Prince Alfred" (1036), and "The Death of King Edward the Confessor" (1065).

The term chronicle is slightly misleading as there is no single master text. At present there are nine known versions or fragments of the original "Anglo-Saxon Chronicle" in existence. All of the extant versions vary (sometimes greatly) in content and quality and crucially all of the surviving manuscripts are copies, so it is not known for certain where or when the first version of the Chronicle was composed. However, it is now generally agreed that the original version was written in the late 9th century by a scribe in Wessex. After the original Chronicle was compiled, copies were made and distributed to various monasteries. Additional copies were made for further distribution or to replace lost manuscripts, and some copies were updated independently of each other. Some of these later copies are those that have survived.

The translation that has been used for this electronic version is not a translation of any one Chronicle; rather, it is a conflation of readings from many different versions containing primarily the translation of Rev. James Ingram from 1828. The footnotes are those of Rev. Ingram and are supplied for the sake of completeness. There are additions to this translation by Dr J.A. Giles in 1847 which were originally in the form of an appendix to the Everyman edition. These have been marked by square brackets [ ]. Modern readers should approach those notes with extreme care. In many cases the views expressed by Rev. Ingram are long out of date, having been superseded by almost 175 years of active scholarship. At best, these notes will provide a starting point for inquiry. They should not, however, be treated as authoritative.

The earliest extant manuscript is the Winchester Chronicle which was written by a single scribe up to the year 891. We know this to be the case because the scribe wrote the year number, DCCCXCII, in the margin of the next line and subsequent material was written by other scribes. This strongly suggests that the composition of the Chronicle took place no later than 892; further evidence is provided by Bishop Asser's use of a version of the Chronicle in his work Life of King Alfred, which is known to have been composed in 893. It is also known that the Winchester manuscript is at least two removes from the original Chronicle; as a result, there is no proof that the Chronicle was compiled at Winchester.

It is also difficult to fix the date of composition for the original manuscript, but it is generally thought that the Chronicle was composed during the reign of Alfred the Great (871–99), as Alfred deliberately tried to revive learning and culture during his reign, and encouraged the use of English as a written language. The Chronicle, as well as the distribution of copies to other centres of learning, may be a consequence of the changes Alfred introduced.

The Chronicle incorporates material from multiple sources. The entry for 755, describing how Cynewulf took the kingship of Wessex from Sigebehrt, is far longer than the surrounding entries, and includes direct speech quotations from the participants in those events. It seems likely that this was taken by the scribe from existing saga material. Early entries, up to the year 110, probably came from one of the small encyclopaedic volumes of world history in circulation at the time the Chronicle was first written. The chronological summary to Bede's Ecclesiastical History was used as a source. The Chronicle gives dates and genealogies for Northumbrian and Mercian kings, and provides a list of Wessex bishops; these are likely to have had separate sources. The entry for 661 records a battle fought by Cenwalh that is said to have been fought "at Easter"; this precision implies a contemporary record, which survived and was re-used by the Chronicle scribe.

Contemporary annals began to be kept in Wessex during the 7th century. The material compiled in Alfred's reign included annals relating to Kentish, South Saxon, Mercian and, particularly, West Saxon history, but, with the exception of the Cynewulf entry, does not gather momentum until it comes to the Danish invasions of the late 8th century onwards.

It is thought that the Chronicle grew out of the tradition of compiling the Easter Tables, drawn up to help the clergy determine the dates of feasts in future years: a page consisted of a sequence of horizontal lines followed by astronomical data, with a space for short notes of events to distinguish one year from another. As the Chronicle developed, it lost its list-like appearance, and such notes took up more space, becoming more like historical records. Many later entries, especially those written by contemporaries, contained a great deal of historical narrative under the year headings.

As with any historical source, the Chronicle has to be treated with some caution. For example, between 514 and 544 the Chronicle makes reference to Wihtgar, who is supposedly buried on the Isle of Wight at "Wihtgar's stronghold" (which is "Wihtgaræsbyrg" in the original) and he purportedly gave his name to the island. However, the name of the "Isle of Wight" derives from the Latin "Vectis", not from Wihtgar. The actual name of the fortress was probably "Wihtwarabyrg", "the stronghold of the inhabitants of Wight", and either the chronicler or an earlier source misinterpreted this as referring to Wihtgar.

Of the nine surviving manuscripts, seven are written entirely in Old English (also known as Anglo-Saxon). One, known as the Bilingual Canterbury Epitome, is in Old English with a translation of each annal into Latin. Another, the Peterborough Chronicle, is in Old English except for the last entry, which is in early Middle English. The oldest (Corp. Chris. MS 173) is known as the Winchester Chronicle or the Parker Chronicle (after Matthew Parker, an Archbishop of Canterbury who once owned it). Six of the manuscripts were printed in an 1861 edition for the Rolls Series by Benjamin Thorpe with the text laid out in columns labelled A to F. Following this convention, the three additional manuscripts are often called G, H and I. The surviving manuscripts are listed opposite.

The manuscripts are all thought to derive from a common original, but the connections between the texts are more complex than simple inheritance via copying. The following is a summary of the relationships that are known.

A² was a copy of A, made in Winchester, probably between

Version	Chronicle name	Location	Manuscript
A	Winchester (or Parker) Chronicle	Parker Library, Corpus Christi College	173
B	Abingdon Chronicle I	British Library	Cotton Tiberius A. vi
C	Abingdon Chronicle II	British Library	Cotton Tiberius B. i
D	Worcester Chronicle	British Library	Cotton Tiberius B. iv
E	Peterborough (or Laud) Chronicle	Bodleian Library	Laud misc. 636
F	Bilingual Canterbury Epitome	British Library	Cotton Domitian viii
G or A² or W	A copy of the Winchester Chronicle	British Library	Cotton Otho B. xi + Otho B. x
H	Cottonian Fragment	British Library	Cotton Domitian ix
I	An Easter Table Chronicle	British Library	Cotton Caligula A. xv

1001 and 1013.

B was used in the compilation of C at Abingdon, in the mid-11th century. However, the scribe for C also had access to another version, which has not survived.

D includes material from Bede's Ecclesiastical History and from a set of 8th-century Northumbrian annals and is thought to have been copied from a northern version that has not survived.

E has material that appears to derive from the same sources as D but does not include some additions that appear only in D, such as the Mercian Register. This manuscript was composed at the monastery in Peterborough, some time after a fire there in 1116 that probably destroyed their copy of the Chronicle; E appears to have been created thereafter as a copy of a Kentish version, probably from Canterbury.

F appears to include material from the same Canterbury version that was used to create E.

Asser's Life of King Alfred, which was written in 893, includes a translation of the Chronicle's entries from 849 to 887. Only A, of surviving manuscripts, could have been in existence by 893, but there are places where Asser departs from the text in A, so it is possible that Asser used a version that has not survived.

Æthelweard wrote a translation of the Chronicle into Latin in the late 10th century; the version he used probably came from the same branch in the tree of relationships that A comes from.

Asser's text agrees with A and with Æthelweard's text in some places against the combined testimony of B, C, D and E, implying that there is a common ancestor for the latter four manuscripts.

At Abingdon, some time between 1120 and 1140, an unknown author wrote a Latin chronicle known as the Annals of St Neots. This work includes material from a copy of the Chronicle, but it is very difficult to tell which version because the annalist was selective about his use of the material. It may have been a northern revision of the text, or a Latin derivative of that recension.

The dating of the events recorded also requires extreme care. In addition to dates that are simply inaccurate, scribes occasionally made mistakes that caused further errors. For example, in the D manuscript, the scribe omits the year 1044 from the list on the left hand side. The annals copied down are therefore incorrect from 1045 to 1052, which has two entries. A more difficult problem is the question of the date at which a new year began, since the modern custom of starting the year on 1 January was not universal at that time. The entry for 1091 in E begins at Christmas and continues throughout the year; it is clear that this entry follows the old custom of starting the year at Christmas. Some other entries appear to begin the year on 25 March, such as the year 1044 in the C manuscript, which ends with Edward the Confessor's marriage on 23 January, while the entry for 22 April is recorded under 1045. There are also years which appear to start in September.

The manuscripts were produced in different places, and each manuscript reflects the biases of its scribes. It has been argued that the Chronicle should be regarded as propaganda, produced by Alfred's court and written with the intent of glorifying Alfred and creating loyalty. This is not universally accepted, but the origins of the manuscripts clearly colour both the description of interactions between Wessex and other kingdoms, and the descriptions of the Vikings' depredations. An example can be seen in the entry for 829, which describes Egbert's invasion of Northumbria. According to the Chronicle, after Egbert conquered Mercia and Essex, he became a "bretwalda", implying overlordship of all of England. Then when he marched into Northumbria, the Northumbrians offered him "submission and peace". The Northumbrian chronicles incorporated into Roger of Wendover's 13th-century history give a different picture: "When Egbert had obtained all the southern kingdoms, he led a large army into Northumbria, and laid waste that province with severe pillaging, and made King Eanred pay tribute."

Occasionally the scribes' biases can be seen by comparing different versions of the manuscript they created. For example, Ælfgar, earl of East Anglia, and son of Leofric, the earl of Mercia, was exiled briefly in 1055. The C, D and E manuscripts say the following:

C: "Earl Ælfgar, son of Earl Leofric, was outlawed without any fault..."

D: "Earl Ælfgar, son of Earl Leofric, was outlawed well-nigh without fault..."

E: "Earl Ælfgar was outlawed because it was thrown at him that he was traitor to the king and all the people of the land. And he admitted this before all the men who were gathered there, although the words shot out against his will."

Another example that mentions Ælfgar shows a different kind of unreliability in the Chronicle: that of omission. Ælfgar was Earl of Mercia by 1058, and in that year was exiled again. This time only D has anything to say: "Here Earl Ælfgar was expelled, but he soon came back again, with violence, through the help of Gruffydd. And here came a raiding ship-army from Norway; it is tedious to tell how it all happened." In this case other sources exist to clarify the picture: a major Norwegian attempt was made on England, but E says nothing at all, and D scarcely mentions it. It has sometimes been argued that when the Chronicle is silent, other sources that report major events must be mistaken, but this example demonstrates that the Chronicle does omit important events.

All the manuscripts described above share a chronological error between the years 756 and 845, but it is apparent that the composer of the Annals of St Neots was using a copy that did not have this error and which must have preceded them. Æthelweard's copy did have the chronological error but it had not lost a whole sentence from annal 885; all the surviving manuscripts have lost this sentence. Hence the error and the missing sentence must have been introduced in separate copying steps, implying that none of the surviving manuscripts are closer than two removes from the original version.

A: The Winchester Chronicle

The Winchester (or Parker) Chronicle is the oldest manuscript of the Chronicle that survives. It was begun at Old Minster, Winchester, towards the end of Alfred's reign. The manuscript begins with a genealogy of Alfred, and the first chronicle entry is for the year 60 BC. The section containing the Chronicle takes up folios 1-32. Unlike the other manuscripts, A is of early enough composition to show entries dating back to the late 9th century in the hands of different scribes as the entries were made. The first scribe's hand is dateable to the late 9th or very early 10th century; his entries cease in late 891, and the following entries were made at intervals throughout the 10th century by several scribes. The eighth scribe wrote the annals for the years 925–955, and was clearly at Winchester when he wrote them since he adds some material related to events there; he also uses ceaster, or "city", to mean Winchester. The manuscript becomes independent of the other recensions after the entry for 975. The book, which also had a copy of the Laws of Alfred and Ine bound in after the entry for 924, was transferred to Canterbury some time in the early 11th century, as evidenced by a list of

This is a page from the Parker chronicle, covering the years 455-490.

books that Archbishop Parker gave to Corpus Christi. While at Canterbury, some interpolations were made; this required some erasures in the manuscript. The additional entries appear to have been taken from a version of the manuscript from which E descends. The last entry in the vernacular is for 1070. After this comes the Latin Acta Lanfranci, which covers church events from 1070–1093. This is followed by a list of popes and the

H.   DCCCLXXI. Her com se here to Readingum on Westseaxe. 7 þæs ymbe .III. niht ridon
twegen eorlas up. þa gemette Æþelwulf ealdorman hie on Englafelda. 7 him þær wiþ gefeaht.
7 sige nam. 7 heora þeah oþer þær ofslægen
þæs nama wæs Sidroc. Ða ymb .IIII. niht æþered
cyning. 7 ælfred his broþer þær mycle fyrd
to Readingum gelæddon. 7 wiþ þone here gefuhton. 7 þær wæs mycel wæl geslægen on gehwæþe
hand. 7 eadelwulf ealdorman wearþ ofslægen.
7 þa deniscan ahton wælstowe gewald. 7 þæs
ymb .IIII. nyht gefeaht æþered cyning 7 ælfred
his broþor wiþ ealne þone here on æscesdune.
7 hi wærun on twam gefylcum on oþrum wæs
bagsecg. 7 healfdene þa hæþenan cyningas. 7 on
oþrum wærun þa eorlas. 7 þa feaht se cyning
æþered wiþ þara cyninga gewuman. 7 þær
wearþ se cyning bagsecg ofslægen. 7 ælfred
his broþor wiþ þara eorla gewuman. 7 þær

A page from the C text of the Anglo-Saxon Chronicle. This entry is for 871,
a year of battles between Wessex and the Vikings.

Archbishops of Canterbury to whom they sent the pallium. The manuscript was acquired by Matthew Parker, Archbishop of Canterbury (1559–1575) and master of Corpus Christi College, Cambridge, following the dissolution of the monasteries, and bequeathed to the college on his death. It now forms part of the Parker Library.

This manuscript is included in full in this ebook.

B: The Abingdon Chronicle I

B was written by a single scribe in the second half of the 10th century. The Chronicle takes up folios 1-34 . It begins with an entry for 60 BC and ends with the entry for 977. A manuscript that is now separate (British Library MS. Cotton Tiberius Aiii, f. 178) was originally the introduction to this chronicle; it contains a genealogy, as does A, but extends it to the late 10th century. B was at Abingdon in the mid-11th century, because it was used in the composition of C. Shortly after this it went to Canterbury, where interpolations and corrections were made. As with A, it ends with a list of popes and the archbishops of Canterbury to whom they sent the pallium..

C: The Abingdon Chronicle II

C includes additional material from local annals at Abingdon, where it was composed. The section containing the Chronicle (folios 115-64) is preceded by King Alfred's Old English translation of Orosius's world history, followed by a menologium and some gnomic verses of the laws of the natural world and of humanity. Then follows a copy of the chronicle, beginning with 60 BC; the first scribe copied up to the entry for 490, and a second scribe took over up to the entry for 1048. B and C are identical between 491 and 652, but differences thereafter make it clear that the second scribe was also using another copy of the Chronicle. This scribe also inserted, after the annal for 915, the Mercian Register, which covers the years 902–924, and which focuses on Aethelflaed. The manuscript

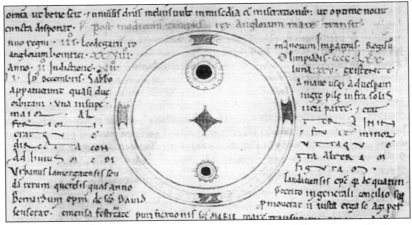

A drawing of a sunspot in the Chronicle of John of Worcester, who is believed to have used an original copy the Anglo-Saxon Chronicle as a source. He died circa 1140.

continues to 1066 and stops in the middle of the description of the Battle of Stamford Bridge. In the 12th century a few lines were added to complete the account.

D: The Worcester Chronicle

D appears to have been written in the middle of the 11th century. After 1033 it includes some records from Worcester, so it is generally thought to have been composed there. Five different scribes can be identified for the entries up to 1054, after which it appears to have been worked on at intervals. The text includes material from Bede's Ecclesiastical History and from a set of 8th-century Northumbrian annals. It is thought that some of the entries may have been composed by Archbishop Wulfstan. D contains more information than other manuscripts on northern and Scottish affairs, and it has been speculated that it was a copy intended for the Anglicised Scottish court. From 972 to 1016, the sees of York and Worcester were both held by the same person - Oswald from 972, Ealdwulf from 992, and Wulfstan from 1003, and this may explain why a northern recension was to be found at Worcester. By the 16th century, parts of the manuscript were lost; eighteen pages were inserted containing substitute entries from other sources, including A, B, C, and E. These pages were written by John Joscelyn, who was secretary to Matthew Parker.

E: The Peterborough Chronicle

In 1116, a fire at the monastery at Peterborough destroyed most of the buildings. The copy of the Chronicle kept there may have been lost at that time or later, but in either case shortly thereafter a fresh copy was made, apparently copied from a Kentish version—most likely to have been from Canterbury. The manuscript was written at one time and by a single scribe, down to the annal for 1121. The scribe added material relating to Peterborough Abbey which is not in other versions. The Canterbury original which he copied was similar, but not identical, to D: the Mercian Register does not appear, and a poem about the Battle of Brunanburh in 937, which appears in most of the other surviving copies of the Chronicle, is not recorded. The same scribe then continued the annals through to 1131; these entries were made at intervals, and thus are presumably contemporary records. Finally, a second scribe, in 1154, wrote an account of the years 1132–1154; but his dating is known to be unreliable. This last entry is in Middle English, rather than Old English. E was once owned by William Laud, Archbishop of Canterbury 1633–1654, so is also known as the Laud Chronicle. The manuscript contains occasional glosses in Latin, and is referred to (as "the Saxon storye of Peterborowe church") in an antiquarian book from 1566. According to Joscelyn, Nowell had a transcript of the manuscript. Previous owners include William Camden18 and William Lisle; the latter probably passed the manuscript on to Laud.

F: The Canterbury Bilingual Epitome

At about 1100, a copy of the Chronicle was written at Christ Church, Canterbury, probably by one of the scribes who made notes in A. This version is written in both Old English and Latin;

each entry in Old English was followed by the Latin version. The version the scribe copied (on folios 30-70) is similar to the version used by the scribe in Peterborough who wrote E, though it seems to have been abridged. It includes the same introductory material as D and, along with E, is one of the two chronicles that does not include the "Battle of Brunanburh" poem. The manuscript has many annotations and interlineations, some made by the original scribe and some by later scribes, including Robert Talbot.

A²/G: Copy of the Winchester Chronicle

A² was copied from A at Winchester in the eleventh century and follows a 10th-century copy of an Old English translation of Bede's Ecclesiastical History. The last annal copied was 1001, so the copy was made no earlier than that; an episcopal list appended to A² suggests that the copy was made by 1013. This manuscript was almost completely destroyed in the 1731 fire at Ashburnham House, where the Cotton Library was housed. Of the original 34 leaves, seven remain, ff. 39-47 in the manuscript. However, a transcript had been made by Laurence Nowell, a 16th century antiquary, which was used by Abraham Wheloc in an edition of the Chronicle printed in 1643. Because of this, it is also sometimes known as W, after Wheloc. The appellations A, A², and G derive from Plummer, Smith, and Thorpe, respectively.

H: Cottonian Fragment

H consists of a single leaf, containing annals for 1113 and 1114. In the entry for 1113 it includes the phrase "he came to Winchester"; hence it is thought likely that the manuscript was written at Winchester. There is not enough of this manuscript for reliable relationships to other manuscripts to be established. Ker notes that the entries may have been written contemporarily.

I: Easter Table Chronicle

A list of Chronicle entries accompanies a table of years,

Brittene igland is ehta hund mila lang. ⁊ twa hund brad. ⁊ her synd on þis iglande fif geþeode. englisc. ⁊ brittisc. ⁊ wilsc. ⁊ scyttisc. ⁊ pyhtisc. ⁊ boc leden. Erest weron bugend þises landes brittes. þa coman of armenia. ⁊ gesætan suðewearde bryttene ærost. Þa gelamp hit þ pyhtas coman suþan of scithian. mid langum scipum na manegum. ⁊ þa coman ærost on norþ ybernian up. ⁊ þær bædon scottas þ hi ðer mostan wunian. ac hi noldan heom lyfan. forðan hi cwedon þa scottas. we eow magon þeah hwaðere ræd gelæron. we witan oþer egland her be eastan. þer ge magon eardian gif ge willað. ⁊ gif hwa eow wið stent. we eow fultumiað. þ ge hit magon gegangan. Ða ferdon þa pihtas. ⁊ ge ferdon þis land norþan weard. ⁊ suþanweard hit hef don brittas. swa we ær cwedon. And þa pyhtas heom abæ don wif æt scottum. on þa geræd þ hi ge curon heora kyne cin aa on þa wif healfa. þ hi heoldon swa lange syððan. ⁊ þa gelamp hit imbe geara runa. þ scotta sum dæl ge wat of ybernian on bryttene. ⁊ þes lan des sum dæl ge eodon. ⁊ wes heora heretoga reoda ge haten. from þa heo synd genemnode dæl reodi. Six tigum wintru ær þe crist were acenned. gai iuli? romana kasere mid hund ehtatigum scipum ge sohte bryttene. þer he wes ærost ge swenced mid grummum ge feohte. ⁊ micelne dæl his heres forlædde. ⁊ þa he

Liber Guil: Laud Archiepi Cant: & Cancellar. Vniuersit: Oxon. 1638.

The initial page of the Peterborough Chronicle. The manuscript is an autograph of the monastic scribes of Peterborough. The opening sections were likely scribed around 1150.

19

found on folios 133-37 in a badly burned manuscript containing miscellaneous notes on charms, the calculation of dates for church services, and annals pertaining to Christ Church, Canterbury. Most of the Chronicle's entries pertain to Christ Church, Canterbury. Until 1109 (the death of Anselm of Canterbury) they are in English, all but one of the following entries are in Latin. Part of I was written by a scribe soon after 1075 in the same hand and ink as the rest of the Caligula MS. After 1085, the annals are in various contemporary hands. The original annalist's entry for the Norman conquest is limited to "Her forðferde eadward kyng"; a later hand added the coming of William the Conqueror, " her com willelm." At one point this manuscript was at St Augustine's Abbey, Canterbury.

Lost manuscripts

Two manuscripts are recorded in an old catalogue of the library of Durham; they are described as cronica duo Anglica. In addition, Parker included a manuscript called Hist. Angliae Saxonica in his gifts but the manuscript that included this, now Cambridge University Library MS. Hh.1.10, has lost 52 of its leaves, including all of this copy of the chronicle.

The three main Anglo-Norman historians, John of Worcester, William of Malmesbury, and Henry of Huntingdon, each had a copy of the Chronicle, which they adapted for their own purposes. Simeon of Durham also had a copy of the Chronicle. Some later medieval historians also used the Chronicle, and others took their material from those who had used it, and so the Chronicle became "central to the mainstream of English historical tradition".

Henry of Huntingdon used a copy of the chronicle that was very similar to E. There is no evidence in his work of any of the entries in E after 1121, so although his manuscript may have been actually been E, it may also have been a copy—either one taken of E prior to the entries he makes no use of, or a manuscript from which E was copied, with the copying taking place prior to the date of the last annal he uses. Henry also made use of the C manuscript.

The Waverley annals made use of a manuscript that was similar to E, though it appears that it did not contain the entries focused on Peterborough. The manuscript of the chronicle translated by Geoffrey Gaimar's cannot be identified accurately, though according to historian Dorothy Whitelock it was "a rather better text than 'E' or 'F'. Gaimar implies that there was a copy at Winchester in his day (the middle of the 12th century); Whitelock suggests that there is evidence that a manuscript that has not survived to the present day was at Winchester in the mid-tenth century. If it survived to Gaimar's time that would explain why A was not kept up to date, and why A could be given to the monastery at Canterbury.

John of Worcester's Chronicon ex chronicis appears to have had a manuscript that was either A or similar to it; he makes use of annals that do not appear in other versions, such as entries concerning Edward the Elder's campaigns and information about Winchester towards the end of the chronicle. His account is often similar to that of D, though there is less attention paid to Margaret of Scotland, an identifying characteristic of D. He had the Mercian register, which appears only in C and D; and he includes material from annals 979–982 which only appears in C. It is possible he had a manuscript that was an ancestor of D. He also had sources which have not been identified, and some of his statements have no earlier surviving source.

A manuscript similar to E was available to William of Malmesbury, though it is unlikely to have been E as that manuscript is known to have still been in Peterborough after the time William was working, and he does not make use of any of the entries in E that are specifically related to Peterborough. It is likely he had either the original from which E was copied, or a copy of that original. He mentions that the chronicles do not give any information on the murder of Alfred Atheling, but since this is covered in both C and D it is apparent he had no access to those manuscripts. On occasion he appears to show some knowledge of D but it is possible that his information was taken from John of Worcester's account. He also omits any reference to a battle fought by Cenwealh in 652; this battle is mentioned in A, B, and C, but not in E. He does mention a battle fought by Cenwealh at Wirtgernesburg, which is not in any of the extant manuscripts, so it is possible he had a copy now lost.

History of editions and availability

An important early printed edition of the Chronicle appeared in 1692, by Edmund Gibson, an English jurist and divine who became Bishop of Lincoln in that year. Titled Chronicum Saxonicum, it printed Latin and Old English versions of the text in parallel columns and became the standard edition until the 19th century. It was superseded in 1861 by Benjamin Thorpe's Rolls edition, which printed six versions in columns, labelled A to F, thus giving the manuscripts the letters which are now used to refer to them.

John Earle wrote two of the Saxon Chronicles Parallel (1865). Charles Plummer edited this book, producing a Revised Text with notes, appendices, and glossary in two volumes in 1892 and 1899. This edition of the A and E texts, with material from other versions, was widely used; it was reprinted in 1952.

SELECTED BIBLIOGRAPHY:

Original Text

- Classen, E. and Harmer, F.E. (eds.): "An Anglo-Saxon Chronicle from British Museum, Cotton MS. Tiberius B iv." (Manchester, 1926)
- Flower, Robin and Smith, Hugh (eds.): "The Peterborough Chronicle and Laws" (Early English Text Society, Original Series 208, Oxford, 1941).
- Taylor, S. (ed.): "The Anglo-Saxon Chronicle: MS B" (Cambridge, 1983)

Other translations

- Garmonsway, G.N.: "The Anglo-Saxon Chronicle" (Everyman Press, London, 1953, 1972). HIGHLY RECOMMENDED. Contains side-by-side translations of all nine known texts.

Recommended reading

- Bede: "A History of the English Church and People" , translated by Leo Sherley-Price (Penguin Classics, London, 1955, 1968).
- Poole, A.L.: "Domesday Book to Magna Carta" (Oxford University Press, Oxford, 1951, 1953)
- Stenton, Sir Frank W.: "Anglo-Saxon England" (Oxford University Press, Oxford, 1943, 1947, 1971)

Introduction by the
Rev. James Ingram, 1823

ENGLAND may boast of two substantial monuments of its early history; to either of which it would not be easy to find a parallel in any nation, ancient or modern. These are, the Record of Doomsday[1] and the "Saxon Chronicle"[2]. The former, which is little more than a statistical survey, but contains the most authentic information relative to the descent of property and the comparative importance of the different parts of the kingdom at a very interesting period, the wisdom and liberality of the British Parliament long since deemed worthy of being printed[3] among the Public Records, by Commissioners appointed for that purpose. The other work, though not treated with absolute neglect, has not received that degree of attention which every person who feels an interest in the events and transactions of former times would naturally expect. In the first place, it has never been printed entire, from a collation of all the MSS. But of the extent of the two former editions, compared with the present, the reader may form some idea, when he is told that Professor Wheloc's "Chronologia Anglo-Saxonica", which was the first attempt[4] of the kind, published at Cambridge in 1644, is comprised in less than 62 folio pages, exclusive of the Latin appendix. The improved edition by Edmund Gibson, afterwards Bishop of London, printed at Oxford in 1692, exhibits nearly four times the quantity of the former; but is very far from

---

1 *Whatever was the origin of this title, by which it is now distinguished, in an appendix to the work itself it is called "Liber de Wintonia," or "The Winchester-Book," from its first place of custody.*

2 *This title is retained, in compliance with custom, though it is a collection of chronicles, rather than one uniform work, as the received appellation seems to imply.*

3 *In two volumes folio, with the following title: "Domesday-Book, seu Liber Censualis Willelmi Primi Regis Angliae, inter Archlyos Regni in Domo Capitulari Westmonasterii asservatus: jubente rege augustissimo Georgio Tertio praelo mandatus typis MDCCLXXXIII"*

4 *Gerard Langbaine had projected such a work, and had made considerable progress in the collation of MSS., when he found himself anticipated by Wheloc.*

being the entire[5] chronicle, as the editor considered it. The text of the present edition, it was found, could not be compressed within a shorter compass than 374 pages, though the editor has suppressed many notes and illustrations, which may be thought necessary to the general reader. Some variations in the MSS. may also still remain unnoticed; partly because they were considered of little importance, and partly from an apprehension, lest the commentary, as it sometimes happens, should seem an unwieldy burthen, rather than a necessary appendage, to the text. Indeed, till the editor had made some progress in the work, he could not have imagined that so many original and authentic materials of our history still remained unpublished.

To those who are unacquainted with this monument of our national antiquities, two questions appear requisite to be answered: — "What does it contain?" and, "By whom was it written?" The indulgence of the critical antiquary is solicited, whilst we endeavour to answer, in some degree, each of these questions.

To the first question we answer, that the "Saxon Chronicle" contains the original and authentic testimony of contemporary writers to the most important transactions of our forefathers, both by sea and land, from their first arrival in this country to the year 1154. Were we to descend to particulars, it would require a volume to discuss the great variety of subjects which it embraces. Suffice it to say, that every reader will here find many interesting facts relative to our architecture, our agriculture, our coinage, our commerce, our naval and military glory, our laws, our liberty, and our religion. In this edition, also, will be found numerous specimens of Saxon poetry, never before printed, which might form the ground-work of an introductory volume to Warton's elaborate annals of English Poetry. Philosophically

5 *"Nunc primum integrum edidit" is Gibson's expression in the title-page. He considers Wheloc's MSS. as fragments, rather than entire chronicles: "quod integrum nacti jam discimus." These MSS., however, were of the first authority, and not less entire, as far as they went, than his own favourite "Laud". But the candid critic will make allowance for the zeal of a young Bachelor of Queen's, who, it must be remembered, had scarcely attained the age of twenty-three when this extraordinary work was produced.*

considered, this ancient record is the second great phenomenon in the history of mankind. For, if we except the sacred annals of the Jews, contained in the several books of the Old Testament, there is no other work extant, ancient or modern, which exhibits at one view a regular and chronological panorama of a PEOPLE, described in rapid succession by different writers, through so many ages, in their own vernacular LANGUAGE. Hence it may safely be considered, nor only as the primaeval source from which all subsequent historians of English affairs have principally derived their materials, and consequently the criterion by which they are to be judged, but also as the faithful depository of our national idiom; affording, at the same time, to the scientific investigator of the human mind a very interesting and extraordinary example of the changes incident to a language, as well as to a nation, in its progress from rudeness to refinement.

But that the reader may more clearly see how much we are indebted to the "Saxon Chronicle", it will be necessary to examine what is contained in other sources of our history, prior to the accession of Henry II., the period wherein this invaluable record terminates.

The most ancient historian of our own island, whose work has been preserved, is Gildas, who flourished in the latter part of the sixth century. British antiquaries of the present day will doubtless forgive me, if I leave in their original obscurity the prophecies of Merlin, and the exploits of King Arthur, with all the Knights of the Round Table, as scarcely coming within the verge of history. Notwithstanding, also, the authority of Bale, and of the writers whom he follows, I cannot persuade myself to rank Joseph of Arimathea, Arviragus, and Bonduca, or even the Emperor Constantine himself, among the illustrious writers of Great Britain. I begin, therefore, with Gildas; because, though he did not compile a regular history of the island, he has left us, amidst a cumbrous mass of pompous rhapsody and querulous declamation some curious descriptions of the character and manners of the inhabitants; not only the Britons and Saxons, but the Picts and Scots[6]. There are also some parts of his work, almost literally transcribed by Bede, which confirm the brief statements of the "Saxon Chronicle"[7]. But there is, throughout, such a want of precision and simplicity, such a barrenness of facts amidst a multiplicity of words, such a scantiness of names of places and persons, of dates, and other circumstances, that we are obliged to have recourse to the Saxon Annals, or to Venerable Bede, to supply the absence of those two great lights of history—Chronology and Topography.

The next historian worth notice here is Nennius, who is supposed to have flourished in the seventh century: but the work ascribed to him is so full of interpolations and corruptions, introduced by his transcribers, and particularly by a simpleton who is called Samuel, or his master Beulanus, or both, who appear to have lived in the ninth century, that it is difficult to say how much of this motley production is original and authentic. Be that as it may, the writer of the copy printed by Gale bears ample testimony to the "Saxon Chronicle", and says expressly, that he compiled his history partly from the records of the Scots and Saxons[8]. At the end is a confused but very curious appendix, containing that very genealogy, with some brief notices of Saxon affairs, which the fastidiousness of Beulanus, or of his amanuensis, the aforesaid Samuel, would not allow him to transcribe. This writer, although he professes to be the first historiographer[9] of the Britons, has sometimes repeated

---

6 *The reader is forcibly reminded of the national dress of the Highlanders in the following singular passage: "furciferos magis vultus pilis, quam corporum pudenda, pudendisque proxima, vestibus tegentes."*

7 *See particularly capp. xxiii. and xxvi. The work which follows, called the "Epistle of Gildas", is little more than a cento of quotations from the Old and New Testament.*

8 *"De historiis Scotorum Saxonumque, licet inimicorum," etc. "Hist. Brit. ap." Gale, XV. Script. p. 93. See also p. 94 of the same work; where the writer notices the absence of all written memorials among the Britons, and attributes it to the frequent recurrence of war and pestilence. A new edition has been prepared from a Vatican MS. with a translation and notes by the Rev. W. Gunn, and published by J. and A. Arch.*

9 *"Malo me historiographum quam neminem," etc.*

the very words of Gildas[10]; whose name is even prefixed to some copies of the work. It is a puerile composition, without judgment, selection, or method[11]; filled with legendary tales of Trojan antiquity, of magical delusion, and of the miraculous exploits of St. Germain and St. Patrick: not to mention those of the valiant Arthur, who is said to have felled to the ground in one day, single-handed, eight hundred and forty Saxons! It is remarkable, that this taste for the marvelous, which does not seem to be adapted to the sober sense of Englishmen, was afterwards revived in all its glory by Geoffrey of Monmouth in the Norman age of credulity and romance.

We come now to a more cheering prospect; and behold a steady light reflected on the "Saxon Chronicle" by the "Ecclesiastical History" of Bede; a writer who, without the intervention of any legendary tale, truly deserves the title of Venerable[12]. With a store of classical learning not very common in that age, and with a simplicity of language seldom found in monastic Latinity, he has moulded into something like a regular form the scattered fragments of Roman, British, Scottish, and Saxon history. His work, indeed, is professedly ecclesiastical; but, when we consider the prominent station which the Church had at this time assumed in England, we need not be surprised if we find therein the same intermixture of civil, military, and ecclesiastical affairs, which forms so remarkable a feature in the "Saxon Chronicle". Hence Gibson concludes, that many passages of the latter description were derived from the work of Bede[13]. He thinks the same of the description of Britain, the notices of the Roman emperors, and the detail of the first arrival of the Saxons. But, it may be observed, those passages

---

10 He considered his work, perhaps, as a lamentation of declamation, rather than a history. But Bede dignifies him with the title of "historicus," though he writes "fiebili sermone."

11 But it is probable that the work is come down to us in a garbled and imperfect state.

12 There is an absurd story of a monk, who in vain attempting to write his epitaph, fell asleep, leaving it thus: "Hac sunt in fossa Bedae. ossa:" but, when he awoke, to his great surprise and satisfaction he found the long-sought epithet supplied by an angelic hand, the whole line standing thus: "Hac sunt in fossa Bedae venerabilis ossa."

13 See the preface to his edition of the "Saxon Chronicle".

to which he alludes are not to be found in the earlier MSS. The description of Britain, which forms the introduction, and refers us to a period antecedent to the invasion of Julius Caesar; appears only in three copies of the "Chronicle"; two of which are of so late a date as the Norman Conquest, and both derived from the same source. Whatever relates to the succession of the Roman emperors was so universally known, that it must be considered as common property: and so short was the interval between the departure of the Romans and the arrival of the Saxons, that the latter must have preserved amongst them sufficient memorials and traditions to connect their own history with that of their predecessors. Like all rude nations, they were particularly attentive to genealogies; and these, together with the succession of their kings, their battles, and their conquests, must be derived originally from the Saxons themselves, and not from Gildas, or Nennius, or Bede[14]. Gibson himself was so convinced of this, that he afterwards attributes to the "Saxon Chronicle" all the knowledge we have of those early times[15]. Moreover, we might ask, if our whole dependence had been centered in Bede, what would have become of us after his death?[16] Malmsbury indeed asserts, with some degree of vanity, that you will not easily find a Latin historian of English affairs between Bede and himself[17]; and in the fullness of self-complacency professes his determination, "to season with Roman salt the barbarisms of his native tongue!" He affects great contempt for Ethelwerd, whose work will be considered hereafter; and he well knew how unacceptable any praise of the "Saxon Annals" would be to the Normans, with whom he was connected[18]. He thinks it

---

14 *This will be proved more fully when we come to speak of the writers of the "Saxon Chronicle".*

15 *Preface, "ubi supra".*

16 *He died A.D. 734, accordingW to our chronicle; but some place his death to the following year.*

17 *This circumstance alone proves the value of the "Saxon Chronicle". In the "Edinburgh Chronicle" of St. Cross, printed by H. Wharton, there is a chasm from the death of Bede to the year 1065; a period of 330 years.*

18 *The cold and reluctant manner in which he mentions the "Saxon Annals", to which he was so much indebted, can only be ascribed to this cause in him, as well as in the other Latin historians. See his prologue to the first book, "De Gestis Regum," etc.*

necessary to give his reasons, on one occasion, for inserting from these very "Annals" what he did not find in Bede; though it is obvious, that the best part of his materials, almost to his own times, is derived from the same source.

The object of Bishop Asser, the biographer of Alfred, who comes next in order, was to deliver to posterity a complete memorial of that sovereign, and of the transactions of his reign. To him alone are we indebted for the detail of many interesting circumstances in the life and character of his royal patron[19]; but most of the public transactions will be found in the pages of the "Saxon Chronicle": some passages of which he appears to have translated so literally, that the modern version of Gibson does not more closely represent the original. In the editions of Parker, Camden, and Wise, the last notice of any public event refers to the year 887. The interpolated copy of Gale, called by some Pseudo-Asserius, and by others the Chronicle of St. Neot's, is extended to the year 914[20]. Much difference of opinion exists respecting this work; into the discussion of which it is not our present purpose to enter. One thing is remarkable: it contains the vision of Drihtelm, copied from Bede, and that of Charles King of the Franks, which Malmsbury thought it worth while to repeat in his "History of the Kings of England". What Gale observes concerning the "fidelity" with which these annals of Asser are copied by Marianus, is easily explained. They both translated from the "Saxon Chronicle", as did also Florence of Worcester, who interpolated Marianus; of whom we shall speak hereafter.

But the most faithful and extraordinary follower of the "Saxon Annals" is Ethelwerd; who seems to have disregarded almost all other sources of information. One great error,

19 *If there are additional anecdotes in the Chronicle of St. Neot's, which is supposed to have been so called by Leland because he found the MS. there, it must be remembered that this work is considered an interpolated Asser.*

20 *The death of Asser himself is recorded in the year 909; but this is no more a proof that the whole work is spurious, than the character and burial of Moses, described in the latter part of the book of "Deuteronomy", would go to prove that the Pentateuch was not written by him. See Bishop Watson's "Apology for the Bible".*

however, he committed; for which Malmsbury does nor spare him. Despairing of the reputation of classical learning, if he had followed the simplicity of the Saxon original, he fell into a sort of measured and inverted prose, peculiar to himself; which, being at first sufficiently obscure, is sometimes rendered almost unintelligible by the incorrect manner in which it has been printed. His authority, nevertheless, in an historical point of view, is very respectable. Being one of the few writers untainted by monastic prejudice[21], he does not travel out of his way to indulge in legendary tales and romantic visions. Critically considered, his work is the best commentary on the "Saxon Chronicle" to the year 977; at which period one of the MSS. which he seems to have followed, terminates. Brevity and compression seem to have been his aim, because the compilation was intended to be sent abroad for the instruction of a female relative of high rank in Germany[22], at her request. But there are, nevertheless, some circumstances recorded which are not to be found elsewhere; so that a reference to this epitome of Saxon history will be sometimes useful in illustrating the early part of the "Chronicle"; though Gibson, I know not on what account, has scarcely once quoted it.

During the sanguinary conflicts of the eleventh century, which ended first in the temporary triumph of the Danes, and afterwards in the total subjugation of the country by the Normans, literary pursuits, as might be expected, were so much neglected, that scarcely a Latin writer is to be found: but the "Saxon Chronicle" has preserved a regular and minute detail of occurrences, as they passed along, of which subsequent historians were glad to avail themselves. For nearly a century after the Conquest, the

---

21 *Malmsbury calls him "noble and magnificent," with reference to his rank; for he was descended from King Alfred: but he forgets his peculiar praise—that of being the only Latin historian for two centuries; though, like Xenophon, Caesar, and Alfred, he wielded the sword as much as the pen.*

22 *This was no less a personage than Matilda, the daughter of Otho the Great, Emperor of Germany, by his first Empress Eadgitha or Editha; who is mentioned in the "Saxon Chronicle", A.D. 925, though not by name, as given to Otho by her brother, King Athelstan. Ethelwerd adds, in his epistle to Matilda, that Athelstan sent two sisters, in order that the emperor might take his choice; and that he preferred the mother of Matilda.*

Saxon annalists appear to have been chiefly eye-witnesses of the transactions which they relate[23]. The policy of the Conqueror led him by degrees to employ Saxons as well as Normans: and William II. found them the most faithful of his subjects: but such an influx of foreigners naturally corrupted the ancient language; till at length, after many foreign and domestic wars, tranquillity being restored on the accession of Henry II, literature revived; a taste for composition increased; and the compilation of Latin histories of English and foreign affairs, blended and diversified with the fabled romance and legendary tale, became the ordinary path to distinction. It is remarkable, that when the "Saxon Chronicle" ends, Geoffrey of Monmouth begins. Almost every great monastery about this time had its historian: but some still adhered to the ancient method. Florence of Worcester, an interpolator of Marianus, as we before observed, closely follows Bede, Asser, and the "Saxon Chronicle"[24]. The same may be observed of the annals of Gisburne, of Margan, of Meiros, of Waverley, etc.; some of which are anonymous compilations, whilst others have the name of an author, or rather transcriber; for very few aspired to the character of authors or original historians. Thomas Wikes, a canon of Oseney, who compiled a Latin chronicle of English affairs from the Conquest to the year 1304, tells us expressly, that he did this, not because he could add much to the histories of Bede, William of Newburgh, and Matthew Paris, but "propter minores, quibus non suppetit copia librorum."[25] Before the invention of printing, it was necessary that numerous copies of historical works should be transcribed, for the instruction of those who had not access to libraries. The transcribers frequently added something of their own, and abridged or omitted what they thought less interesting. Hence

23 See particularly the character of William I. p. 294, written by one who was in his court. The compiler of the "Waverley Annals" we find literally translating it more than a century afterwards:— "nos dicemus, qui eum vidimus, et in curia ejus aliquando fuimus," etc.—Gale, ii. 134.

24 His work, which is very faithfully and diligently compiled, ends in the year 1117; but it is continued by another hand to the imprisonment of King Stephen.

25 "Chron. ap." Gale, ii. 21.

the endless variety of interpolators and deflorators of English history. William of Malmsbury, indeed, deserves to be selected from all his competitors for the superiority of his genius; but he is occasionally inaccurate, and negligent of dates and other minor circumstances; insomuch that his modern translator has corrected some mistakes, and supplied the deficiencies in his chronology, by a reference to the "Saxon Chronicle". Henry of Huntingdon, when he is not transcribing Bede, or translating the "Saxon Annals", may be placed on the same shelf with Geoffrey of Monmouth.

As I have now brought the reader to the period when our "Chronicle" terminates, I shall dismiss without much ceremony the succeeding writers, who have partly borrowed from this source; Simon of Durham, who transcribes Florence of Worcester, the two priors of Hexham, Gervase, Hoveden, Bromton, Stubbes, the two Matthews, of Paris and Westminster, and many others, considering that sufficient has been said to convince those who may not have leisure or opportunity to examine the matter themselves, that however numerous are the Latin historians of English affairs, almost everything original and authentic, and essentially conducive to a correct knowledge of our general history, to the period above mentioned, may be traced to the "Saxon Annals".

It is now time to examine, who were probably the writers of these "Annals". I say probably, because we have very little more than rational conjecture to guide us.

The period antecedent to the times of Bede, except where passages were afterwards inserted, was perhaps little else, originally, than a kind of chronological table of events, with a few genealogies, and notices of the death and succession of kings and other distinguished personages. But it is evident from the preface of Bede and from many passages in his work, that he received considerable assistance from Saxon bishops, abbots, and others; who not only communicated certain traditionary facts "viva voce", but also transmitted to him many written documents. These, therefore, must have been the early chronicles of Wessex, of Kent, and of the other provinces of the Heptarchy; which formed together the ground-work of his history. With greater honesty than most of his followers, he has given us the names of those learned persons who assisted him with this local information. The first is Alcuinus or Albinus, an abbot of Canterbury, at whose instigation he undertook the work; who sent by Nothelm, afterwards archbishop of that province, a full account of all ecclesiastical transactions in Kent, and in the contiguous districts, from the first conversion of the Saxons. From the same source he partly derived his information respecting the provinces of Essex, Wessex, East Anglia, and Northumbria. Bishop Daniel communicated to him by letter many particulars concerning Wessex, Sussex, and the Isle of Wight. He acknowledges assistance more than once "ex scriptis priorum"; and there is every reason to believe that some of these preceding records were the "Anglo-Saxon Annals"; for we have already seen that such records were in existence before the age of Nennius. In proof of this we may observe, that even the phraseology sometimes partakes more of the Saxon idiom than the Latin. If, therefore, it be admitted, as there is every reason to conclude from the foregoing remarks, that certain succinct and chronological arrangements of historical facts had taken place in several provinces of the Heptarchy before the time of Bede, let us inquire by whom they were likely to have been made.

In the province of Kent, the first person on record, who is celebrated for his learning, is Tobias, the ninth bishop of Rochester, who succeeded to that see in 693. He is noticed by Bede as not only furnished with an ample store of Greek and Latin literature, but skilled also in the Saxon language and erudition[26]. It is probable, therefore, that he left some proofs of this attention to his native language and as he died within

26 "Virum Latina, Graec, et Saxonica lingua atque eruditione multipliciter instructum."—Bede, "Ecclesiastical History", v. 8. "Chron. S. Crucis Edinb. ap.", Wharton, i. 157.

a few years of Bede, the latter would naturally avail himself of his labours. It is worthy also of remark, that Bertwald, who succeeded to the illustrious Theodore of Tarsus in 690, was the first English or Saxon archbishop of Canterbury. From this period, consequently, we may date that cultivation of the vernacular tongue which would lead to the composition of brief chronicles[27], and other vehicles of instruction, necessary for the improvement of a rude and illiterate people. The first chronicles were, perhaps, those of Kent or Wessex; which seem to have been regularly continued, at intervals, by the archbishops of Canterbury, or by their direction[28], at least as far as the year 1001, or by even 1070; for the Benet MS., which some call the Plegmund MS., ends in the latter year; the rest being in Latin. From internal evidence indeed, of an indirect nature, there is great reason to presume, that Archbishop Plegmund transcribed or superintended this very copy of the "Saxon Annals" to the year 891[29]; the year in which he came to the see; inserting, both before and after this date, to the time of his death in 923, such additional materials as he was well qualified to furnish from his high station and learning, and the confidential intercourse which he enjoyed in the court of King Alfred. The total omission of his own name, except by another hand, affords indirect evidence of some importance in support of this conjecture. Whether King Alfred himself was the author of a distinct and separate chronicle of Wessex, cannot now be determined. That he furnished additional supplies of historical matter to the older chronicles is, I conceive, sufficiently obvious to every reader who will take the trouble of examining the subject. The argument of Dr. Beeke, the present Dean of Bristol, in an obliging letter to the editor on this subject, is

27 *The materials, however, though not regularly arranged, must be traced to a much higher source.*

28 *Josselyn collated two Kentish MSS. of the first authority; one of which he calls the History or Chronicle of St. Augustine's, the other that of Christ Church, Canterbury. The former was perhaps the one marked in our series "C.T." A VI.; the latter the Benet or Plegmund MS.*

29 *Wanley observes, that the Benet MS. is written in one and the same hand to this year, and in hands equally ancient to the year 924; after which it is continued in different hands to the end. Vid. "Cat." p. 130.*

not without its force;—that it is extremely improbable, when we consider the number and variety of King Alfred's works, that he should have neglected the history, of his own country. Besides a genealogy of the kings of Wessex from Cerdic to his own time, which seems never to have been incorporated with any MS. of the "Saxon Chronicle", though prefixed or annexed to several, he undoubtedly preserved many traditionary facts; with a full and circumstantial detail of his own operations, as well as those of his father, brother, and other members of his family; which scarcely any other person than himself could have supplied. To doubt this would be as incredulous a thing as to deny that Xenophon wrote his "Anabasis", or Caesar his "Commentaries". From the time of Alfred and Plegmund to a few years after the Norman Conquest, these chronicles seem to have been continued by different hands, under the auspices of such men as Archbishops Dunstan, Aelfric, and others, whose characters have been much misrepresented by ignorance and scepticism on the one hand; as well as by mistaken zeal and devotion on the other. The indirect evidence respecting Dunstan and Aelfric is as curious as that concerning Plegmund; but the discussion of it would lead us into a wide and barren field of investigation; nor is this the place to refute the errors of Hickes, Cave, and Wharton, already noticed by Wanley in his preface. The chronicles of Abingdon, of Worcester, of Peterborough, and others, are continued in the same manner by different hands; partly, though not exclusively, by monks of those monasteries, who very naturally inserted many particulars relating to their own local interests and concerns; which, so far from invalidating the general history, render it more interesting and valuable. It would be a vain and frivolous attempt ascribe these latter compilations to particular persons[30], where there were evidently so many contributors; but that they were successively furnished by contemporary writers, many of whom were eye-witnesses of

---

30 Hickes supposed the Laud or Peterborough Chronicle to have been compiled by Hugo Candidus
(Albus, or White), or some other monk of that house.

36

the events and transactions which they relate, there is abundance of internal evidence to convince us. Many instances of this the editor had taken some pains to collect, in order to lay them before the reader in the preface; but they are so numerous that the subject would necessarily become tedious; and therefore every reader must be left to find them for himself. They will amply repay him for his trouble, if he takes any interest in the early history of England, or in the general construction of authentic history of any kind. He will see plagarisms without end in the Latin histories, and will be in no danger of falling into the errors of Gale and others; not to mention those of our historians who were not professed antiquaries, who mistook that for original and authentic testimony which was only translated. It is remarkable that the "Saxon Chronicle" gradually expires with the Saxon language, almost melted into modern English, in the year 1154. From this period almost to the Reformation, whatever knowledge we have of the affairs of England has been originally derived either from the semi-barbarous Latin of our own countrymen, or from the French chronicles of Froissart and others.

The revival of good taste and of good sense, and of the good old custom adopted by most nations of the civilised world—that of writing their own history in their own language—was happily exemplified at length in the laborious works of our English chroniclers and historians.

Many have since followed in the same track; and the importance of the whole body of English History has attracted and employed the imagination of Milton, the philosophy of Hume, the simplicity of Goldsmith, the industry of Henry, the research of Turner, and the patience of Lingard. The pages of these writers, however, accurate and luminous as they generally are, as well as those of Brady, Tyrrell, Carte, Rapin, and others, not to mention those in black letter, still require correction from the "Saxon Chronicle"; without which no person, however learned, can possess anything beyond a superficial acquaintance with the elements of English History, and of the British Constitution.

Some remarks may here be requisite on the chronology of the "Saxon Chronicle". In the early part of it[31] the reader will observe a reference to the grand epoch of the creation of the world. So also in Ethelwerd, who closely follows the "Saxon Annals". It is allowed by all, that considerable difficulty has occurred in fixing the true epoch of Christ's nativity[32], because the Christian aera was not used at all till about the year 532[33], when it was introduced by Dionysius Exiguus; whose code of canon law, joined afterwards with the decretals of the popes, became as much the standard of authority in ecclesiastical matters as the pandects of Justinian among civilians. But it does not appear that in the Saxon mode of computation this system of chronology was implicitly followed. We mention this circumstance, however, not with a view of settling the point of difference, which would not be easy, but merely to account for those variations observable in different MSS.; which arose, not only from the common mistakes or inadvertencies of transcribers, but from the liberty which the original writers themselves sometimes assumed in this country, of computing the current year according to their own ephemeral or local custom. Some began with the Incarnation or Nativity of Christ; some with the Circumcision, which accords with the solar year of the Romans as now restored; whilst others commenced with the Annunciation; a custom which became very prevalent in honour of the Virgin Mary, and was not formally abolished here till the year 1752; when the Gregorian calendar, commonly called the New Style, was substituted by Act of Parliament for the

---

31 See A.D. xxxiii., the aera of Christ's crucifixion, p. 23, and the notes below.

32 See Playfair's "System of Chronology", p. 49.

33 Playfair says 527: but I follow Bede, Florence of Worcester, and others, who affirm that the great paschal cycle of Dionysius commenced from the year of our Lord's incarnation 532—the year in which the code of Justinian was promulgated. "Vid. Flor. an." 532, 1064, and 1073. See also M. West. "an." 532.

Dionysian. This diversity of computation would alone occasion some confusion; but in addition to this, the INDICTION, or cycle of fifteen years, which is mentioned in the latter part of the "Saxon Chronicle", was carried back three years before the vulgar aera, and commenced in different places at four different periods of the year! But it is very remarkable that, whatever was the commencement of the year in the early part of the "Saxon Chronicle", in the latter part the year invariably opens with Midwinter-day or the Nativity. Gervase of Canterbury, whose Latin chronicle ends in 1199, the aera of "legal" memory, had formed a design, as he tells us, of regulating his chronology by the Annunciation; but from an honest fear of falsifying dates he abandoned his first intention, and acquiesced in the practice of his predecessors; who for the most part, he says, began the new year with the Nativity[34].

Having said thus much in illustration of the work itself, we must necessarily be brief in our account of the present edition. It was contemplated many years since, amidst a constant succession of other occupations; but nothing was then projected beyond a reprint of Gibson, substituting an English translation for the Latin. The indulgence of the Saxon scholar is therefore requested, if we have in the early part of the chronicle too faithfully followed the received text. By some readers no apology of this kind will be deemed necessary; but something may be expected in extenuation of the delay which has retarded the publication. The causes of that delay must be chiefly sought in the nature of the work itself. New types were to be cast; compositors to be instructed in a department entirely new to them; manuscripts to be compared, collated, transcribed; the text to be revised throughout; various readings of great intricacy to be carefully presented, with considerable additions from unpublished sources; for, however unimportant some may at first sight appear, the most trivial may be of use. With such and

---

34 *"Vid. Prol. in Chron." Bervas. "ap. X." Script. p. 1338.*

other difficulties before him, the editor has, nevertheless, been blessed with health and leisure sufficient to overcome them; and he may now say with Gervase the monk at the end of his first chronicle, "Finito libro reddatur gratia Christo."[35]

Of the translation it is enough to observe, that it is made as literal as possible, with a view of rendering the original easy to those who are at present unacquainted with the Saxon language. By this method also the connection between the ancient and modern language will be more obvious. The same method has been adopted in an unpublished translation of Gibson's "Chronicle" by the late Mr. Cough, now in the Bodleian Library. But the honour of having printed the first literal version of the "Saxon Annals" was reserved for a learned LADY, the Elstob of her age[36]; whose Work was finished in the year 1819. These translations, however, do not interfere with that in the present edition; because they contain nothing but what is found in the printed texts, and are neither accompanied with the original, nor with any collation of MSS.

---

35 *Often did the editor, during the progress of the work, sympathise with the printer; who, in answer to his urgent importunities to hasten the work, replied once in the classical language of Manutius: "Precor, ut occupationibus meis ignoscas; premor enim oneribus, et typographiae cura, ut vix sustineam." Who could be angry after this?*

36 *Miss Gurney, of Keswick, Norfolk. The work, however, was not published.*

The Anglo-Saxon Chronicle

The island Britain[1] is 800 miles long, and 200 miles broad. And there are in the island five nations; English, Welsh (or British)[2], Scottish, Pictish, and Latin. The first inhabitants were the Britons, who came from Armenia[3], and first peopled Britain southward. Then happened it, that the Picts came south from Scythia, with long ships, not many; and, landing first in the northern part of Ireland, they told the Scots that they must dwell there. But they would not give them leave; for the Scots told them that they could not all dwell there together; "But," said the Scots, "we can nevertheless give you advice. We know another island here to the east. There you may dwell, if you will; and whosoever withstandeth you, we will assist you, that you may gain it." Then went the Picts and entered this land northward. Southward the Britons possessed it, as we before said. And the Picts obtained wives of the Scots, on condition that they chose their kings always on the female side[4]; which they have continued to do, so long since. And it happened, in the run of years, that some party of Scots went from Ireland into Britain, and acquired some portion of this land. Their leader was called Reoda[5], from whom they are named Dalreodi (or Dalreathians).

Sixty winters ere that Christ was born, Caius Julius, emperor

---

1 This introductory part of the "Chronicle" to An. I. first printed by Gibson from the Laud MS. only, has been corrected by a collation of two additional MSS. in the British Museum, "Cotton Tiberius B" lv. and "Domitianus A" viii. Some defects are also here supplied. The materials of this part are to be found in Pliny, Solinus, Orosius, Gildas, and Bede. The admeasurement of the island, however inaccurate, is from the best authorities of those times, and followed by much later historians.

2 Gibson, following the Laud MS. has made six nations of five, by introducing the British and Welsh as two distinct tribes.

3 "De tractu Armoricano."—Bede, "Ecclesiastical History" i. I. The word Armenia occurring a few lines above in Bede, it was perhaps inadvertently written by the Saxon compiler of the "Chronicle" instead of Armorica.

4 In case of a disputed succession, "Ubi res veniret in dabium," etc.—Bede, "Ecclesiastical History" i. I.

5 Reada, Aelfr.; Reuda, Bede, Hunt. etc. Perhaps it was originally Reutha or Reotha.

SAXON ENGLAND
according to the
SAXON CHRONICLE

of the Romans, with eighty ships sought Britain. There he was
first beaten in a dreadful fight, and lost a great part of his army.
Then he let his army abide with the Scots[6], and went south into
Gaul. There he gathered six hundred ships, with which he went
back into Britain. When they first rushed together, Caesar's

---

6 *This is an error, arising from the inaccurately written MSS. of Orosius and Bede; where "in
Hybernia" and "in Hiberniam" occur for "in hiberna". The error is retained in Wheloc's Bede.*

tribune, whose name was Labienus[7], was slain. Then took the Welsh sharp piles, and drove them with great clubs into the water, at a certain ford of the river called Thames. When the Romans found that, they would not go over the ford. Then fled the Britons to the fastnesses of the woods; and Caesar, having after much fighting gained many of the chief towns, went back into Gaul[8].

[B.C. 60. Before the incarnation of Christ sixty years, Gaius Julius the emperor, first of the Romans, sought the land of Britain; and he crushed the Britons in battle, and overcame them; and nevertheless he was unable to gain any empire there.]

A.D. 1. Octavianus reigned fifty-six winters; and in the forty-second year of his reign Christ was born. Then three astrologers from the east came to worship Christ; and the children in Bethlehem were slain by Herod in persecution of Christ.

A.D. 3. This year died Herod, stabbed by his own hand; and Archelaus his son succeeded him. The child Christ was also this year brought back again from Egypt.

A.D. 6. From the beginning of the world to this year were agone five thousand and two hundred winters.

A.D. 11. This year Herod the son of Antipater undertook the government in Judea.

A.D. 12. This year Philip and Herod divided Judea into four kingdoms.

[A.D. 12. This year Judea was divided into four tetrarchies.]

A.D. 16. This year Tiberius succeeded to the empire.

---

7 Labienus = Laberius. Venerable Bede also, and Orosius, whom he follows verbatim, have "Labienus". It is probably a mistake of some very ancient scribe, who improperly supplied the abbreviation "Labius" (for "Laberius") by "Labienus".

8 Of these early transactions in Britain King Alfred supplies us with a brief but circumstantial account in his Saxon paraphrase of "Orosius".

A.D. 26. This year Pilate began to reign over the Jews.

A.D. 30. This year was Christ baptized; and Peter and Andrew were converted, together with James, and John, and Philip, and all the twelve apostles.

A.D. 33. This year was Christ crucified;[9] about five thousand two hundred and twenty six winters from the beginning of the world.[10]

A.D. 34. This year was St. Paul converted, and St. Stephen stoned.

A.D. 35. This year the blessed Peter the apostle settled an episcopal see in the city of Antioch.

A.D. 37. This year[11] Pilate slew himself with his own hand.

A.D. 39. This year Caius undertook the empire.

A.D. 44. This year the blessed Peter the apostle settled an episcopal see at Rome; and James, the brother of John, was slain by Herod.

A.D. 45. This year died Herod, who slew James one year ere his own death.

A.D. 46. This year Claudius, the second of the Roman emperors who invaded Britain, took the greater part of the island into his power, and added the Orkneys to rite dominion of the Romans. This was in the fourth year of his reign. And in the same year[12] happened the great famine in Syria which Luke mentions in the book called "The Acts of the Apostles". After Claudius Nero succeeded to the empire, who almost lost the island Britain through his incapacity.

---

9 "8 die Aprilis", Flor. M. West.

10 Gibbon regrets this chronology, i.e. from the creation of the world, which he thinks preferable to the vulgar mode from the Christian aera. But how vague and uncertain the scale which depends on a point so remote and undetermined as the precise time when the world was created. If we examine the chronometers of different writers we shall find a difference, between the maximum and the minimum, of 3368 years. The Saxon chronology seems to be founded on that of Eusebius, which approaches the medium between the two extremes.

11 An. 42, Flor. This act is attributed by Orosius, and Bede who follows him, to the threatening conduct of Caligula, with a remark, that it was he (Pilate) who condemned our Lord to death.

12 An. 48, Flor. See the account of this famine in King Alfred's "Orosius".

Caesar's invasion of Britain (by Edward Armitage)

[A.D. 46. This year the Emperor Claudius came to Britain, and subdued a large part of the island; and he also added the island of Orkney to the dominion of the Romans.]

A.D. 47. This year Mark, the evangelist in Egypt beginneth to write the gospel.

[A.D. 47. This was in the fourth year of his reign, and in this same year was the great famine in Syria which Luke speaks of in the book called "Actus Apostolorum".]

[A.D. 47. This year Claudius, king of the Romans, went with an army into Britain, and subdued the island, and subjected all the Picts and Welsh to the rule of the Romans.]

A.D. 50. This year Paul was sent bound to Rome.

A.D. 62. This year James, the brother of Christ, suffered.

A.D. 63. This year Mark the evangelist departed this life.

A.D. 69. This year Peter and Paul suffered.

A.D. 70. This year Vespasian undertook the empire.

A.D. 71. This year Titus, son of Vespasian, slew in Jerusalem eleven hundred thousand Jews.

A.D. 81. This year Titus came to the empire, after Vespasian, who said that he considered the day lost in which he did no good.

A.D. 83. This year Domitian, the brother of Titus, assumed the government.

A.D. 84. This year John the evangelist in the island Patmos wrote the book called "The Apocalypse".

A.D. 90. This year Simon, the apostle, a relation of Christ, was crucified: and John the evangelist rested at Ephesus.

A.D. 92. This year died Pope Clement.

A.D. 110. This year Bishop Ignatius suffered.

A.D. 116. This year Hadrian the Caesar began to reign.

A.D. 145. This year Marcus Antoninus and Aurelius his brother succeeded to the empire.

[A.D. 167. This year Eleutherius succeeded to the popedom, and held it fifteen years; and in the same year Lucius, king of the Britons, sent and begged baptism of him. And he soon sent it him, and they continued in the true faith until the time of Diocletian.]

A.D. 189. This year Severus came to the empire; and went with his army into Britain, and subdued in battle a great part of the island. Then wrought he a mound of turf, with a broad wall thereupon, from sea to sea, for the defence of the Britons. He reigned seventeen years; and then ended his days at York. His son Bassianus succeeded him in the empire. His other son, who perished, was called Geta. This year Eleutherius undertook the bishopric of Rome, and held it honourably for fifteen winters. To him Lucius, king of the Britons, sent letters, and prayed that he might be made a Christian. He obtained his request; and they continued afterwards in the right belief until the reign of Diocletian.

A.D. 199. In this year was found the holy rood.[13]

---

13 *Those writers who mention this discovery of the holy cross, by Helena the mother of Constantine, disagree so much in their chronology, that it is a vain attempt to reconcile them to*

A.D. 283. This year suffered Saint Alban the Martyr.

A.D. 343. This year died St. Nicolaus.

A.D. 379. This year Gratian succeeded to the empire.

A.D. 381. This year Maximus the Caesar came to the empire. He was born in the land of Britain, whence he passed over into Gaul. He there slew the Emperor Gratian; and drove his brother, whose name was Valentinian, from his country (Italy). The same Valentinian afterwards collected an army, and slew Maximus; whereby he gained the empire. About this time arose the error of Pelagius over the world.

A.D. 418. This year the Romans collected all the hoards of gold[14] that were in Britain; and some they hid in the earth, so that no man afterwards might find them, and some they carried away with them into Gaul.

A.D. 423. This year Theodosius the younger succeeded to the empire.

A.D. 429. This year Bishop Palladius was sent from Pope Celesrinus to the Scots, that he might establish their faith.

A.D. 430. This year Patricius was sent from Pope Celestinus to preach baptism to the Scots.

[A.D. 430. This year Patrick was sent by Pope Celestine to preach baptism to the Scots.]

A.D. 435. This year the Goths sacked the city of Rome; and never since have the Romans reigned in Britain. This was about eleven hundred and ten winters after it was built. They reigned altogether in Britain four hundred and seventy winters since Gaius Julius first sought that land.

A.D. 443. This year sent the Britons over sea to Rome, and begged assistance against the Picts; but they had none, for

truth or to each other. This and the other notices of ecclesiastical matters, whether Latin or Saxon, from the year 190 to the year 380 of the Laud MS. and 381 of the printed Chronicle, may be safely considered as interpolations, probably posterior to the Norman Conquest.

14   This is not to be understood strictly; gold being used as a general term for money or coin of every description; great quantities of which, it is well known, have been found at different times, and in many different places, in this island: not only of gold, but of silver, brass, copper, etc.

the Romans were at war with Atila, king of the Huns. Then sent they to the Angles, and requested the same from the nobles of that nation.

A.D. 444. This year died St. Martin.

A.D. 448. This year John the Baptist showed his head to two monks, who came from the eastern country to Jerusalem for the sake of prayer, in the place that whilom was the palace of Herod.[15]

A.D. 449. This year Marcian and Valentinian assumed the empire, and reigned seven winters. In their days Hengest and Horsa, invited by Wurtgern, king of the Britons to his assistance, landed in Britain in a place that is called Ipwinesfleet; first of all to support the Britons, but they afterwards fought against them. The king directed them to fight against the Picts; and they did so; and obtained the victory wheresoever they came. They then sent to the Angles, and desired them to send more assistance. They described the worthlessness of the Britons, and the richness of the land. They then sent them greater support. Then came the men from three powers of Germany; the Old Saxons, the Angles, and the Jutes. From the Jutes are descended the men of Kent, the Wightwarians (that is, the tribe that now dwelleth in the Isle of Wight), and that kindred in Wessex that men yet call the kindred of the Jutes. From the Old Saxons came the people of Essex and Sussex and Wessex. From Anglia, which has ever since remained waste between the Jutes and the Saxons, came the East Angles, the Middle Angles, the Mercians, and all of those north of the Humber. Their leaders were two brothers, Hengest and Horsa; who were the sons of Wihtgils; Wihtgils was the son of Witta, Witta of Wecta, Wecta of Woden. From this Woden arose all our royal kindred, and that of the Southumbrians also.

---

15 *An interpolated legend, from the "Gesta Pontificum", repeated by Bede, Florence, Matth. West., Fordun, and others. The head was said to be carried to Edessa.*

Illumination of a 15th century manuscript of Historia Regum Britanniae showing king of the Britons Vortigern watching the fight between two dragons

[A.D. 449. And in their days Vortigern invited the Angles thither, and they came to Britain in three ceols, at the place called Wippidsfleet.]

A.D. 455. This year Hengest and Horsa fought with Wurtgern the king on the spot that is called Aylesford. His brother Horsa being there slain, Hengest afterwards took to the kingdom with his son Esc.

A.D. 457. This year Hengest and Esc fought with the Britons on the spot that is called Crayford, and there slew four thousand men. The Britons then forsook the land of Kent, and in great consternation fled to London.

A.D. 465. This year Hengest and Esc fought with the Welsh, nigh Wippedfleet; and there slew twelve leaders, all Welsh. On their side a thane was there slain, whose name was Wipped.

Hengist and Horsa. "The Arrival of the First Ancestors of Englishmen out of Germany into Britain", from A Restitution of Decayed Intelligence by Richard Verstegan (1605)

A.D. 473. This year Hengest and Esc fought with the Welsh, and took immense Booty. And the Welsh fled from the English like fire.

A.D. 477. This year came Ella to Britain, with his three sons, Cymen, and Wlenking, and Cissa, in three ships; landing at a place that is called Cymenshore. There they slew many of the Welsh; and some in flight they drove into the wood that is called Andred'sley.

A.D. 482. This year the blessed Abbot Benedict shone in this world, by the splendour of those virtues which the blessed Gregory records in the book of Dialogues.

A.D. 485. This year Ella fought with the Welsh nigh Mecred's-Burnsted.

A.D. 488. This year Esc succeeded to the kingdom; and was king of the men of Kent twenty-four winters.

A.D. 490. This year Ella and Cissa besieged the city of Andred, and slew all that were therein; nor was one Briten left there afterwards.

A.D. 495. This year came two leaders into Britain, Cerdic and Cynric his son, with five ships, at a place that is called Cerdic's-ore. And they fought with the Welsh the same day. Then he died, and his son Cynric succeeded to the government, and held it six and twenty winters. Then he died; and Ceawlin, his son, succeeded, who reigned seventeen years. Then he died; and Ceol succeeded to the government, and reigned five years. When he died, Ceolwulf, his brother, succeeded, and reigned seventeen years. Their kin goeth to Cerdic. Then succeeded Cynebils, Ceolwulf's brother's son, to the kingdom; and reigned one and thirty winters. And he first of West-Saxon kings received baptism. Then succeeded Cenwall, who was the son of Cynegils, and reigned one and thirty winters. Then held Sexburga, his queen, the government one year after him. Then succeeded Escwine to the kingdom, whose kin goeth to Cerdic, and held it two years. Then succeeded Centwine, the son of Cynegils, to the kingdom of the West-Saxons, and reigned nine years. Then succeeded Ceadwall to the government, whose kin goeth to Cerdic, and held it three years. Then succeeded Ina to the kingdom of the West-Saxons, whose kin goeth to Cerdic, and reigned thirty-seven winters. Then succeeded Ethelheard, whose kin goeth to Cerdic, and reigned sixteen years. Then succeeded Cuthred, whose kin goeth to Cerdic, and reigned sixteen winters. Then succeeded Sigebriht, whose kin goeth to Cerdic, and reigned one year. Then succeeded Cynwulf, whose kin goeth to Cerdic, and reigned one and thirty winters. Then succeeded Brihtric, whose kin goeth to Cerdic, and reigned sixteen years. Then succeeded Egbert to the kingdom, and held it seven and thirty winters, and seven months. Then succeeded Ethelwulf, his son, and reigned eighteen years and a half. Ethelwulf was the son of Egbert, Egbert of Ealmund, Ealmund of Eafa, Eafa of Eoppa, Eoppa of Ingild, Ingild of Cenred (Ina of Cenred, Cuthburga of Cenred, and Cwenburga of Cenred), Cenred of Ceolwald, Ceolwald of Cuthwulf, Cuthwulf of Cuthwine, Cuthwine of Celm, Celm of Cynric, Cynric of Creoda, Creoda of Cerdic. Then succeeded Ethelbald, the son of Ethelwulf, to the kingdom, and held it five years. Then succeeded Ethelbert, his brother, and reigned five years. Then succeeded Ethelred, his brother, to the kingdom, and held it five years. Then succeeded Alfred, their brother, to the government. And then had elapsed of his age three and twenty winters, and three hundred and ninety-six winters from the time when his kindred first gained the land of Wessex from the Welsh. And he held the kingdom a year and a half less than thirty winters. Then succeeded Edward, the son of Alfred, and reigned twenty-four winters. When he died, then succeeded Athelstan, his son, and reigned fourteen years and seven weeks and three days. Then succeeded Edmund, his brother, and reigned six years and a half, wanting two nights. Then succeeded Edred, his brother, and reigned nine years and six weeks. Then succeeded Edwy, the son of Edmund, and reigned three years and thirty-six weeks, wanting two days. When he died, then succeeded Edgar, his brother, and reigned sixteen years and eight weeks and two nights. When he died, then succeeded Edward, the son of Edgar, and reigned—

A.D. 501. This year Porta and his two sons, Beda and Mela, came into Britain, with two ships, at a place called Portsmouth. They soon landed, and slew on the spot a young Briton of very high rank.

A.D. 508. This year Cerdic and Cynric slew a British king, whose name was Natanleod, and five thousand men with him. After this was the land named Netley, from him, as far as Charford.

A.D. 509. This year St. Benedict, the abbot, father of all the monks,[16] ascended to heaven.

A.D. 514. This year came the West-Saxons into Britain, with three ships, at the place that is called Cerdic's-ore. And Stuff and Wihtgar fought with the Britons, and put them to flight.

A.D. 519. This year Cerdic and Cynric undertook the government of the West-Saxons; the same year they fought with the Britons at a place now called Charford. From that day have reigned the children of the West-Saxon kings.

A.D. 527. This year Cerdic and Cynric fought with the Britons in the place that is called Cerdic's-ley.

A.D. 530. This year Cerdic and Cynric took the isle of Wight, and slew many men in Carisbrook.

A.D. 534. This year died Cerdic, the first king of the West-Saxons. Cynric his son succeeded to the government, and reigned afterwards twenty-six winters. And they gave to their two nephews, Stuff and Wihtgar, the whole of the Isle of Wight.

A.D. 538. This year the sun was eclipsed, fourteen days before the calends of March, from before morning until nine.

A.D. 540. This year the sun was eclipsed on the twelfth day

---

16 *Merely of those called from him "Benedictines". But the compiler of the Cotton MS., who was probably a monk of that order, seems not to acknowledge any other. Matthew of Westminster places his death in 536.*

before the calends of July; and the stars showed themselves full nigh half an hour over nine.

A.D. 544. This year died Wihtgar; and men buried him at Carisbrook.

A.D. 547. This year Ida began his reign; from whom first arose the royal kindred of the Northumbrians. Ida was the son of Eoppa, Eoppa of Esa, Esa of Ingwy, Ingwy of Angenwit, Angenwit of Alloc, Alloc of Bennoc, Bennoc of Brand, Brand of Balday, Balday of Woden. Woden of Fritholaf, Fritholaf of Frithowulf, Frithowulf of Finn, Finn of Godolph, Godolph of Geata. Ida reigned twelve years. He built Bamburgh-Castle, which was first surrounded with a hedge, and afterwards with a wall.

A.D. 552. This year Cynric fought with the Britons on the spot that is called Sarum, and put them to flight. Cerdic was the father of Cynric, Cerdic was the son of Elesa, Elesa of Esla, Esla of Gewis, Gewis of Wye, Wye of Frewin, Frewin of Frithgar, Frithgar of Brand, Brand of Balday, Balday of Woden. In this year Ethelbert, the son of Ermenric, was born, who on the two and thirtieth year of his reign received the rite of baptism, the first of all the kings in Britain.

A.D. 556. This year Cynric and Ceawlin fought with the Britons at Beranbury.

A.D. 560. This year Ceawlin undertook the government of the West-Saxons; and Ella, on the death of Ida, that of the Northumbrians; each of whom reigned thirty winters. Ella was the son of Iff, Iff of Usfrey, Usfrey of Wilgis, Wilgis of Westerfalcon, Westerfalcon of Seafowl, Seafowl of Sebbald, Sebbald of Sigeat, Sigeat of Swaddy, Swaddy of Seagirt, Seagar of Waddy, Waddy of Woden, Woden of Frithowulf. This year Ethelbert came to the kingdom of the Cantuarians, and held it fifty-three winters. In his days the holy Pope Gregory sent us baptism. That was in the two and thirtieth year of his reign. And Columba, the mass-priest, came to the Picts, and converted them to the belief of Christ. They are the dwellers by the northern moors. And their king gave him the island of Hii, consisting of five hides, as they say, where Columba built a monastary. There he was abbot two and thirty winters; and there he died, when he was seventy-seven years old. The place his successors yet have. The Southern Picts were long before baptized by Bishop Ninnia, who was taught at Rome. His church or monastery is at Hwiterne, hallowed in the name of St. Martin, where he resteth with many holy men. Now, therefore, shall there be ever in Hii an abbot, and no bishop; and to him shall be subject all the bishops of the Scots; because Columba was an abbot—no bishop.

[A.D. 565. This year Columba the presbyter came from the Scots among the Britons, to instruct the Picts, and he built a monastery in the island of Hii.]

A.D. 568. This year Ceawlin, and Cutha the brother of Ceawlin, fought with Ethelbert, and pursued him into Kent. And they slew two aldermen at Wimbledon, Oslake and Cnebba.

A.D. 571. This year Cuthulf fought with the Britons at Bedford, and took four towns, Lenbury, Aylesbury, Benson, and Ensham. And this same year he died.

A.D. 577. This year Cuthwin and Ceawlin fought with the Britons, and slew three kings, Commail, and Condida, and Farinmail, on the spot that is called Derham, and took from them three cities, Gloucester, Cirencester, and Bath.

A.D. 583. This year Mauricius succeeded to the empire of the Romans.

A.D. 584. This year Ceawlin and Cutha fought with the Britons on the spot that is called Fretherne. There Cutha was slain. And Ceawlin took many towns, as well as immense booty and wealth. He then retreated to his own people.

A.D. 588. This year died King Ella; and Ethelric reigned after him five years.

A.D. 591. This year there was a great slaughter of Britons at Wanborough; Ceawlin was driven from his kingdom, and Ceolric reigned six years.

A.D. 592. This year Gregory succeeded to the papacy at Rome.

A.D. 593. This year died Ceawlin, and Cwichelm, and Cryda; and Ethelfrith succeeded to the kingdom of the Northumbrians. He was the son of Ethelric; Ethelric of Ida.

A.D. 596. This year Pope Gregory sent Augustine to Britain with very many monks, to preach the word of God to the English people.

A.D. 597. This year began Ceolwulf to reign over the West-Saxons; and he constantly fought and conquered, either with the Angles, or the Welsh, or the Picts, or the Scots. He was the son of Cutha, Cutha of Cynric, Cynric of Cerdic, Cerdic of Elesa, Elesa of Gewis, Gewis of Wye, Wye of Frewin, Frewin of Frithgar, Frithgar of Brand, Brand of Balday, and Balday of Woden. This year came Augustine and his companions to England.[17]

A.D. 601. This year Pope Gregory sent the pall to Archbishop Augustine in Britain, with very many learned doctors to assist him; and Bishop Paulinus converted Edwin, king of the Northumbrians, to baptism.

A.D. 603. This year Aeden, king of the Scots, fought with the Dalreathians, and with Ethelfrith, king of the Northumbrians, at Theakstone; where he lost almost all his army. Theobald also, brother of Ethelfrith, with his whole armament, was slain. None of the Scottish kings durst afterwards bring an army against this nation. Hering, the son of Hussa, led the army thither.

---

17 For an interesting and minute account of the arrival of Augustine and his companions in the Isle of Thanet, their entrance into Canterbury, and their general reception in England, vid. Bede, "Hist. Eccles." i. 25, and the following chapters, with the Saxon translation by King Alfred. The succeeding historians have in general repeated the very words of Bede.

St Augustine by Philippe de Champaigne, 1645-1650

[A.D. 603. This year Aethan, King of the Scots, fought against
the Dalreods and against Ethelfrith, king of the North-
humbrians, at Daegsanstane [Dawston?], and they slew
almost all his army. There Theodbald, Ethelfrith's brother,
was slain with all his band. Since then no king of the Scots
has dared to lead an army against this nation. Hering, the son
of Hussa, led the enemy thither.]

A.D. 604. This year Augustine consecrated two bishops,
Mellitus and Justus. Mellitus he sent to preach baptism to

the East-Saxons. Their king was called Seabert, the son of Ricola, Ethelbert's sister, whom Ethelbert placed there as king. Ethelbert also gave Mellitus the bishopric of London; and to Justus he gave the bishopric of Rochester, which is twenty-four miles from Canterbury.

[A.D. 604. This year Augustine consecrated two bishops, Mellitus and Justus. He sent Mellitus to preach baptism to the East-Saxons, whose king was called Sebert, son of Ricole, the sister of Ethelbert, and whom Ethelbert had there appointed king. And Ethelbert gave Mellitus a bishop's see in London, and to Justus he gave Rochester, which is twenty-four miles from Canterbury.]

A.D. 606. This year died Gregory; about ten years since he sent us baptism. His father was called Gordianus, and his mother Silvia.

A.D. 607. This year Ceolwulf fought with the South-Saxons. And Ethelfrith led his army to Chester; where he slew an innumerable host of the Welsh; and so was fulfilled the prophecy of Augustine, wherein he saith "If the Welsh will not have peace with us, they shall perish at the hands of the Saxons." There were also slain two hundred priests,[18] who came thither to pray for the army of the Welsh. Their leader was called Brocmail, who with some fifty men escaped thence.

A.D. 611. This year Cynegils succeeded to the government in Wessex, and held it one and thirty winters. Cynegils was the son of Ceol, Ceol of Cutha, Cutha of Cynric.

A.D. 614. This year Cynegils and Cwichelm fought at Bampton, and slew two thousand and forty-six of the Welsh.

A.D. 616. This year died Ethelbert, king of Kent, the first of

---

18 It was originally, perhaps, in the MSS. ICC. The abbreviation for 1,200; which is the number of the slain in Bede. The total number of the monks of Bangor is said to have been 2,100; most of whom appear to have been employed in prayer on this occasion, and only fifty escape by flight. Vide Bede, "Hist. Eccles." ii. 2, and the tribe of Latin historians who copy him.

English kings that received baptism: he was the son of
Ermenric. He reigned fifty-six winters, and was succeeded
by his son Eadbald. And in this same year had elapsed from
the beginning of the world five thousand six hundred and
eighteen winters. This Eadbald renounced his baptism, and
lived in a heathen manner; so that he took to wife the relict
of his father. Then Laurentius, who was archbishop in Kent,
meant to depart southward over sea, and abandon everything.
But there came to him in the night the apostle Peter, and
severely chastised him,[19] because he would so desert the flock
of God. And he charged him to go to the king, and teach him
the right belief. And he did so; and the king returned to the
right belief. In this king's days the same Laurentius, who was
archbishop in Kent after Augustine, departed this life on the
second of February, and was buried near Augustine. The holy
Augustine in his lifetime invested him bishop, to the end that
the church of Christ, which yet was new in England, should
at no time after his decease be without an archbishop. After
him Mellitus, who was first Bishop of London, succeeded
to the archbishopric. The people of London, where Mellitus
was before, were then heathens: and within five winters of
this time, during the reign of Eadbald, Mellitus died. To him
succeeded Justus, who was Bishop of Rochester, whereto he
consecrated Romanus bishop.

[A.D. 616. In that time Laurentius was archbishop, and for the
sorrowfulness which he had on account of the king's unbelief
he was minded to forsake this country entirely, and go over
sea; but St. Peter the apostle scourged him sorely one night,
because he wished thus to forsake the flock of God, and
commanded him to teach boldly the true faith to the king; and
he did so, and the king turned to the right (faith). In the days
of this same king, Eadbald, this Laurentius died. The holy

---

19 *Literally, "swinged, or scourged him." Both Bede and Alfred begin by recording the matter as
a vision, or a dream; whence the transition is easy to a matter of fact, as here stated by the Norman
interpolators of the "Saxon Annals".*

Augustine, while yet in sound health, ordained him bishop, in order that the community of Christ, which was yet new in England, should not after his decease be at any time without an archbishop. After him Mellitus, who had been previously Bishop of London, succeeded to the archbishopric. And within five years of the decease of Laurentius, while Eadbald still reigned, Mellitus departed to Christ.]

A.D. 617. This year was Ethelfrith, king of the Northumbrians, slain by Redwald, king of the East-Angles; and Edwin, the son of Ella, having succeeded to the kingdom, subdued all Britain, except the men of Kent alone, and drove out the Ethelings, the sons of Ethelfrith, namely, Enfrid. Oswald, Oswy, Oslac, Oswood. Oslaf, and Offa.

A.D. 624. This year died Archbishop Mellitus.

A.D. 625. This year Paulinus was invested bishop of the Northumbrians, by Archbishop Justus, on the twelfth day before the calends of August.

[A.D. 625. This year Archbishop Justus consecrated Paulinus bishop of the North-humbrians.]

A.D. 626. This year came Eamer from Cwichelm, king of the West-Saxons, with a design to assassinate King Edwin; but he killed Lilla his thane, and Forthere, and wounded the king. The same night a daughter was born to Edwin, whose name was Eanfleda. Then promised the king to Paulinus, that he would devote his daughter to God, if he would procure at the hand of God, that he might destroy his enemy, who had sent the assassin to him. He then advanced against the West-Saxons with an army, felled on the spot five kings, and slew many of their men. This year Eanfleda, the daughter of King Edwin, was baptized, on the holy eve of Pentecost. And the king within twelve months was baptized, at Easter, with all his people. Easter was then on the twelfth of April. This was done at York, where he had ordered a church to be built of timber, which was hallowed in the name of St. Peter. There the king gave the bishopric to Paulinus; and there he afterwards ordered a larger church to be built of stone. This year Penda began to reign; and reigned thirty winters. He had seen fifty winters when he began to reign. Penda was the son of Wybba, Wybba of Creoda, Creoda of Cynewald, Cynewald of Cnebba, Cnebba of Icel, Icel of Eomer, Eomer of Angelthew, Angelthew of Offa, Offa of Wearmund, Wearmund of Whitley, Whitley of Woden.

A.D. 627. This year was King Edwin baptized at Easter, with all his people, by Paulinus, who also preached baptism in Lindsey, where the first person who believed was a certain rich man, of the name of Bleek, with all his people. At this time Honorius succeeded Boniface in the papacy, and sent hither to Paulinus the pall; and Archbishop Justus having departed this life on the tenth of November, Honorius was consecrated at Lincoln Archbishop of Canterbury by Paulinus; and Pope Honorius sent him the pall. And he sent an injunction to the Scots, that they should return to the right celebration of Easter.

[A.D. 627. This year, at Easter, Paulinus baptized Edwin king of the North-humbrians, with his people; and earlier within the same year, at Pentecost, he had baptized Eanfled, daughter of the same king.]

A.D. 628. This year Cynegils and Cwichelm fought with Penda at Cirencester, and afterwards entered into a treaty there.

A.D. 632. This year was Orpwald baptized.

A.D. 633. This year King Edwin was slain by Cadwalla and Penda, on Hatfield moor, on the fourteenth of October. He reigned seventeen years. His son Osfrid was also slain with him. After this Cadwalla and Penda went and ravaged all the land of the Northumbrians; which when Paulinus saw, he took Ethelburga, the relict of Edwin, and went by ship to

Kent. Eadbald and Honorius received him very honourably, and gave him the bishopric of Rochester, where he continued to his death.

A.D. 634. This year Osric, whom Paulinus baptized, succeeded to the government of Deira. He was the son of Elfric, the uncle of Edwin. And to Bernicia succeeded Eanfrith, son of Ethelfrith. This year also Bishop Birinus first preached baptism to the West-Saxons, under King Cynegils. The said Birinus went thither by the command of Pope Honorius; and he was bishop there to the end of his life. Oswald also this year succeeded to the government of the Northumbrians, and reigned nine winters. The ninth year was assigned to him on account of the heathenism in which those lived who reigned that one year betwixt him and Edwin.

A.D. 635. This year King Cynegils was baptized by Bishop Birinus at Dorchester; and Oswald, king of the Northumbrians, was his sponsor.

A.D. 636. This year King Cwichelm was baptized at Dorchester, and died the same year. Bishop Felix also preached to the East-Angles the belief of Christ.

A.D. 639. This year Birinus baptized King Cuthred at Dorchester, and received him as his son.

A.D. 640. This year died Eadbald, King of Kent, after a reign of twenty-five winters. He had two sons, Ermenred and Erkenbert; and Erkenbert reigned there after his father. He overturned all the idols in the kingdom, and first of English kings appointed a fast before Easter. His daughter was called Ercongota—holy damsel of an illustrious sire! whose mother was Sexburga, the daughter of Anna, king of the East-Angles. Ermenred also begat two sons, who were afterwards martyred by Thunnor.

A.D. 642. This year Oswald, king of the Northumbrians, was slain by Penda, king of the Southumbrians, at Mirfield, on the fifth day of August; and his body was buried at Bardney. His holiness and miracles were afterwards displayed on manifold occasions throughout this island; and his hands remain still uncorrupted at Barnburgh. The same year in which Oswald was slain, Oswy his brother succeeded to the government of the Northumbrians, and reigned two less than thirty years.

A.D. 643. This year Kenwal succeeded to the kingdom of the West-Saxons, and held it one and thirty winters. This Kenwal ordered the old[20] church at Winchester to be built in the name of St. Peter. He was the son of Cynegils.

A.D. 644. This year died at Rochester, on the tenth of October, Paulinus, who was first Archbishop at York, and afterwards at Rochester. He was bishop nineteen winters, two months, and one and twenty days. This year the son of Oswy's uncle (Oswin), the son of Osric, assumed the government of Deira, and reigned seven winters.

A.D. 645. This year King Kenwal was driven from his dominion by King Penda.

A.D. 646. This year King Kenwal was baptized.

A.D. 648. This year Kenwal gave his relation Cuthred three thousand hides of land by Ashdown. Cuthred was the son of Cwichelm, Cwichelm of Cynegils.

A.D. 650. This year Egelbert, from Gaul, after Birinus the Romish bishop, obtained the bishopric of the West-Saxons.

[A.D. 650. This year Birinus the bishop died, and Agilbert the Frenchman was ordained.]

A.D. 651. This year King Oswin was slain, on the twentieth day of August; and within twelve nights afterwards died Bishop Aidan, on the thirty-first of August.

A.D. 652. This year Kenwal fought at Bradford by the Avon.

---

20 *This epithet appears to have been inserted in some copies of the "Saxon Chronicle" so early as the tenth century; to distinguish the "old" church or minster at Winchester from he "new", consecrated A.D. 903.*

A stained glass window from the cloister of Worcester Cathedral showing the death of Penda of Mercia.

A.D. 653. This year, the Middle-Angles under alderman Peada received the right belief.

A.D. 654. This year King Anna was slain, and Botolph began to build that minster at Icanhoe. This year also died Archbishop Honorius, on the thirtieth of September.

A.D. 655. This year Penda was slain at Wingfield, and thirty royal personages with him, some of whom were kings. One of them was Ethelhere, brother of Anna, king of the East-Angles. The Mercians after this became Christians. From the beginning of the world had now elapsed five thousand eight hundred and fifty winters, when Peada, the son of Penda, assumed the government of the Mercians. In his time came together himself and Oswy, brother of King Oswald, and said, that they would rear a minster to the glory of Christ, and the honour of St. Peter. And they did so, and gave it the name of Medhamsted; because there is a well there, called Meadswell. And they began the groundwall, and wrought thereon; after which they committed the work to a monk, whose name was Saxulf. He was very much the friend of God, and him also loved all people. He was nobly born in the world, and rich: he is now much richer with Christ. But King Peada reigned no while; for he was betrayed by his own queen, in Easter-tide. This year Ithamar, Bishop of Rochester, consecrated Deus-dedit to Canterbury, on the twenty-sixth day of March.

A.D. 656. This year was Peada slain; and Wulfhere, son of Penda, succeeded to the kingdom of the Mercians. In his time waxed the abbey of Medhamsted very rich, which his brother had begun. The king loved it much, for the love of his brother Peada, and for the love of his wed-brother Oswy, and for the love of Saxulf the abbot. He said, therefore, that he would dignify and honour it by the counsel of his brothers, Ethelred and Merwal; and by the counsel of his sisters, Kyneburga and Kyneswitha; and by the counsel of the archbishop, who was called Deus-dedit; and by the counsel of all his peers, learned and lewd, that in his kingdom were. And he so did. Then sent the king after the abbot, that he should immediately come to him. And he so did. Then said the king to the abbot: "Beloved Saxulf, I have sent after thee for the good of my soul; and I will plainly tell thee for why. My brother Peada and my beloved friend Oswy began a minster, for the love of Christ and St. Peter: but my brother, as Christ willed, is departed from this life; I will therefore intreat thee, beloved friend, that they earnestly proceed on their work; and I will find thee thereto gold and silver, land and possessions, and all that thereto behoveth." Then went the abbot home, and began to work. So he sped, as Christ permitted him; so that in a few years was that minster ready. Then, when the king heard say that, he was very glad; and bade men send through all the nation, after all his thanes; after the archbishop, and after bishops: and after his earls; and after all those that loved God; that they should come to him. And he fixed the day when men should hallow the minster. And when they were hallowing the minster, there was the king, Wulfere, and his brother Ethelred, and his sisters, Kyneburga and Kyneswitha. And the minster was hallowed by Archbishop Deusdedit of Canterbury; and the Bishop of Rochester, Ithamar; and the Bishop of London, who was called Wina; and the Bishop of the Mercians, whose name was Jeruman; and Bishop Tuda. And there was Wilfrid, priest, that after was bishop; and there were all his thanes that were in his kingdom. When the minster was hallowed, in the name of St. Peter, and St. Paul, and St. Andrew, then stood up the king before all his thanes, and said with a loud voice: "Thanks be to the high almighty God for this worship that here is done; and I will this day glorify Christ and St. Peter, and I will that you all confirm my words.—I Wulfere give to-day to St. Peter, and the Abbot Saxulf, and the monks of the minster, these lands, and these waters, and meres, and fens, and weirs, and all the lands that thereabout lye, that are of my kingdom, freely, so that no man have there any ingress, but the abbot and the monks. This is the gift. From Medhamsted to Northborough; and so to the place that is called Foleys; and so all the fen, right to Ashdike; and from Ashdike to the place called Fethermouth; and so in a right line ten miles long to Ugdike; and so to Ragwell; and from Ragwell five miles to the main river that goeth to Elm and to Wisbeach; and so about three miles to Trokenholt; and from Trokenholt right through all the fen to Derworth; that is twenty miles long; and so to Great Cross; and from Great Cross through a clear water called Bradney; and thence six miles to Paxlade; and so forth through all the meres and fens that lye toward Huntingdon-port; and the meres and lakes Shelfermere and Wittlesey mere, and all the others that thereabout lye; with land and with houses that are on the east side of Shelfermere; thence all the fens to Medhamsted; from Medhamsted all to Welmsford; from Welmsford to Clive; thence to Easton; from Easton to Stamford; from Stamford as the water runneth to the aforesaid Northborough."—These are the lands and the fens that the king gave unto St. Peter's minster.—Then quoth the king: "It is little—this gift— but I will that they hold it so royally and so freely, that there be taken there from neither gild nor gable, but for the monks alone. Thus I will free this minster; that it be not subject except to Rome alone; and hither I will that we seek St. Peter, all that to Rome cannot go." During these words the abbot desired that he would gant him his request. And the king granted it. "I have here (said he) some good monks that would lead their life in retirement, if they wist where. Now here is an island, that is called Ankerig; and I will request, that we may there build a minster to the honour of St. Mary; that they may dwell there who will lead their lives in peace and tranquillity." Then answered the king, and quoth thus: "Beloved Saxulf, not that only which thou desirest, but all things that I know thou desirest in our Lord's behalf, so I approve, and grant. And I bid thee, brother Ethelred, and my sisters, Kyneburga and Kyneswitha, for the release of your souls, that you be witnesses, and that you subscribe it with your fingers. And I pray all that come after me, be they my sons, be they my brethren, or kings that come after me, that our gift may stand; as they would be partakers of the life everlasting, and as they would avoid everlasting punishment. Whoso lesseneth our gift, or the gift of other good men, may the heavenly porter lessen him in the kingdom of heaven; and whoso advanceth it, may the heavenly porter advance him in the kingdom of heaven." These are the witnesses that were there, and that subscribed it with their fingers on the cross of Christ, and confirmed it with their tongues. That was, first the king, Wulfere, who confirmed it first with his word, and afterwards wrote with his finger on the cross of Christ, saying thus: "I Wulfere, king, in the presence of kings, and of earls, and of captains, and of thanes, the witnesses of my gift, before the Archbishop Deus-dedit, I confirm it with the cross of Christ." (+)—"And I Oswy, king of the Northumbrians, the friend of this minster, and o[oe] the Abbot Saxulf, commend it with the cross of Christ." (+)—"And I Sighere, king, ratify it with the cross of Christ." (+)—"And I Sibbi, king, subscribe it with the cross of Christ." (+)—"And I Ethelred, the king's brother, granted the same with the cross of Christ." (+)—"And we, the king's sisters, Kyneburga and Kyneswitha, approve it."—"And I Archbishop of Canterbury, Deus-dedit, ratify it."—Then confirmed it all the others that were there with the cross of Christ (+): namely, Ithamar, Bishop of Rochester; Wina, Bishop of London; Jeruman, Bishop of the Mercians; and Tuda, bishop; and Wilfrid, priest, who was afterwards bishop;

and Eoppa, priest, whom the king, Wulfere, sent to preach christianity in the Isle of Wight; and Saxulf, abbot; and Immine, alderman, and Edbert, alderman, and Herefrith, alderman, and Wilbert, alderman, and Abo, alderman; Ethelbald, Brord, Wilbert, Elmund, Frethegis. These, and many others that were there, the king's most loyal subjects, confirmed it all. This charter was written after our Lord's Nativity 664—the seventh year of King Wulfere—the ninth year of Archbishop Deus-dedir. Then they laid God's curse, and the curse of all saints, and all christian folks, on whosoever undid anything that there was done. "So be it," saith all. "Amen."—When this thing was done, then sent the king to Rome to the Pope Vitalianus that then was, and desired, that he would ratify with his writ and with his blessing, all this aforesaid thing. And the pope then sent his writ, thus saying: "I Vitalianus, pope, grant thee, King Wulfere, and Deus-dedit, archbishop, and Abbot Saxulf, all the things that you desire. And I forbid, that any king, or any man, have any ingress, but the abbot alone; nor shall he be Subject to any man, except the Pope of Rome and the Archbishop of Canterbury. If any one breaketh anything of this, St. Peter with his sword destroy him. Whosoever holdeth it, St. Peter with heaven's key undo him the kingdom of heaven."—Thus was the minster of Medhamsted begun, that was afterwards called Peter-borough. Afterwards came another archbishop to Canterbury, who was called Theodorus; a very good man and wise; and held his synod with his bishops and with his clerk. There was Wilfrid, bishop of the Mercians, deprived of his bishopric; and Saxulf, abbot, was there chosen bishop; and Cuthbald, monk of the same minster, was chosen abbot. This synod was holden after our Lord's Nativity six hundred and seventy-three winters.

A.D. 658. This year Kenwal fought with the Welsh at Pen, and pursued them to the Parret. This battle was fought after his return from East-Anglia, where he was three years in exile. Penda had driven him thither and deprived him of his kingdom, because he had discarded his sister.

A.D. 660. This year Bishop Egelbert departed from Kenwal; and Wina held the bishopric three years. And Egbert accepted the bishopric of Paris, in Gaul, by the Seine.

A.D. 661. This year, at Easter, Kenwal fought at Pontesbury; and Wulfere, the son of Penda, pursued him as far as Ashdown. Cuthred, the son of Cwichelm, and King Kenbert, died in one year. Into the Isle of Wight also Wulfere, the son of Penda, penetrated, and transferred the inhabitants to Ethelwald, king of the South-Saxons, because Wulfere adopted him in baptism. And Eoppa, a mass-priest, by command of Wilfrid and King Wulfere, was the first of men who brought baptism to the people of the Isle of Wight.

A.D. 664. This year the sun was eclipsed, on the eleventh of May; and Erkenbert, King of Kent, having died, Egbert his son succeeded to the kingdom. Colman with his companions this year returned to his own country. This same year there was a great plague in the island Britain, in which died Bishop Tuda, who was buried at Wayleigh—Chad and Wilferth were consecrated—And Archbishop Deus-dedit died.

A.D. 667. This year Oswy and Egbert sent Wighard, a priest, to Rome, that he might be consecrated there Archbishop of Canterbury; but he died as soon as he came thither.

[A.D. 667. This year Wighard went to Rome, even as King Oswy, and Egbert had sent him.]

A.D. 668. This year Theodore was consecrated archbishop, and sent into Britain.

A.D. 669. This year King Egbert gave to Bass, a mass-priest, Reculver—to build a minster upon.

A.D. 670. This year died Oswy, King of Northumberland, on the fifteenth day before the calends of March; and Egferth his son reigned after him. Lothere, the nephew of Bishop Egelbert, succeeded to the bishopric over the land of the West-Saxons, and held it seven years. He was consecrated by Archbishop Theodore. Oswy was the son of Ethelfrith, Ethelfrith of Ethelric, Ethelric of Ida, Ida of Eoppa.

A.D. 671. This year happened that great destruction among the fowls.

A.D. 672. This year died King Cenwal; and Sexburga his queen held the government one year after him.

A.D. 673. This year died Egbert, King of Kent; and the same year there was a synod at Hertford; and St. Etheldritha began that monastery at Ely.

A.D. 674. This year Escwin succeeded to the kingdom of Wessex. He was the son of Cenfus, Cenfus of Cenferth, Cenferth of Cuthgils, Cuthgils of Ceolwulf, Ceolwulf of Cynric, Cynric of Cerdic.

A.D. 675. This year Wulfere, the son of Penda, and Escwin, the son of Cenfus, fought at Bedwin. The same year died Wulfere, and Ethelred succeeded to the government. In his time sent he to Rome Bishop Wilfrid to the pope that then was, called Agatho, and told him by word and by letter, how his brothers Peada and Wulfere, and the Abbot Saxulf, had wrought a minster, called Medhamsted; and that they had freed it, against king and against bishop, from every service; and he besought him that he would confirm it with his writ and with his blessing. And the pope sent then his writ to England, thus saying: "I Agatho, Pope of Rome, greet well the worthy Ethelred, king of the Mercians, and the Archbishop Theodorus of Canterbury, and Saxulf, the bishop of the Mercians, who before was abbot, and all the abbots that are in England; God's greeting and my blessing. I have heard the petition of King Ethelred, and of the Archbishop Theodorus, and of the Bishop Saxulf, and of the Abbot Cuthbald; and

I will it, that it in all wise be as you have spoken it. And I ordain, in behalf of God, and of St. Peter, and of all saints, and of every hooded head, that neither king, nor bishop, nor earl, nor any man whatever, have any claim, or gable, or gild, or levy, or take any service of any kind, from the abbey of Medhamsted. I command also, that no shire-bishop be so bold as to hold an ordination or consecration within this abbacy, except the abbot intreat him, nor have there any claim to proxies, or synodals, or anything whatever of any kind. And I will, that the abbot be holden for legate of Rome over all that island; and whatever abbot is there chosen by the monks that he be consecrated by the Archbishop of Canterbury. I will and decree, that, whatever man may have made a vow to go to Rome, and cannot perform it, either from infirmity, or for his lord's need, or from poverty, or from any other necessity of any kind whatever, whereby he cannot come thither, be he of England, or of whatever other island he be, he may come to that minster of Medhamsted, and have the same forgiveness of Christ and St. Peter, and of the abbot, and of the monks, that he should have if he went to Rome. Now bid I thee, brother Theodorus, that thou let it be proclaimed through all England, that a synod be gathered, and this writ be read and observed. Also I tell thee, Bishop Saxulf, that, as thou desirest it, that the minster be free, so I forbid thee, and all the bishops that after thee come, from Christ and from all his saints, that ye have no demand from that minster, except so much as the abbot will. Now will I say in a word, that, whoso holdeth this writ and this decree, then be he ever dwelling with God Almighty in the kingdom of heaven. And whoso breaketh it, then be he excommunicated, and thrust down with Judas, and with all the devils in hell, except he come to repentance. Amen!" This writ sent the Pope Agatho, and a hundred and twenty-five bishops, by Wilfrid, Archbishop of York, to England.

This was done after our Lord's Nativity 680, the sixth year of King Ethelred. Then the king commanded the Archbishop Theodorus, that he should appoint a general Wittenmoot at the place called Hatfield. When they were there collected, then he allowed the letter to be read that the pope sent thither; and all ratified and confirmed it. Then said the king: "All things that my brother Peada, and my brother Wulfere, and my sisters, Kyneburga and Kyneswitha, gave and granted to St. Peter and the abbot, these I will may stand; and I will in my day increase it, for their souls and for my soul. Now give I St. Peter to-day into his minster, Medhamsted, these lands, and all that thereto lyeth; that is, Bredon, Repings, Cadney, Swineshead, Hanbury, Lodeshall, Scuffanhall, Cosford, Stratford, Wattleburn, Lushgard, Ethelhun-island, Bardney. These lands I give St. Peter just as freely as I possessed them myself; and so, that none of my successors take anything therefrom. Whoso doeth it, have he the curse of the Pope of Rome, and the curse of all bishops, and of all those that are witnesses here. And this I confirm with the token of Christ." (+) "I Theodorus, Archbishop of Canterbury, am witness to this charter of Medhamsted; and I ratify it with my hand, and I excommunicate all that break anything thereof; and I bless all that hold it." (+) "I Wilfrid, Archbishop of York, am witness to this charter; and I ratify this same curse." (+) "I Saxulf, who was first abbot, and now am bishop, I give my curse, and that of all my successors, to those who break this."—"I Ostritha, Ethelred's queen, confirm it."—"I Adrian, legate, ratify it."—"I Putta, Bishop of Rochester, subscribe it."—"I Waldhere, Bishop of London, confirm it."—"I Cuthbald, abbot, ratify it; so that, whoso breaketh it, have he the cursing of all bishops and of all christian folk. Amen."

A.D. 676. This year, in which Hedda succeeded to his bishopric, Escwin died; and Centwin obtained the government of the

West-Saxons. Centwin was the son of Cynegils, Cynegils of Ceolwulf. Ethelred, king of the Mercians, in the meantime, overran the land of Kent.

A.D. 678. This year appeared the comet-star in August, and shone every morning, during three months, like a sunbeam. Bishop Wilfrid being driven from his bishopric by King Everth, two bishops were consecrated in his stead, Bosa over the Deirians, and Eata over the Bernicians. About the same time also Eadhed was consecrated bishop over the people of Lindsey, being the first in that division.

A.D. 679. This year Elwin was slain, by the river Trent, on the spot where Everth and Ethelred fought. This year also died St. Etheldritha; and the monastery of Coldingiham was destroyed by fire from heaven.

A.D. 680. This year Archbishop Theodore appointed a synod at Hatfield; because he was desirous of rectifying the belief of Christ; and the same year died Hilda, Abbess of Whitby.

A.D. 681. This year Trumbert was consecrated Bishop of Hexham, and Trumwin bishop of the Picts; for they were at that time subject to this country. This year also Centwin pursued the Britons to the sea.

A.D. 684. This year Everth sent an army against the Scots, under the command of his alderman, Bright, who lamentably plundered and burned the churches of God.

A.D. 685. This year King Everth commanded Cuthbert to be consecrated a bishop; and Archbishop Theodore, on the first day of Easter, consecrated him at York Bishop of Hexham; for Trumbert had been deprived of that see. The same year Everth was slain by the north sea, and a large army with him, on the thirteenth day before the calends of June. He continued king fifteen winters; and his brother Elfrith succeeded him in the government. Everth was the son of Oswy. Oswy of Ethelferth, Ethelferth of Ethelric, Ethelric of Ida, Ida of

Eoppa. About this time Ceadwall began to struggle for a kingdom. Ceadwall was the son of Kenbert, Kenbert of Chad, Chad of Cutha, Cutha of Ceawlin, Ceawlin of Cynric, Cynric of Cerdic. Mull, who was afterwards consigned to the flames in Kent, was the brother of Ceadwall. The same year died Lothhere, King of Kent; and John was consecrated Bishop of Hexham, where he remained till Wilferth was restored, when John was translated to York on the death of Bishop Bosa. Wilferth his priest was afterwards consecrated Bishop of York, and John retired to his monastery[21] in the woods of Delta. This year there was in Britain a bloody rain, and milk and butter were turned to blood.

[A.D. 685. And in this same year Cuthbert was consecrated Bishop of Hexham by Archbishop Theodore at York, because Bishop Tumbert had been driven from the bishopric.]

A.D. 686. This year Ceadwall and his brother Mull spread devastation in Kent and the Isle of Wight. This same Ceadwall gave to St. Peter's minster, at Medhamsted, Hook; which is situated in an island called Egborough. Egbald at this time was abbot, who was the third after Saxulf; and Theodore was archbishop in Kent.

A.D. 687. This year was Mull consigned to the flames in Kent, and twelve other men with him; after which, in the same year, Ceadwall overran the kingdom of Kent.

A.D. 688. This year Ceadwall went to Rome, and received baptism at the hands of Sergius the pope, who gave him the name of Peter; but in the course of seven nights afterwards, on the twelfth day before the calends of May, he died in his crisom-cloths, and was buried in the church of St. Peter. To him succeeded Ina in the kingdom of Wessex, and reigned thirty-seven winters. He founded the monastery of Glastonbury; after which he went to Rome, and continued

---

21 *Beverley-minster, in Yorkshire.*

there to the end of his life. Ina was the son of Cenred, Cenred of Ceolwald; Ceolwald was the brother of Cynegils; and both were the sons of Cuthwin, who was the son of Ceawlin; Ceawlin was the son of Cynric, and Cynric of Cerdic.

[A.D. 688. This year King Caedwalla went to Rome, and received baptism of Pope Sergius, and he gave him the name of Peter, and in about seven days afterwards, on the twelfth before the kalends of May, while he was yet in his baptismal garments, he died: and he was buried in St. Peter's church. And Ina succeeded to the kingdom of the West-Saxons after him, and he reigned twenty-seven years.]

A.D. 690. This year Archbishop Theodore, who had been bishop twenty-two winters, departed this life,[22] and was buried within the city of Canterbury. Bertwald, who before this was abbot of Reculver, on the calends of July succeeded him in the see; which was ere this filled by Romish bishops, but henceforth with English. Then were there two kings in Kent, Wihtred and Webherd.

A.D. 693. This year was Bertwald consecrated archbishop by Godwin, bishop of the Gauls, on the fifth day before the nones of July; about which time died Gifmund, who was Bishop of Rochester; and Archbishop Bertwald consecrated Tobias in his stead. This year also Dryhtelm[23] retired from the world.

A.D. 694. This year the people of Kent covenanted with Ina, and gave him 30,000 pounds in friendship, because they had burned his brother Mull. Wihtred, who succeeded to the kingdom of Kent, and held it thirty-three winters, was the son of Egbert, Egbert of Erkenbert, Erkenbert of Eadbald, Eadbald of Ethelbert. And as soon as he was king, he ordained a great council to meet in the place that is called Bapchild;

---

22 *He was a native of Tarsus in Cilicia, the birth-place of St. Paul.*

23 *This brief notice of Dryhtelm, for so I find the name written in "Cotton Tiberius B iv." is totally unintelligible without a reference to Bede's "Ecclesiastical History", v. 12; where a curious account of him may be found, which is copied by Matthew of Westminster, anno. 699.*

in which presided Wihtred, King of Kent, the Archbishop of Canterbury, Brihtwald, and Bishop Tobias of Rochester; and with him were collected abbots and abbesses, and many wise men, all to consult about the advantage of God's churches that are in Kent. Now began the king to speak, and said, "I will that all the minsters and the churches, that were given and bequeathed to the worship of God in the days of believing kings, my predecessors, and in the days of my relations of King Ethelbert and of those that followed him—shall so remain to the worship of God, and stand fast for evermore. For I Wihtred, earthly king, urged on by the heavenly king, and with the spirit of righteousness annealed, have of our progenitors learned this, that no layman should have any right to possess himself of any church or of any of the things that belong to the church. And, therefore, strongly and truly, we set and decree, and in the name of Almighty God, and of all saints, we forbid all our succeeding kings, and aldermen, and all lawmen, ever, any lordship over churches, and over all their appurtenances, which I or my elders in old days have given for a perpetual inheritance to the glory of Christ and our Lady St. Mary, and the holy apostles. And look! when it happeneth, that bishop, or abbot, or abbess, depart from this life, be it told the archbishop, and with his counsel and injunction be chosen such as be worthy. And the life of him, that shall be chosen to so holy a thing, let the archbishop examine, and his cleanness; and in no wise be chosen any one, or to so holy a thing consecrated, without the archbishop's counsel. Kings shall appoint earls, and aldermen, sheriffs, and judges; but the archbishop shall consult and provide for God's flock: bishops, and abbots, and abbesses, and priests, and deacons, he shall choose and appoint; and also sanctify and confirm with good precepts and example, lest that any of God's flock go astray and perish—"

A.D. 697. This year the Southumbrians slew Ostritha, the queen of Ethelred, the sister of Everth.

A.D. 699. This year the Picts slew Alderman Burt.

A.D. 702. This year Kenred assumed the government of the Southumbrians.

A.D. 703. This year died Bishop Hedda, having held the see of Winchester twenty-seven winters.

A.D. 704. This year Ethelred, the son of Penda, King of Mercia, entered into a monastic life, having reigned twenty-nine winters; and Cenred succeeded to the government.

A.D. 705. This year died Ealdferth, king of the Northumbrians, on the nineteenth day before the calends of January, at Driffield; and was succeeded by his son Osred. Bishop Saxulf also died the same year.

A.D. 709. This year died Aldhelm, who was bishop by Westwood. The land of the West-Saxons was divided into two bishoprics in the first days of Bishop Daniel; who held one whilst Aldhelm held the other. Before this it was only one. Forthere succeeded to Aldhelm; and Ceolred succeeded to the kingdom of Mercia. And Cenred went to Rome; and Offa with him. And Cenred was there to the end of his life. The same year died Bishop Wilferth, at Oundle, but his body was carried to Ripon. He was the bishop whom King Everth compelled to go to Rome.

A.D. 710. This year Acca, priest of Wilferth, succeeded to the bishopric that Wilferth ere held; and Alderman Bertfrith fought with the Picts between Heugh and Carau. Ina also, and Nun his relative, fought with Grant, king of the Welsh; and the same year Hibbald was slain.

A.D. 714. This year died Guthlac the holy, and King Pepin.

A.D. 715. This year Ina and Ceolred fought at Wanborough; and King Dagobert departed this life.

A.D. 716. This year Osred, king of the Northumbrians, was slain

Folio 27r from the Lindisfarne Gospels which contains the incipit from the Gospel of Matthew.
This masterpiece of Anglo-Saxon art was created circa 715.

near the southern borders. He reigned eleven winters after Ealdferth. Cenred then succeeded to the government, and held it two years; then Osric, who held it eleven years. This same year died Ceolred, king of the Mercians. His body lies at Lichfield; but that of Ethelred, the son of Penda, at Bardney. Ethelbald then succeeded to the kingdom of Mercia, and held it one and forty winters. Ethelbald was the son of Alwy,

Alwy of Eawa, Eawa of Webba, whose genealogy is already written. The venerable Egbert about this time converted the monks of Iona to the right faith, in the regulation of Easter, and the ecclesiastical tonsure.

A.D. 718. This year died Ingild, the brother of Ina. Cwenburga and Cuthburga were their sisters. Cuthburga reared the monastery of Wimburn; and, though given in marriage to Ealdferth, King of Northumberland, they parted during their lives.

A.D. 721. This year Bishop Daniel went to Rome; and the same year Ina slew Cynewulf, the etheling. This year also died the holy Bishop John; who was bishop thirty-three years, and eight months, and thirteen days. His body now resteth at Beverley.

A.D. 722. This year Queen Ethelburga destroyed Taunton, which Ina had formerly built; Ealdbert wandered a wretched exile in Surrey and Sussex; and Ina fought with the South-Saxons.

A.D. 725. This year died Wihtred, King of Kent, on the ninth day before the calends of May, after a reign of thirty-two winters. His pedigree is above; and he was succeeded by Eadbert. Ina this year also fought with the South-Saxons, and slew Ealdbert, the etheling, whom he had before driven into exile.

A.D. 727. This year died Tobias, Bishop of Rochester: and Archbishop Bertwald consecrated Aldulf bishop in his stead.

A.D. 728. This year[24] Ina went to Rome, and there gave up the ghost. He was succeeded in the kingdom of Wessex by Ethelhard his relative, who held it fourteen years; but he fought this same year with Oswald the etheling. Oswald was the son of Ethelbald, Ethelbald of Cynebald, Cynebald of

---

24 *Wothnesbeorhge, Ethelw.; Wonsdike, Malmsb.; Wonebirih, H. Hunt; Wodnesbeorh, Flor.; Wodnesbirch, M. West. There is no reason, therefore, to transfer the scene of action to Woodbridge, as some have supposed from an erroneous reading.*

Cuthwin, Cuthwin of Ceawlin.

A.D. 729. This year appeared the comet-star, and St. Egbert died in Iona. This year also died the etheling Oswald; and Osric was slain, who was eleven winters king of Northumberland; to which kingdom Ceolwulf succeeded, and held it eight years. The said Ceolwulf was the son of Cutha, Cutha of Cuthwin, Cuthwin of Leodwald, Leodwald of Egwald, Egwald of Ealdhelm, Ealdhelm of Occa, Occa of Ida, Ida of Eoppa. Archbishop Bertwald died this year on the ides of January. He was bishop thirty-seven winters, and six months, and fourteen days. The same year Tatwine, who was before a priest at Bredon in Mercia, was consecrated archbishop by Daniel Bishop of Winchester, Ingwald Bishop of London, Aldwin Bishop of Lichfield, and Aldulf Bishop of Rochester, on the tenth day of June. He enjoyed the archbishopric about three years.

[A.D. 729. And the same year Osric died; he was king eleven years; then Ceolwulf succeeded to the kingdom, and held it eight years.]

A.D. 733. This year Ethelbald took Somerton; the sun was eclipsed; and Acca was driven from his bishopric.

A.D. 734. This year was the moon as if covered with blood; and Archbishop Tatwine and Bede departed this life; and Egbert was consecrated bishop.

A.D. 735. This year Bishop Egbert received the pall at Rome.[25]

A.D. 736. This year Archbishop Nothelm received the pall from the bishop of the Romans.

A.D. 737. This year Bishop Forthere and Queen Frithogitha went to Rome; and King Ceolwulf received the clerical tonsure, giving his kingdom to Edbert, his uncle's son: who reigned one and twenty winters. Bishop Ethelwold and Acca died

---

25 *The establishment of the "English school" at Rome is attributed to Ina; a full account of which, and of the origin of "Romescot" or "Peter-pence" for the support of it, may be seen in Matthew of Westminster. [NOT VERIFIED]*

this year, and Cynewulf was consecrated bishop. The same year also Ethelbald ravaged the land of the Northumbrians.

A.D. 738. This year Eadbery, the son of Eata the son of Leodwald, succeeded to the Northumbrian kingdom, and held it one and twenty winters. Archbishop Egbert, the son of Eata, was his brother. They both rest under one porch in the city of York.

A.D. 740. This year died King Ethelhard; and Cuthred, his relative, succeeded to the West-Saxon kingdom, which he held fourteen winters, during which time he fought many hard battles with Ethelbald, king of the Mercians. On the death of Archbishop Nothelm, Cuthbert was consecrated archbishop, and Dunn, Bishop of Rochester. This year York was on fire.

A.D. 742. This year there was a large synod assembled at Cliff's-Hoo; and there was Ethelbald, king of Mercia, with Archbishop Cuthbert, and many other wise men.

A.D. 743. This year Ethelbald, king of Mercia, and Cuthred, king of the West-Saxons, fought with the Welsh.

A.D. 744. This year Daniel resigned the see of Winchester; to which Hunferth was promoted. The stars went swiftly shooting; and Wilferth the younger, who had been thirty winters Bishop of York, died on the third day before the calends of May.

A.D. 745. This year died Daniel. Forty-three winters had then elapsed since he received the episcopal function.

A.D. 746. This year was King Selred slain.

A.D. 748. This year was slain Cynric, etheling of the West-Saxons; Edbert, King of Kent, died; and Ethelbert, son of King Wihtred, succeeded to the kingdom.

A.D. 750. This year Cuthred, king of the West-Saxons, fought with the proud chief Ethelhun.

A.D. 752. This year, the twelfth of his reign, Cuthred, king of the West-Saxons, fought at Burford[26] with Ethelbald, king of the Mercians, and put him to flight.

A.D. 753. This year Cuthred, king of the West-Saxons, fought against the Welsh.

A.D. 754. This year died Cuthred, king of the West-Saxons; and Sebright, his relative, succeeded to the kingdom, which he held one year; Cyneard succeeded Humferth in the see of Winchester; and Canterbury was this year on fire.

A.D. 755. This year Cynewulf, with the consent of the West-Saxon council, deprived Sebright, his relative, for unrighteous deeds, of his kingdom, except Hampshire; which he retained, until he slew the alderman who remained the longest with him. Then Cynewulf drove him to the forest of Andred, where he remained, until a swain stabbed him at Privett, and revenged the alderman, Cumbra. The same Cynewulf fought many hard battles with the Welsh; and, about one and thirty winters after he had the kingdom, he was desirous of expelling a prince called Cyneard, who was the brother of Sebright. But he having understood that the king was gone, thinly attended, on a visit to a lady at Merton,[27] rode after him, and beset him therein; surrounding the town without, ere the attendants of the king were aware of him. When the king found this, he went out of doors, and defended himself with courage; till, having looked on the etheling, he rushed out upon him, and wounded him severely. Then were they all fighting against the king, until they had slain him. As soon as the king's thanes in the lady's bower heard the tumult, they ran to the spot, whoever was then ready. The etheling immediately offered them life and rewards; which none of

---

26 *Beorgforda, Ethelw.; Beorhtforda, Flor.; Hereford and Bereford, H. Hunt; Beorford, M. West. This battle of Burford has been considerably amplified by Henry of Huntingdon, and after him by Matthew of Westminster. The former, among other absurdities, talks of "Amazonian" battle-axes. They both mention the banner of the "golden dragon" etc.*

27 *The minuteness of this narrative, combined with the simplicity of it, proves that it was written at no great distance of time from the event. It is the first that occurs of any length in the older MSS. of the "Saxon Chronicle".*

them would accept, but continued fighting together against him, till they all lay dead, except one British hostage, and he was severely wounded. When the king's thanes that were behind heard in the morning that the king was slain, they rode to the spot, Osric his alderman, and Wiverth his thane, and the men that he had left behind; and they met the etheling at the town, where the king lay slain. The gates, however, were locked against them, which they attempted to force; but he promised them their own choice of money and land, if they would grant him the kingdom; reminding them, that their relatives were already with him, who would never desert him. To which they answered, that no relative could be dearer to them than their lord, and that they would never follow his murderer. Then they besought their relatives to depart from him, safe and sound. They replied, that the same request was made to their comrades that were formerly with the king; "And we are as regardless of the result," they rejoined, "as our comrades who with the king were slain." Then they continued fighting at the gates, till they rushed in, and slew the etheling and all the men that were with him; except one, who was the godson of the alderman, and whose life he spared, though he was often wounded. This same Cynewulf reigned one and thirty winters. His body lies at Winchester, and that of the etheling at Axminster. Their paternal pedigree goeth in a direct line to Cerdic. The same year Ethelbald, king of the Mercians, was slain at Seckington; and his body lies at Repton. He reigned one and forty years; and Bernred then succeeded to the kingdom, which he held but a little while, and unprosperously; for King Offa the same year put him to flight, and assumed the government; which he held nine and thirty winters. His son Everth held it a hundred and forty days. Offa was the son of Thingferth, Thingferth of Enwulf, Enwulf of Osmod, Osmod of Eawa, Eawa of Webba, Webba of Creoda, Creoda of Cenwald, Cenwald of

Offa, King of Mercia

Cnebba, Cnebba of Icel, Icel of Eomer, Eomer of Angelthew, Angelthew of Offa, Offa of Wermund, Wermund of Witley, Witley of Woden.

[A.D. 755. This year Cynewulf deprived King Sigebert of his kingdom; and Sigebert's brother, Cynehard by name, slew Cynewulf at Merton; and he reigned thirty-one years. And in the same year Ethelbald, king of the Mercians, was slain at Repton. And Offa succeeded to the kingdom of the Mercians, Bernred being driven out.]

A.D. 757. This year Eadbert, king of the Northumbrians, received the tonsure, and his son Osulf the kingdom; which he held one year. Him his own domestics slew on the ninth day before the kalends of August.

A.D. 758. This year died Archbishop Cuthbert. He held the archbishopric eighteen years.

A.D. 759. This year Bregowin was invested archbishop at Michaelmas, and continued four years. Mull Ethelwold this year succeeded to the Northumbrian kingdom, held it six winters, and then resigned it.

A.D. 760. This year died Ethelbert, King of Kent, who was the son of King Wihtred, and also of Ceolwulf.

A.D. 761. This year was the severe winter; and Mull, king of the Northumbrians, slew Oswin at Edwin's-Cliff, on the eighth day before the ides of August.

A.D. 762. This year died Archbishop Bregowin.

A.D. 763. This year Eanbert was invested archbishop, on the fortieth day over mid-winter; and Frithwald, Bishop of Whitern, died on the nones of May. He was consecrated at York, on the eighteenth day before the calends of September, in the sixth year of the reign of Ceolwulf, and was bishop nine and twenty winters. Then was Petwin consecrated Bishop of Whitern at Adlingfleet, on the sixteenth day before the calends of August.

A.D. 764. This year Archbishop Eanbert received the pall.

A.D. 765. This year Alred succeeded to the kingdom of the Northumbrians, and reigned eight winters.

A.D. 766. This year died Archbishop Egbert at York, on the thirteenth day before the calends of December, who was bishop thirty-six winters; and Frithbert at Hexham, who was bishop there thirty-four winters. Ethelbert was consecrated to York, and Elmund to Hexham.

A.D. 768. This year died King Eadbert, the son of Eata, on the fourteenth day before the calends of September.

A.D. 772. This year died Bishop Mildred.

A.D. 774. This year the Northumbrians banished their king, Alred, from York at Easter-tide; and chose Ethelred, the son of Mull, for their lord, who reigned four winters. This year also appeared in the heavens a red crucifix, after sunset; the Mercians and the men of Kent fought at Otford; and wonderful serpents were seen in the land of the South-Saxons.

A.D. 775. This year Cynewulf and Offa fought near Bensington, and Offa took possession of the town. In the days of this king, Offa, there was an abbot at Medhamsted, called Beonna; who, with the consent of all the monks of the minster, let to farm, to Alderman Cuthbert, ten copyhold lands at Swineshead, with leasow and with meadow, and with all the appurtenances; provided that the said Cuthbert gave the said abbot fifty pounds therefore, and each year entertainment for one night, or thirty shillings in money;[28] provided also, that after his decease the said lands should revert to the monastery. The king, Offa, and King Everth, and Archbishop Hibbert, and Bishop Ceolwulf, and Bishop Inwona, and Abbot Beonna, and many other bishops, and abbots, and rich men, were witnesses to this. In the days of this same Offa was an alderman, of the name of Brorda, who requested the king for his sake to free his own monastery, called Woking, because he would give it to Medhamsted and St. Peter, and the abbot that then was, whose name was Pusa. Pusa succeeded Beonna; and the king loved him much. And the king freed the monastery of Woking, against king, against bishop, against earl, and against all men' so that no man should have any claim there, except St. Peter and the abbot. This was done at the king's town called Free-Richburn.

A.D. 776. This year died Bishop Petwin, on the thirteenth day before the calends of October, having been bishop fourteen winters. The same year Ethelbert was consecrated Bishop of Whitern, at York, on the seventeenth day before the calends of July.

A.D. 778. This year Ethelbald and Herbert slew three high-sheriffs—Eldulf, the son of Bosa, at Coniscliff; Cynewulf and Eggo at Helathyrn—on the eleventh day before the

28 *Penga in the original, i.e. "of pence", or "in pence"; because the silver penny, derived from the Roman "denarius", as the standard coin in this country for more than a thousand years. It was also used as a weight, being the twentieth part of an ounce.*

calends of April. Then Elwald, having banished Ethelred from his territory, seized on his kingdom, and reigned ten winters.

A.D. 780. This year a battle was fought between the Old-Saxons and the Franks; and the high-sheriffs of Northumbria committed to the flames Alderman Bern at Silton, on the ninth day before the calends of January. The same year Archbishop Ethelbert died at York, and Eanbald was consecrated in his stead; Bishop Cynewulf retired to Holy-island; Elmund, Bishop of Hexham, died on the seventh day before the ides of September, and Tilbert was consecrated in his stead, on the sixth day before the nones of October; Hibbald was consecrated Bishop of Holy-island at Sockbury; and King Elwald sent to Rome for a pall in behoof of Archbishop Eanbald.

A.D. 782. This year died Werburga, Queen of Ceolred, and Bishop Cynewulf, in Holy-island; and the same year there was a synod at Acley.

A.D. 784. This year Cyneard slew King Cynewulf, and was slain himself, and eighty-four men with him. Then Bertric undertook the government of the West-Saxons, and reigned sixteen years. His body is deposited at Wareham; and his pedigree goeth in a direct line to Cerdic. At this time reigned Elmund king in Kent, the father of Egbert; and Egbert was the father of Athulf.

A.D. 785. This year died Bothwin, Abbot of Ripon, and a litigious synod was holden at Chalk-hythe; Archbishop Eanbert resigned some part of his bishopric, Hibbert was appointed bishop by King Offa, and Everth was consecrated king. In the meantime legates were sent from Rome to England by Pope Adrian, to renew the blessings of faith and peace which St. Gregory sent us by the mission of Bishop Augustine, and they were received with every mark of honour and respect.

A.D. 787. This year King Bertric took Edburga the daughter of Offa to wife. And in his days came first three ships of the Northmen from the land of robbers. The reve[29] then rode thereto, and would drive them to the king's town; for he knew not what they were; and there was he slain. These were the first ships of the Danish men that sought the land of the English nation.

A.D. 788. This year there was a synod assembled at Fingall in Northumberland, on the fourth day before the nones of September; and Abbot Albert departed this life.

A.D. 789. This year Elwald, king of the Northumbrians, was slain by Siga, on the eleventh day before the calends of October; and a heavenly light was often seen on the spot where he was slain. He was buried in the church of Hexham; and Osred, the son of Alred, who was his nephew, succeeded him in the government. This year there was a synod assembled at Acley.

A.D. 790. This year Archbishop Eanbert died, and Abbot Ethelherd was chosen archbishop the same year. Osred, king of the Northumbrians, was betrayed and banished from his kingdom, and Ethelred, the son of Ethelwald, succeeded him.

A.D. 791. This year Baldulf was consecrated Bishop of Whitern, on the sixteenth day before the calends of August, by Archbishop Eanbald and Bishop Ethelbert.

A.D. 792. This year Offa, King of Mercia, commanded that King Ethelbert should be beheaded; and Osred, who had been king of the Northumbrians, returning home after his exile, was apprehended and slain, on the eighteenth day before the calends of October. His body is deposited at Tinemouth. Ethelred this year, on the third day before the calends of October, took unto himself a new wife, whose name was Elfleda.

A.D. 793. This year came dreadful fore-warnings over the land

---

29 *Since called "sheriff"; i.e. the reve, or steward, of the shire. "Exactor regis".—Ethelw.*

Saint Aiden of Lindisfarne. The monastery was attacked by the vikings in 793.

of the Northumbrians, terrifying the people most woefully: these were immense sheets of light rushing through the air, and whirlwinds, and fiery, dragons flying across the firmament. These tremendous tokens were soon followed by a great famine: and not long after, on the sixth day before the ides of January in the same year, the harrowing inroads of heathen men made lamentable havoc in the church of God in Holy-island, by rapine and slaughter. Siga died on the eighth day before the calends of March.

A.D. 794. This year died Pope Adrian; and also Offa, King of Mercia, on the fourth day before the ides of August, after he had reigned forty winters. Ethelred, king of the Northumbrians, was slain by his own people, on the thirteenth day before the calends of May; in consequence of which, Bishops Ceolwulf and Eadbald retired from the land. Everth took to the government of Mercia, and died the same year. Eadbert, whose other name was Pryn, obtained the kingdom of Kent; and Alderman Ethelherd died on the calends of August. In the meantime, the heathen armies spread devastation among the Northumbrians, and plundered the monastery of King Everth at the mouth of the Wear. There, however, some of their leaders were slain; and some of their ships also were shattered to pieces by the violence of the weather; many of the crew were drowned; and some, who escaped alive to the shore, were soon dispatched at the mouth of the river.

A.D. 795. This year was the moon eclipsed, between cock-crowing and dawn,[30] on the fifth day before the calends of April; and Erdulf succeeded to the Northumbrian kingdom on the second before the ides of May. He was afterwards consecrated and raised to his throne, at York, on the seventh day before the calends of June, by Archbishop Eanbald, and Bishops Ethelbert, Hibbald, and Baldulf.

A.D. 796. This year died Archbishop Eanbald, on the fourth day before the ides of August; and his body is deposited at York. The same year also died Bishop Ceolwulf; and another Eanbald was consecrated to the see of the former, on the nineteenth day before the calends of September. About the same time Cynewulf, King of Mercia, made inroads upon the inhabitants of Kent as far as the marsh; and the

---

30 *This is the Grecian method of computation; between the hours of three and six in the morning. It must be recollected, that before the distribution of time into hours, minutes, and seconds, the day and night were divided into eight equal portions, containing three hours each; and this method was continued long afterwards by historians.*

Mercians seized Edbert Pryn, their king, led him bound into Mercia, and suffered men to pick out his eyes, and cut off his hands.[31] And Ethelard, Archbishop of Canterbury, held a synod, wherein he ratified and confirmed, by command of Pope Leo, all things concerning God's monasteries that were fixed in Witgar's days, and in other king's days, saying thus: "I Ethelard, the humble Archbishop of Canterbury, with the unanimous concurrence of the whole synod, and of all the congregations of all the minsters, to which in former days freedom was given by faithful men, in God's name and by his terrible judgment do decree, as I have command from Pope Leo, that henceforth none dare to choose them lords from lewd men over God's inheritance; but, as it is in the writ that the pope has given, or holy men have settled, our fathers and our teachers, concerning holy minsters, so they continue untainted without any resistance. If there is any man that will not observe this decree of God, of our pope, and of us, but overlooketh it, and holdeth it for nought, let them know, that they shall give an account before the judgment-seat of God. And I Ethelard, archbishop, with twelve bishops, and with three and twenty abbots, this same with the rood-token of Christ confirm and fasten."

[A.D. 796. This year Offa, king of the Mercians, died on the fourth before the kalends of August; he reigned forty years.]

A.D. 797. This year the Romans cut out the tongue of Pope Leo, put out his eyes, and drove him from his see; but soon after, by the assistance of God, he could see and speak, and became pope as he was before. Eanbald also received the pall on the sixth day before the ides of September, and Bishop Ethelherd died on the third before the calends of November.

---

31 *This wanton act of barbarity seems to have existed only in the depraved imagination of the Norman interpolator of the "Saxon Annals", who eagerly and impatiently dispatches the story thus, in order to introduce the subsequent account of the synod at Bapchild, so important in his eyes. Hoveden and Wallingford and others have repeated the idle tale; but I have not hitherto found it in any historian of authority.*

A.D. 798. This year a severe battle was fought in the Northumbrian territory, during Lent, on the fourth day before the nones of April, at Whalley; wherein Alric, the son of Herbert, was slain, and many others with him.

A.D. 799. This year Archbishop Ethelbert, and Cynbert, Bishop of Wessex, went to Rome. In the meantime Bishop Alfun died at Sudbury, and was buried at Dunwich. After him Tidfrith was elected to the see; and Siric, king of the East Saxons, went to Rome. In this year the body of Witburga was found entire, and free from decay, at Dercham, after a lapse of five and fifty years from the period of her decease.

A.D. 800. This year was the moon eclipsed, at eight in the evening, on the seventeenth day before the calends of February; and soon after died King Bertric and Alderman Worr. Egbert succeeded to the West-Saxon kingdom; and the same day Ethelmund, alderman of the Wiccians, rode over the Thames at Kempsford; where he was met by Alderman Woxtan, with the men of Wiltshire, and a terrible conflict ensued, in which both the commanders were slain, but the men of Wiltshire obtained the victory.

[A.D. 801. This year Beornmod was ordained Bishop of Rochester.]

A.D. 802. This year was the moon eclipsed, at dawn, on the thirteenth day before the calends of January; and Bernmod was consecrated Bishop of Rochester.

A.D. 803. This year died Hibbald, Bishop of Holy-island, on the twenty-fourth of June, and Egbert was consecrated in his stead, on the thirteenth of June following. Archbishop Ethelherd also died in Kent, and Wulfred was chosen archbishop in his stead. Abbot Forthred, in the course of the same year, departed this life.

A.D. 804. This year Archbishop Wulfred received his pall.

A.D. 805. This year died King Cuthred in Kent, and Abbess

The Holy Roman Emperor Charlemagne, by Albrecht Dürer

Colburga, and Alderman Herbert.

A.D. 806. This year was the moon eclipsed, on the first of September; Erdwulf, king of the Northumbrians, was banished from his dominions; and Eanbert, Bishop of Hexham, departed this life. This year also, on the next day before the nones of June, a cross was seen in the moon, on a Wednesday, at the dawn; and afterwards, during the same year, on the third day before the calends of September, a wonderful circle was displayed about the sun.

A.D. 807. This year was the sun eclipsed, precisely at eleven in the morning, on the seventeenth day before the calends of August.

A.D. 812. This year died the Emperor Charlemagne, after a reign of five and forty winters; and Archbishop Wulfred, accompanied by Wigbert, Bishop of Wessex, undertook a journey to Rome.

A.D. 813. This year Archbishop Wulfred returned to his own see, with the blessing of Pope Leo; and King Egbert spread devastation in Cornwall from east to west.

A.D. 814. This year died Leo, the noble and holy pope; and Stephen succeeded him in the papal government.

A.D. 816. This year died Pope Stephen; and Paschalis was consecrated pope after him. This same year the school of the English nation at Rome was destroyed by fire.

A.D. 819. This year died Cenwulf, King of Mercia; and Ceolwulf[32] succeeded him. Alderman Eadbert also departed this life.

A.D. 821. This year Ceolwulf was deprived of his kingdom.

A.D. 822. This year two aldermen were slain, whose names were

---

32   St. Kenelm is said to have succeeded Cenwulf: "In the foure and twentithe yere of his kingdom Kenulf wente out of this worlde, and to the joye of hevene com; It was after that oure Lord in his moder alygte Eigte hondred yet and neygentene, by a countes rigte, Seint Kenelm his yonge sone in his sevende yere Kyng was ymad after him, theg he yong were." – "Vita S. Kenelmi, MS. Coll. Trin Oxon." No. 57. Arch.

Burhelm and Mucca; and a synod was holden at Cliff's-Hoo.

A.D. 823. This year a battle was fought between the Welsh in Cornwall and the people of Devonshire, at Camelford; and in the course of the same year Egbert, king of the West-Saxons, and Bernwulf, King of Mercia, fought a battle at Wilton, in which Egbert gained the victory, but there was great slaughter on both sides. Then sent he his son Ethelwulf into Kent, with a large detachment from the main body of the army, accompanied by his bishop, Elstan, and his alderman, Wulfherd; who drove Baldred, the king, northward over the Thames. Whereupon the men of Kent immediately submitted to him; as did also the inhabitants of Surrey, and Sussex, and Essex; who had been unlawfully kept from their allegiance by his relatives. The same year also, the king of the East-Angles, and his subjects besought King Egbert to give them peace and protection against the terror of the Mercians; whose king, Bernwulf, they slew in the course of the same year.

A.D. 825. This year Ludecan, King of Mercia, was slain, and his five aldermen with him; after which Wiglaf succeeded to the kingdom.

A.D. 827. This year was the moon eclipsed, on mid-winter's mass-night; and King Egbert, in the course of the same year, conquered the Mercian kingdom, and all that is south of the Humber, being the eighth king who was sovereign of all the British dominions. Ella, king of the South-Saxons, was the first who possessed so large a territory; the second was Ceawlin, king of the West-Saxons: the third was Ethelbert, King of Kent; the fourth was Redwald, king of the East-Angles; the fifth was Edwin, king of the Northumbrians; the sixth was Oswald, who succeeded him; the seventh was Oswy, the brother of Oswald; the eighth was Egbert, king of the West-Saxons. This same Egbert led an army against the Northumbrians as far as Dore, where they met him, and

both of the pirates and of the others. Soon after this, the same harvest, went King Edward with the West-Saxon army to Passham; and sat there the while that men fortified the town of Towcester with a stone wall. And there returned to him Earl Thurferth, and the captains, and all the army that belonged to Northampton northward to the Welland, and sought him for their lord and protector. When this division of the army went home, then went another out, and marched to the town of Huntingdon; and repaired and renewed it, where it was broken down before, by command of King Edward. And all the people of the country that were left submitted to King Edward, and sought his peace and protection. After this, the same year, before Martinmas, went King Edward with the West-Saxon army to Colchester; and repaired and renewed the town, where it was broken down before. And much people turned to him, both in East-Anglia and in Essex, that were before under the power of the Danes. And all the army in East-Anglia swore union with him; that they would all that he would, and would protect all that he protected, either by sea or land. And the army that belonged to Cambridge chose him separately for their lord and protector, and confirmed the same with oaths, as he had advised. This year King Edward repaired the town of Gladmouth; and the same year King Sihtric slew Neil his brother.

A.D. 922. This year, betwixt gang-days and midsummer, went King Edward with his army to Stamford, and ordered the town to be fortified on the south side of the river. And all the people that belonged to the northern town submitted to him, and sought him for their lord. It was whilst he was tarrying there, that Ethelfleda his sister died at Tamworth, twelve nights before midsummer. Then rode he to the borough of Tamworth; and all the population in Mercia turned to him, who before were subject to Ethelfleda. And the kings in North-Wales, Howel, and Cledauc, and Jothwel, and all the people of North-Wales, sought him for their lord. Then went he thence to Nottingham, and secured that borough, and ordered it to be repaired, and manned both with English and with Danes. And all the population turned to him, that was settled in Mercia, both Danish and English.

A.D. 923. This year went King Edward with an army, late in the harvest, to Thelwall; and ordered the borough to be repaired, and inhabited, and manned. And he ordered another army also from the population of Mercia, the while he sat there to go to Manchester in Northumbria, to repair and to man it. This year died Archbishop Plegmund; and King Reynold won York.

A.D. 924. This year, before midsummer, went King Edward with an army to Nottingham; and ordered the town to be repaired on the south side of the river, opposite the other, and the bridge over the Trent betwixt the two towns. Thence he went to Bakewell in Peakland; and ordered a fort to be built as near as possible to it, and manned. And the King of Scotland, with all his people, chose him as father and lord; as did Reynold, and the son of Eadulf, and all that dwell in Northumbria, both English and Danish, both Northmen and others; also the king of the Strathclydwallians, and all his people.

[A.D. 924. This year Edward was chosen for father and for lord by the king of the Scots, and by the Scots, and King Reginald, and by all the North-humbrians, and also the king of the Strath-clyde Britons, and by all the Strath-clyde Britons.]

[A.D. 924. This year King Edward died among the Mercians at Farndon; and very shortly, about sixteen days after this, Elward his son died at Oxford; and their bodies lie at Winchester. And Athelstan was chosen king by the Mercians, and consecrated at Kingston. And he gave his sister to Ofsae (Otho), son of the king of the Old-Saxons.]

A.D. 925. This year died King Edward at Farndon in Mercia; and Elward his son died very soon after this, in Oxford. Their bodies lie at Winchester. And Athelstan was chosen king in Mercia, and consecrated at Kingston. He gave his sister to Otho, son of the king of the Old-Saxons. St. Dunstan was now born; and Wulfhelm took to the archbishopric in Canterbury. This year King Athelstan and Sihtric king of the Northumbrians came together at Tamworth, the sixth day before the calends of February, and Athelstan gave away his sister to him.

[A.D. 925. This year Bishop Wulfhelm was consecrated. And that same year King Edward died.]

A.D. 926. This year appeared fiery lights in the northern part of the firmament; and Sihtric departed; and King Athelstan took to the kingdom of Northumbria, and governed all the kings that were in this island: — First, Howel, King of West-Wales; and Constantine, King of the Scots; and Owen, King of Monmouth; and Aldred, the son of Eadulf, of Bamburgh. And with covenants and oaths they ratified their agreement in the place called Emmet, on the fourth day before the ides of July; and renounced all idolatry, and afterwards returned in peace.

A.D. 927. This year King Athelstan expelled King Guthfrith; and Archbishop Wulfhelm went to Rome.

A.D. 928. William took to Normandy, and held it fifteen years.

[A.D. 931. This year died Frithstan, Bishop of Winchester, and Brinstan was blessed in his place.]

A.D. 932. This year Burnstan was invested Bishop of Winchester on the fourth day before the calends of June; and he held the bishopric two years and a half.

A.D. 933. This year died Bishop Frithestan; and Edwin the atheling was drowned in the sea.

A.D. 934. This year went King Athelstan into Scotland, both

with a land-force and a naval armament, and laid waste a great part of it; and Bishop Burnstan died at Winchester at the feast of All Saints.

A.D. 935. This year Bishop Elfheah took to the bishopric of Winchester.

[A.D. 937. This year King Athelstan and Edmund his brother led a force to Brumby, and there fought against Anlaf; and, Christ helping, had the victory: and they there slew five kings and seven earls.]

A.D. 938. Here Athelstan king, of earls the lord, rewarder of heroes, and his brother eke, Edmund atheling, elder of ancient race, slew in the fight, with the edge of their swords, the foe at Brumby! The sons of Edward their board-walls clove, and hewed their banners, with the wrecks of their hammers. So were they taught by kindred zeal, that they at camp oft 'gainst any robber their land should defend, their hoards and homes. Pursuing fell the Scottish clans; the men of the fleet in numbers fell; 'midst the din of the field the warrior swate. Since the sun was up in morning-tide, gigantic light! glad over grounds, God's candle bright, eternal Lord!— 'till the noble creature sat in the western main: there lay many of the Northern heroes under a shower of arrows, shot over shields; and Scotland's boast, a Scythian race, the mighty seed of Mars! With chosen troops, throughout the day, the West-Saxons fierce press'd on the loathed bands; hew'd down the fugitives, and scatter'd the rear, with strong mill-sharpen'd blades, The Mercians too the hard hand-play spared not to any of those that with Anlaf over the briny deep in the ship's bosom sought this land for the hardy fight. Five kings lay on the field of battle, in bloom of youth, pierced with swords. So seven eke of the earls of Anlaf; and of the ship's-crew unnumber'd crowds. There was dispersed the little band of hardy Scots, the dread of northern hordes; urged to the noisy deep by unrelenting fate! The king of the fleet with his slender craft escaped with his life on the felon flood;— and so too Constantine, the valiant chief, returned to the north in hasty flight. The hoary Hildrinc cared not to boast among his kindred. Here was his remnant of relations and friends slain with the sword in the crowded fight. His son too he left on the field of battle, mangled with wounds, young at the fight. The fair-hair'd youth had no reason to boast of the slaughtering strife. Nor old Inwood and Anlaf the more with the wrecks of their army could laugh and say, that they on the field of stern command better workmen were, in the conflict of banners, the clash of spears, the meeting of heroes, and the rustling of weapons, which they on the field of slaughter played with the sons of Edward. The northmen sail'd in their nailed ships, a dreary remnant, on the roaring sea; over deep water Dublin they sought, and Ireland's shores, in great disgrace. Such then the brothers both together king and atheling, sought their country, West-Saxon land, in right triumphant. They left behind them raw to devour, the sallow kite, the swarthy raven with horny nib, and the hoarse vultur, with the eagle swift to consume his prey; the greedy gos-hawk, and that grey beast the wolf of the weald. No slaughter yet was greater made e'er in this island, of people slain, before this same, with the edge of the sword; as the books inform us of the old historians; since hither came from the eastern shores the Angles and Saxons, over the broad sea, and Britain sought,— fierce battle-smiths, o'ercame the Welsh, most valiant earls, and gained the land.

A.D. 941. This year King Athelstan died in Glocester, on the sixth day before the calends of November, about forty-one winters, bating one night, from the time when King Alfred died. And Edmund Atheling took to the kingdom. He was then eighteen years old. King Athelstan reigned fourteen years and ten weeks. This year the Northumbrians abandoned their allegiance, and chose Anlaf of Ireland for their king.

A Victorian depiction of King Edmund

[A.D. 941. This year King Edmund received King Anlaf at baptism; and that same year, a good long space after, he received King Reginald at the bishop's hands.]

A.D. 942. Here Edmund king, of Angles lord, protector of friends, author and framer of direful deeds. o'erran with speed the Mercian land. whete'er the course of Whitwell-spring, or Humber deep, The broad brim-stream, divides five towns. Leicester and Lincoln. Nottingham and Stamford, and Derby eke. In thraldom long to Norman Danes they bowed through need, and dragged the chains of heathen men; till, to his glory, great Edward's heir, Edmund the king, refuge of warriors, their fetters broke.

A.D. 943. This year Anlaf stormed Tamworth; and much slaughter was made on either hand; but the Danes had the victory, and led away with them much plunder. There was Wulfrun taken, in the spoiling of the town. This year King Edmund beset King Anlaf and Archbishop Wulfstan in Leicester; and he might have conquered them, were it not that they burst out of the town in the night. After this Anlaf obtained the friendship of King Edmund, and King Edmund then received King Anlaf in baptism; and he made him royal presents. And the same year, after some interval, he received King Reynold at episcopal hands. This year also died King Anlaf.

A.D. 944. This year King Edmund reduced all the land of the Northumbrians to his dominion, and expelled two kings, Anlaf the son of Sihtric, and Reynold the son of Guthferth.

A.D. 945. This year King Edmund overran all Cumberland; and let it all to Malcolm king of the Scots, on the condition that he became his ally, both by sea and land.

A.D. 946. This year King Edmund died, on St. Augustine's mass day. That was widely known, how he ended his days: — that Leof stabbed him at Pucklechurch. And Ethelfleda of Damerham, daughter of Alderman Elgar, was then his queen. And he reigned six years and a half: and then succeeded to the kingdom Edred Atheling his brother, who soon after reduced all the land of the Northumbrians to his dominion; and the Scots gave him oaths, that they would do all that he desired.

A.D. 947. This year came King Edred to Tadden's-cliff; and there Archbishop Wulfstan and all the council of the Northumbrians bound themselves to an allegiance with the king. And within a little space they abandoned all, both allegiance and oaths.

A.D. 948. This year King Edred overran all Northumberland; because they had taken Eric for their king; and in the pursuit of plunder was that large minster at Rippon set on fire, which St. Wilferth built. As the king returned homeward, he overtook the enemy at York; but his main army was behind at Chesterford. There was great slaughter made; and the king was so wroth, that he would fain return with his force, and lay waste the land withal; but when the council of the

Northumbrians understood that, they then abandoned Eric, and compromised the deed with King Edred.

A.D. 949. This year came Anlaf Curran to the land of the Northumbrians.

A.D. 951. This year died Elfeah, Bishop of Winchester, on St. Gregory's mass day.

A.D. 952. This year the Northumbrians expelled King Anlaf, and received Eric the son of Harold. This year also King Edred ordered Archbishop Wulfstan to be brought into prison at Jedburgh; because he was oft bewrayed before the king: and the same year the king ordered a great slaughter to be made in the town of Thetford, in revenge of the abbot, whom they had formerly slain.

A.D. 954. This year the Northumbrians expelled Eric; and King Edred took to the government of the Northumbrians. This year also Archbishop Wulfstan received a bishopric again at Dorchester.

A.D. 955. This year died King Edred, on St. Clement's mass day, at Frome.[40] He reigned nine years and a half; and he rests in the old minster. Then succeeded Edwy, the son of King Edmund, to the government of the West-Saxons; and Edgar Atheling, his brother, succeeded to the government of the Mercians. They were the sons of King Edmund and of St. Elfgiva.

[A.D. 955. And Edwy succeeded to the kingdom of the West-Saxons, and Edgar his brother succeeded to the kingdom of the Mercians: and they were the sons of King Edmund and of S. Elfgiva.]

A.D. 956. This year died Wulfstan, Archbishop of York, on the seventeenth day before the calends of January; and he was buried at Oundle; and in the same year was Abbot Dunstan

---

40 So I understand the word. Gibson, from Wheloc, says—"in aetatis vigore;" a fact contradicted by the statement of almost every historian. Names of places seldom occur in old MSS. with capital initials.

driven out of this land over sea.

A.D. 958. This year Archbishop Oda separated King Edwy and Elfgiva; because they were too nearly related.

A.D. 959. This year died King Edwy, on the calends of October; and Edgar his brother took to the government of the West-Saxons, Mercians, and Northumbrians. He was then sixteen years old. It was in this year he sent after St. Dunstan, and gave him the bishopric of Worcester; and afterwards the bishopric of London. In his days it prosper'd well; and God him gave, that he dwelt in peace the while that he lived. Whate'er he did, whate'er he plan'd, he earn'd his thrift. He also rear'd God's glory wide, and God's law lov'd, with peace to man, above the kings that went before in man's remembrance. God so him sped, that kings and earls to all his claims submissive bow'd; and to his will without a blow he wielded all as pleased himself. Esteem'd he was both far and wide in distant lands; because he prized the name of God, and God's law traced, God's glory rear'd, both far and wide, on every side. Wisely he sought in council oft his people's good, before his God, before the world. One misdeed he did, too much however, that foreign tastes he loved too much; and heathen modes into this land he brought too fast; outlandish men hither enticed; and to this earth attracted crowds of vicious men. But God him grant, that his good deeds be weightier far than his misdeeds, to his soul's redemption on the judgment-day.

A.D. 961. This year departed Odo, the good archbishop, and St. Dunstan took to the archbishopric. This year also died Elfgar, a relative of the king, in Devonshire; and his body lies at Wilton: and King Sifferth killed himself; and his body lies at Wimborn. This year there was a very great pestilence; when the great fever was in London; and St. Paul's minster was consumed with fire, and in the same year was afterwards restored. In this year Athelmod. the masspriest, went to

Rome, and there died on the eighteenth before the calends of September.

A.D. 963. This year died Wulfstan, the deacon, on Childermass-day;[41] and afterwards died Gyric, the mass-priest. In the same year took Abbot Athelwold to the bishopric of Winchester; and he was consecrated on the vigil of St. Andrew, which happened on a Sunday. On the second year after he was consecrated, he made many minsters; and drove out the clerks[42] from the bishopric, because they would hold no rule, and set monks therein. He made there two abbacies; one of monks, another of nuns. That was all within Winchester. Then came he afterwards to King Edgar, and requested that he would give him all the minsters that heathen men had before destroyed; for that he would renew them. This the king cheerfully granted; and the bishop came then first to Ely, where St. Etheldritha lies, and ordered the minster to be repaired; which he gave to a monk of his, whose name was Britnoth, whom he consecrated abbot: and there he set monks to serve God, where formerly were nuns. He then bought many villages of the king, and made it very rich. Afterwards came Bishop Athelwold to the minster called Medhamsted, which was formerly ruined by heathen folk; but he found there nothing but old walls, and wild woods. In the old walls at length he found hid writings which Abbot Hedda had formerly written;—how King Wulfhere and Ethelred his brother had wrought it, and how they freed it against king and against bishop, and against all worldly service; and how Pope Agatho confirmed it with his writ, as also Archbishop Deusdedit. He then ordered the minster to be rebuilt; and set there an abbot, who was called Aldulf; and made monks, where before was nothing. He then came to the king, and let him look at the writings which before were found; and

41 i.e. the feast of the Holy Innocents; a festival of great antiquity.
42 i.e. the secular clergy, who observed no rule; opposed to the regulars, or monks.

the king then answered and said: "I Edgar grant and give to-day, before God and before Archbishop Dunstan, freedom to St. Peter's minster at Medhamsted, from king and from bishop; and all the thorps that thereto lie; that is, Eastfield, and Dodthorp, and Eye, and Paston. And so I free it, that no bishop have any jurisdiction there, but the abbot of the minster alone. And I give the town called Oundle, with all that thereto lieth, called Eyot-hundred, with market and toll; so freely, that neither king, nor bishop, nor earl, nor sheriff, have there any jurisdiction; nor any man but the abbot alone, and whom he may set thereto. And I give to Christ and St. Peter, and that too with the advice of Bishop Athelwold, these lands;—that is, Barrow, Warmington, Ashton, Kettering, Castor, Eylesworth, Walton, Witherington, Eye, Thorp, and a minster at Stamford. These lands and al the others that belong to the minster I bequeath clear; that is, with sack and sock, toll and team, and infangthief; these privileges and all others bequeath I clear to Christ and St. Peter. And I give the two parts of Whittlesey-mere, with waters and with wears and fens; and so through Meerlade along to the water that is called Nen; and so eastward to Kingsdelf. And I will that there be a market in the town itself, and that no other be betwixt Stamford and Huntingdon. And I will that thus be given the toll;—first, from Whittlesey-mere to the king's toll of Norman-cross hundred; then backward again from Whittlesey-mere through Meerlade along to the Nen, and as that river runs to Crowland; and from Crowland to Must, and from Must to Kingsdelf and to Whittlesey-mere. And I will that all the freedom, and all the privileges, that my predecessors gave, should remain; and I write and confirm this with the rood-token of Christ." (+)—Then answered Dunstan, the Archbishop of Canterbury, and said: "I grant, that all the things that here are given and spoken, and all the things that thy predecessors and mine have given, shall remain firm; and whosoever breaketh it, then give I him God's curse, and that of all saints, and of all hooded heads, and mine, unless he come to repentance. And I give expressly to St. Peter my mass-hackle, and my stole, and my reef, to serve Christ." "I Oswald, Archbishop of York, confirm all these words through the holy rood on which Christ was crucified." (+) "I Bishop Athelwold bless all that maintain this, and I excommunicate all that break it, unless they come to repentance."—Here was Bishop Ellstan, Bishop Athulf, and Abbot Eskwy, and Abbot Osgar, and Abbot Ethelgar, and Alderman Elfere; Alderman Ethelwin, Britnoth and Oslac aldermen, and many other rich men; and all confirmed it and subscribed it with the cross of Christ. (+) This was done in the year after our Lord's Nativity 972, the sixteenth year of this king. Then bought the Abbot Aldulf lands rich and many, and much endowed the minster withal; and was there until Oswald, Archbishop of York, was dead; and then he was chosen to be archbishop. Soon after another abbot was chosen of the same monastery, whose name was Kenulf, who was afterwards Bishop of Winchester. He first made the wall about the minster, and gave it then the name of Peterborough, which before was Medhamsted. He was there till he was appointed Bishop of Winchester, when another abbot was chosen of the same monastery, whose name was Elfsy, who continued abbot fifty winters afterwards. It was he who took up St. Kyneburga and St. Kyneswitha, that lay at Castor, and St. Tibba, that lay at Ryhall; and brought them to Peterborough, and offered them all to St. Peter in one day, and preserved them all the while he was there.

[A.D. 963. This year, by King Edgar, St. Ethelwold was chosen to the bishoprick at Winchester. And the Archbishop of Canterbury, St. Dunstan, consecrated him bishop on the first Sunday of Advent; that was on the third before the kalends of December.]

A.D. 964. This year drove King Edgar the priests of Winchester out of the old minster, and also out of the new minster; and from Chertsey; and from Milton; and replaced them with monks. And he appointed Ethelgar abbot to the new minster, and Ordbert to Chertsey, and Cyneward to Milton.

[A.D. 964. This year were the canons driven out of the Old-minster by King Edgar, and also from the New-minster, and from Chertsey and from Milton; and he appointed thereto monks and abbots: to the New-minster Ethelgar, to Chertsey Ordbert, to Milton Cyneward.]

A.D. 965. This year King Edgar took Elfrida for his queen, who was daughter of Alderman Ordgar.

A.D. 966. This year Thored, the son of Gunner, plundered Westmorland; and the same year Oslac took to the aldermanship.

A.D. 969. This year King Edgar ordered all Thanet-land to be plundered.

A.D. 970. This year died Archbishop Oskytel; who was first consecrated diocesan bishop at Dorchester, and afterwards it was by the consent of King Edred and all his council that he was consecrated Archbishop of York. He was bishop two and twenty winters; and he died on Alhallow-mas night, ten nights before Martinmas, at Thame. Abbot Thurkytel, his relative, carried the bishop's body to Bedford, because he was the abbot there at that time.

A.D. 971. This year died Edmund Atheling, and his body lies at Rumsey.

[A.D. 972. This year Edgar the etheling was consecrated king at Bath, on Pentecost's mass-day, on the fifth before the ides of May, the thirteenth year since he had obtained the kingdom; and he was then one less than thirty years of age. And soon after that, the king led all his ship-forces to Chester; and there came to meet him six kings, and they all plighted their

141

The Baptism of Christ from the Benedictional of Saint Æthelwold, 970s.

troth to him, that they would be his fellow-workers by sea and by land.]

A.D. 973. Here was Edgar, of Angles lord, with courtly pomp hallow'd to king at Akemancester, the ancient city; whose modern sons, dwelling therein, have named her BATH. Much bliss was there by all enjoyed on that happy day, named Pentecost by men below. A crowd of priests, a throng of monks, I understand, in counsel sage, were gather'd there.

Then were agone ten hundred winters of number'd years from the birth of Christ, the lofty king, guardian of light, save that thereto there yet was left of winter-tale, as writings say, seven and twenty. So near had run of the lord of triumphs a thousand years, when this was done. Nine and twenty hard winters there of irksome deeds had Edmund's son seen in the world, when this took place, and on the thirtieth was hallow'd king.[43] Soon after this the king led all his marine force to Chester; and there came to meet him six kings; and they all covenanted with him, that they would be his allies by sea and by land.

A.D. 975. Here ended his earthly dreams Edgar, of Angles king; chose him other light, serene and lovely, spurning this frail abode, a life that mortals here call lean he quitted with disdain. July the month, by all agreed in this our land, whoever were in chronic lore correctly taught; the day the eighth, when Edgar young, rewarder of heroes, his life—his throne—resigned. Edward his son, unwaxen child, of earls the prince, succeeded then to England's throne. Of royal race ten nights before departed hence Cyneward the good— prelate of manners mild. Well known to me in Mercia then, how low on earth God's glory fell on every side: chaced from the land, his servants fled,— their wisdom scorned; much grief to him whose bosom glow'd with fervent love of great Creation's Lord! Neglected then the God of wonders, victor of victors, monarch of heaven,— his laws by man transgressed! Then too was driv'n Oslac beloved an exile far from his native land over the rolling waves,— over the ganet-bath, over the water-throng, the abode of the whale,— fair-hair'd hero, wise and eloquent, of home bereft! Then too was seen, high in the heavens, the star on his station, that far

---

43 *This poetical effusion on the coronation, or rather consecration, of King Edgar, as well as the following on his death, appears to be imitated in Latin verse by Ethelwerd at the end of his curious chronicle. This seems at least to prove that they were both written very near the time, as also the eulogy on his reign, inserted 959.*

and wide wise men call— lovers of truth and heav'nly lore—
"cometa" by name. Widely was spread God's vengeance
then throughout the land, and famine scour'd the hills. May
heaven's guardian, the glory of angels, avert these ills, and
give us bliss again; that bliss to all abundance yields from
earth's choice fruits, throughout this happy isle.[44]

[A.D. 975. The eighth before the ides of July. Here Edgar died,
ruler of Angles, West-Saxons' joy, and Mercians' protector.
Known was it widely throughout many nations. "Thaet"
offspring of Edmund, o'er the ganet's-bath, honoured far,
Kings him widely bowed to the king, as was his due by kind.
No fleet was so daring, nor army so strong, that 'mid the
English nation took from him aught, the while that the noble
king ruled on his throne. And this year Edward, Edgar's
son, succeeded to the kingdom; and then soon, in the same
year, during harvest, appeared "cometa" the star; and then
came in the following year a very great famine, and very
manifold commotions among the English people. In his days,
for his youth, God's gainsayers God's law broke; Eldfere,
ealdorman, and others many; and rule monastic quashed, and
minsters dissolved, and monks drove out, and God's servants
put down, whom Edgar, king, ordered erewhile the holy
bishop Ethelwold to stablish; and widows they plundered,
many times and oft: and many unrighteousnesses, and evil
unjust-deeds arose up afterwards: and ever after that it greatly
grew in evil. And at that rime, also, was Oslac the great earl
banished from England.]

A.D. 976. This year was the great famine in England.

---

44 *The following passage from Cotton Tiberius B iv., relating to the accession of Edward the Martyr, should be added here—*

In his days, On account of his youth, The opponents of God Broke through God's laws; Alfhere alderman, And others many; And marr'd monastic rules; Minsters they razed, And monks drove away, And put God's laws to flight— Laws that King Edgar Commanded the holy Saint Ethelwold bishop Firmly to settle— Widows they stript Oft and at random. Many breaches of right And many bad laws Have arisen since; And after-times Prove only worse. Then too was Oslac The mighty earl Hunted from England's shores.

A.D. 977. This year was that great council at Kirtlington,[45] after Easter; and there died Bishop Sideman a sudden death, on the eleventh day before the calends of May. He was Bishop of Devonshire; and he wished that his resting-place should be at Crediton, his episcopal residence; but King Edward and Archbishop Dunstan ordered men to carry him to St. Mary's minster that is at Abingdon. And they did so; and he is moreover honourably buried on the north side in St. Paul's porch.

A.D. 978. This year all the oldest counsellors of England fell at Calne from an upper floor; but the holy Archbishop Dunstan stood alone upon a beam. Some were dreadfully bruised: and some did not escape with life. This year was King Edward slain, at eventide, at Corfe-gate, on the fifteenth day before the calends of April. And he was buried at Wareham without any royal honour. No worse deed than this was ever done by the English nation since they first sought the land of Britain. Men murdered him but God has magnified him. He was in life an earthly king—he is now after death a heavenly saint. Him would not his earthly relatives avenge—but his heavenly father has avenged him amply. The earthly homicides would wipe out his memory from the earth—but the avenger above has spread his memory abroad in heaven and in earth. Those, Who would not before bow to his living body, now bow on their knees to His dead bones. Now we may conclude, that the wisdom of men, and their meditations, and their counsels, are as nought against the appointment of God. In this same year succeeded Ethelred Etheling, his brother, to the government; and he was afterwards very readily, and with great joy to the counsellors of England, consecrated king at Kingston. In the same year also died Alfwold, who was Bishop of Dorsetshire, and whose body lieth in the minster at Sherborn.

A.D. 979. In this year was Ethelred consecrated king, on the

45   Florence of Worcester mentions three synods this year; Kyrtlinege, Calne, and Ambresbyrig.

Ethelred the Unready, from the Chronicle of Abindon

Sunday fortnight after Easter, at Kingston. And there were at his consecration two archbishops, and ten diocesan bishops. This same year was seen a bloody welkin oft-times in the likeness of fire; and that was most apparent at midnight, and so in misty beams was shown; but when it began to dawn, then it glided away.

[A.D. 979. This year was King Edward slain at even-tide, at Corfe-gate, on the fifteenth before the kalends of April, and then was he buried at Wareham, without any kind of kingly honours. There has not been 'mid Angles a worse deed done than this was, since they first Britain-land sought. Men him murdered, but God him glorified. He was in life an earthly king; he is now after death a heavenly saint. Him would not his earthly kinsmen avenge, but him hath his heavenly Father greatly avenged. The earthly murderers would his memory on earth blot out, but the lofty Avenger hath his memory in the heavens and on earth wide-spread. They who would not erewhile to his living body bow down, they now humbly on knees bend to his dead bones. Now we may understand that men's wisdom and their devices, and their councils, are like nought 'gainst God's resolves. This year Ethelred succeeded to the kingdom; and he was very quickly after that, with much joy of the English witan, consecrated king at Kingston.]

A.D. 980. In this year was Ethelgar consecrated bishop, on the sixth day before the nones of May, to the bishopric of Selsey; and in the same year was Southampton plundered by a pirate-army, and most of the population slain or imprisoned. And the same year was the Isle of Thanet overrun, and the county of Chester was plundered by the pirate-army of the North. In this year Alderman Alfere fetched the body of the holy King Edward at Wareham, and carried him with great solemnity to Shaftsbury.

A.D. 981. In this year was St. Petroc's-stow plundered; and in the same year was much harm done everywhere by the sea-coast, both upon Devonshire and Wales. And in the same year died Elfstan, Bishop of Wiltshire; and his body lieth in the minster at Abingdon; and Wulfgar then succeeded to the bishopric. The same year died Womare, Abbot of Ghent.

[A.D. 981. This year came first the seven ships, and ravaged Southampton.]

A.D. 982. In this year came up in Dorsetshire three ships of the pirates, and plundered in Portland. The same year London was burned. In the same year also died two aldermen, Ethelmer in Hampshire, and Edwin in Sussex. Ethelmer's body lieth in Winchester, at New-minster, and Edwin's in the minster at Abingdon. The same year died two abbesses in Dorsetshire; Herelufa at Shaftsbury, and Wulfwina at Wareham. The same year went Otho, emperor of the Romans, into Greece; and there met he a great army of the Saracens, who came up from the sea, and would have proceeded forthwith to plunder the Christian folk; but the emperor fought with them. And there was much slaughter made on either side, but the emperor gained the field of battle. He was there, however, much harassed, ere he returned thence; and as he went homeward, his brother's son died, who was also called Otho; and he was the son of Leodulf Atheling. This Leodulf was the son of Otho the Elder and of the daughter of King Edward.

A.D. 983. This year died Alderman Alfere, and Alfric succeeded to the same eldership; and Pope Benedict also died.

A.D. 984. This year died the benevolent Bishop of Winchester, Athelwold, father of monks; and the consecration of the following bishop, Elfheah, who by another name was called Godwin, was on the fourteenth day before the calends of November; and he took his seat on the episcopal bench on the mass-day of the two apostles Simon and Jude, at Winchester.

A.D. 985. This year was Alderman Alfric driven out of the land; and in the same year was Edwin consecrated abbot of the minster at Abingdon.

A.D. 986. This year the king invaded the bishopric of Rochester; and this year came first the great murrain of cattle in England.

A.D. 987. This year was the port of Watchet plundered.

A.D. 988. This year was Goda, the thane of Devonshire, slain; and a great number with him: and Dunstan, the holy archbishop, departed this life, and sought a heavenly one. Bishop Ethelgar succeeded him in the archbishopric; but he lived only a little while after, namely, one year and three months.

A.D. 989. This year died Abbot Edwin, and Abbot Wulfgar succeeded to the abbacy. Siric was this year invested archbishop, and went afterwards to Rome after his pall.

A.D. 991. This year was Ipswich plundered; and very soon afterwards was Alderman Britnoth[46] slain at Maidon. In this same year it was resolved that tribute should be given, for the first time, to the Danes, for the great terror they occasioned by the sea-coast. That was first 10,000 pounds. The first who advised this measure was Archbishop Siric.

A.D. 992. This year the blessed Archbishop Oswald departed this life, and sought a heavenly one; and in the same year died Alderman Ethelwin. Then the king and all his council resolved, that all the ships that were of any account should be gathered together at London; and the king committed the lead of the land-force to Alderman Elfric, and Earl Thorod, and Bishop Elfstan, and Bishop Escwy; that they should try if they could anywhere without entrap the enemy. Then sent Alderman Elfric, and gave warning to the enemy; and on the night preceding the day of battle he sculked away from the army, to his great disgrace. The enemy then escaped; except the crew of one ship, who were slain on the spot. Then met the enemy the ships from East-Anglia, and from London;

---

46 Vid. "Hist. Eliens." ii. 6. He was a great benefactor to the church of Ely.

and there a great slaughter was made, and they took the ship in which was the alderman, all armed and rigged. Then, after the death of Archbishop Oswald, succeeded Aldulf, Abbot of Peterborough, to the sees of York and of Worcester; and Kenulf to the abbacy of Peterborough.

[A.D. 992. This year Oswald the blessed archbishop died, and Abbot Eadulf succeeded to York and to Worcester. And this year the king and all his witan decreed that all the ships which were worth anything should be gathered together at London, in order that they might try if they could anywhere betrap the army from without. But Aelfric the ealdorman, one of those in whom the king had most confidence, directed the army to be warned; and in the night, as they should on the morrow have joined battle, the selfsame Aelfric fled from the forces; and then the army escaped.]

A.D. 993. This year came Anlaf with three and ninety ships to Staines, which he plundered without, and went thence to Sandwich. Thence to Ipswich, which he laid waste; and so to Maidon, where Alderman Britnoth came against him with his force, and fought with him; and there they slew the alderman, and gained the field of battle; whereupon peace was made with him, and the king received him afterwards at episcopal hands by the advice of Siric, Bishop of Canterbury, and Elfeah of Winchester. This year was Bamborough destroyed, and much spoil was there taken. Afterwards came the army to the mouth of the Humber; and there did much evil both in Lindsey and in Northumbria. Then was collected a great force; but when the armies were to engage, then the generals first commenced a flight; namely, Frene and Godwin and Frithgist. In this same year the king ordered Elfgar, son of Alderman Elfric, to be punished with blindness.

[A.D. 993. In this year came Olave with ninety-three ships to Staines, and ravaged there about, and then went thence to Sandwich, and so thence to Ipswich, and that all overran;

and so to Maldon. And there Britnoth the ealdorman came against them with his forces, and fought against them: and they there slew the ealdorman, and had possession of the place of carnage. And after that peace was made with them; and him (Anlaf) the king afterwards received at the bishop's hands, through the instruction of Siric, bishop of the Kentish-men, and of Aelphege of Winchester.]

A.D. 994. This year died Archbishop Siric: and Elfric, Bishop of Wiltshire, was chosen on Easter-day, at Amesbury, by King Ethelred and all his council. This year came Anlaf and Sweyne to London, on the Nativity of St. Mary, with four and ninety-ships. And they closely besieged the city, and would fain have set it on fire; but they sustained more harm and evil than they ever supposed that any citizens could inflict on them. The holy mother of God on that day in her mercy considered the citizens, and ridded them of their enemies. Thence they advanced, and wrought the greatest evil that ever any army could do, in burning and plundering and manslaughter, not only on the sea-coast in Essex, but in Kent and in Sussex and in Hampshire. Next they took horse, and rode as wide as they would, and committed unspeakable evil. Then resolved the king and his council to send to them, and offer them tribute and provision, on condition that they desisted from plunder. The terms they accepted; and the whole army came to Southampton, and there fixed their winter-quarters; where they were fed by all the subjects of the West-Saxon kingdom. And they gave them 16,000 pounds in money. Then sent the king; after King Anlaf Bishop Elfeah and Alderman Ethelwerd;[47] and, hostages being left with the ships, they led Anlaf with great pomp to the king at Andover. And King Ethelred received him at episcopal hands, and honoured him with royal presents. In return Anlaf promised,

---

47 *This was probably the veteran historian of that name, who was killed in the severe encounter with the Danes at Alton (Aethelingadene) in the year 1001.*

as he also performed, that he never again would come in a hostile manner to England.

A.D. 995. This year appeared the comet-star.

A.D. 996. This year was Elfric consecrated archbishop at Christ church.[48]

A.D. 997. This year went the army about Devonshire into Severn-mouth, and equally plundered the people of Cornwall, North-Wales,[49] and Devon. Then went they up at Watchet, and there much evil wrought in burning and manslaughter. Afterwards they coasted back about Penwithstert on the south side, and, turning into the mouth of the Tamer, went up till they came to Liddyford, burning and slaying everything that they met. Moreover, Ordulf's minster at Tavistock they burned to the ground, and brought to their ships incalculable plunder. This year Archbishop Elfric went to Rome after his staff.

A.D. 998. This year coasted the army back eastward into the mouth of the Frome, and went up everywhere, as widely as they would, into Dorsetshire. Often was an army collected against them; but, as soon as they were about to come together, then were they ever through something or other put to flight, and their enemies always in the end had the victory. Another time they lay in the Isle of Wight, and fed themselves meanwhile from Hampshire and Sussex.

A.D. 999. This year came the army about again into the Thames, and went up thence along the Medway to Rochester; where the Kentish army came against them, and encountered them in a close engagement; but, alas! they too soon yielded and fled; because they had not the aid that they should have had. The Danes therefore occupied the field of battle, and, taking horse, they rode as wide as they would, spoiling and

48 *i.e. at Canterbury. He was chosen or nominated before, by King Ethelred and his council, at Amesbury: vid. an. 994. This notice of his consecration, which is confirmed by Florence of Worcester, is now first admitted into the text on the authority of three MSS.*

49 *Not the present district so-called, but all that north of the Sea of Severn, as opposed to West-Wales, another name for Cornwall.*

overrunning nearly all West-Kent. Then the king with his council determined to proceed against them with sea and land forces; but as soon as the ships were ready, then arose delay from day to day, which harassed the miserable crew that lay on board; so that, always, the forwarder it should have been, the later it was, from one time to another;—they still suffered the army of their enemies to increase;—the Danes continually retreated from the sea-coast;—and they continually pursued them in vain. Thus in the end these expeditions both by sea and land served no other purpose but to vex the people, to waste their treasure, and to strengthen their enemies."

A.D. 1000. This year the king went into Cumberland, and nearly laid waste the whole of it with his army, whilst his navy sailed about Chester with the design of co-operating with his land-forces; but, finding it impracticable, they ravaged Anglesey. The hostile fleet was this summer turned towards the kingdom of Richard.

A.D. 1001. This year there was great commotion in England in consequence of an invasion by the Danes, who spread terror and devastation wheresoever they went, plundering and burning and desolating the country with such rapidity, that they advanced in one march as far as the town of Alton; where the people of Hampshire came against them, and fought with them. There was slain Ethelwerd, high-steward of the king, and Leofric of Whitchurch, and Leofwin, high-steward of the king, and Wulfhere, a bishop's thane, and Godwin of Worthy, son of Bishop Elfsy; and of all the men who were engaged with them eighty-one. Of the Danes there was slain a much greater number, though they remained in possession of the field of battle. Thence they proceeded westward, until they came into Devonshire; where Paley came to meet them with the ships which he was able to collect; for he had shaken off his allegiance to King Ethelred, against all the vows of truth

153

and fidelity which he had given him, as well as the presents which the king had bestowed on him in houses and gold and silver. And they burned Teignton, and also many other goodly towns that we cannot name; and then peace was there concluded with them. And they proceeded thence towards Exmouth, so that they marched at once till they came to Pin-hoo; where Cole, high-steward of the king, and Edsy, reve of the king, came against them with the army that they could collect. But they were there put to flight, and there were many slain, and the Danes had possession of the field of battle. And the next morning they burned the village of Pin-hoo, and of Clist, and also many goodly towns that we cannot name. Then they returned eastward again, till they came to the Isle of Wight. The next morning they burned the town of Waltham, and many other small towns; soon after which the people treated with them, and they made peace.

[A.D. 1001. This year the army came to Exmouth, and then went up to the town, and there continued fighting stoutly; but they were very strenuously resisted. Then went they through the land, and did all as was their wont; destroyed and burnt. Then was collected a vast force of the people of Devon and of the people of Somerset, and they then came together at Pen. And so soon as they joined battle, then the people gave way: and there they made great slaughter, and then they rode over the land, and their last incursion was ever worse than the one before: and then they brought much booty with them to their ships. And thence they went into the Isle of Wight, and there they roved about, even as they themselves would, and nothing withstood them: nor any fleet by sea durst meet them; nor land force either, went they ever so far up. Then was it in every wise a heavy time, because they never ceased from their evil doings.]

A.D. 1002. This year the king and his council agreed that tribute should be given to the fleet, and peace made with them, with

154

the provision that they should desist from their mischief. Then sent the king to the fleet Alderman Leofsy, who at the king's word and his council made peace with them, on condition that they received food and tribute; which they accepted, and a tribute was paid of 24,000 pounds. In the meantime Alderman Leofsy slew Eafy, high-steward of the king; and the king banished him from the land. Then, in the same Lent, came the Lady Elfgive Emma, Richard's daughter, to this land. And in the same summer died Archbishop Eadulf; and also, in the same year the king gave an order to slay all the Danes that were in England. This was accordingly done on the mass-day of St. Brice; because it was told the king, that they would beshrew him of his life, and afterwards all his council, and then have his kingdom without any resistance.

A.D. 1003. This year was Exeter demolished, through the French churl Hugh, whom the lady had appointed her steward there. And the army destroyed the town withal, and took there much spoil. In the same year came the army up into Wiltshire. Then was collected a very great force, from Wiltshire and from Hampshire; which was soon ready on their march against the enemy: and Alderman Elfric should have led them on; but he brought forth his old tricks, and as soon as they were so near, that either army looked on the other, then he pretended sickness, and began to retch, saying he was sick; and so betrayed the people that he should have led: as it is said, "When the leader is sick the whole army is hindered." When Sweyne saw that they were not ready, and that they all retreated, then led he his army into Wilton; and they plundered and burned the town. Then went he to Sarum; and thence back to the sea, where he knew his ships were.

A.D. 1004. This year came Sweyne with his fleet to Norwich, plundering and burning the whole town. Then Ulfkytel agreed with the council in East-Anglia, that it were better to purchase peace with the enemy, ere they did too much

A 15th century illuminated manuscript showing Archbishop Elfheah being asked for advice

harm on the land; for that they had come unawares, and he had not had time to gather his force. Then, under the truce that should have been between them, stole the army up from their ships, and bent their course to Thetford. When Ulfkytel understood that, then sent he an order to hew the ships in pieces; but they frustrated his design. Then he gathered his forces, as secretly as he could. The enemy came to Thetford within three weeks after they had plundered Norwich; and, remaining there one night, they spoiled and burned the town; but, in the morning, as they were proceeding to their ships, came Ulfkytel with his army, and said that they must there come to close quarters. And, accordingly, the two armies met together; and much slaughter was made on both sides. There were many of the veterans of the East-Angles slain; but, if the main army had been there, the enemy had never returned to their ships. As they said themselves, that they never met with worse hand-play in England than Ulfkytel brought them.

A.D. 1005. This year died Archbishop Elfric; and Bishop Elfeah succeeded him in the archbishopric. This year was the great famine in England so severe that no man ere remembered such. The fleet this year went from this land to Denmark, and took but a short respite, before they came again.

A.D. 1006. This year Elfeah was consecrated Archbishop; Bishop Britwald succeeded to the see of Wiltshire; Wulfgeat was deprived of all his property;[50] Wulfeah and Ufgeat were deprived of sight; Alderman Elfelm was slain; and Bishop Kenulf[51] departed this life. Then, over midsummer, came the Danish fleet to Sandwich, and did as they were wont; they barrowed and burned and slew as they went. Then the king ordered out all the population from Wessex and from Mercia; and they lay out all the harvest under arms against the enemy; but it availed nothing more than it had often done before. For all this the enemy went wheresoever they would; and the expedition did the people more harm than either any internal or external force could do. When winter approached, then went the army home; and the enemy retired after Martinmas to their quarters in the Isle of Wight, and provided themselves everywhere there with what they wanted. Then, about midwinter, they went to their ready farm, throughout Hampshire into Berkshire, to Reading. And they did according to their custom,—they lighted their camp-beacons as they advanced. Thence they marched to Wallingford, which they entirely destroyed, and passed one night at Cholsey. They then turned along Ashdown to Cuckamsley-hill, and there awaited better cheer; for it was often said, that if they sought Cuckamsley, they would never

<hr />

50 *See a more full and circumstantial account of these events, with some variation of names, in Florence of Worcester.*

51 *The successor of Elfeah, or Alphege, in the see of Winchester, on the translation of the latter to the archiepiscopal see of Canterbury.*

get to the sea. But they went another way homeward. Then was their army collected at Kennet; and they came to battle there, and soon put the English force to flight; and afterwards carried their spoil to the sea. There might the people of Winchester see the rank and iniquitous foe, as they passed by their gates to the sea, fetching their meat and plunder over an extent of fifty miles from sea. Then was the king gone over the Thames into Shropshire; and there he fixed his abode during midwinter. Meanwhile, so great was the fear of the enemy, that no man could think or devise how to drive them from the land, or hold this territory against them; for they had terribly marked each shire in Wessex with fire and devastation. Then the king began to consult seriously with his council, what they all thought most advisable for defending this land, ere it was utterly undone. Then advised the king and his council for the advantage of all the nation, though they were all loth to do it, that they needs must bribe the enemy with a tribute. The king then sent to the army, and ordered it to be made known to them, that his desire was, that there should be peace between them, and that tribute and provision should be given them. And they accepted the terms; and they were provisioned throughout England.

[A.D. 1006. This year Elphege was consecrated archbishop [of Canterbury].]

A.D. 1007. In this year was the tribute paid to the hostile army; that was, 30,000 pounds. In this year also was Edric appointed alderman over all the kingdom of the Mercians. This year went Bishop Elfeah to Rome after his pall.

A.D. 1008. This year bade the king that men should speedily build ships over all England; that is, a man possessed of three hundred and ten hides to provide on galley or skiff; and a man possessed of eight hides only, to find a helmet and breastplate[52].

52 *This passage, though very important, is rather confused, from the Variations in the MSS.; so that*

A.D. 1009. This year were the ships ready, that we before spoke about; and there were so many of them as never were in England before, in any king's days, as books tell us. And they were all transported together to Sandwich; that they should lie there, and defend this land against any out-force. But we have not yet had the prosperity and the honour, that the naval armament should be useful to this land, any more than it often before was. It was at this same time, or a little earlier, that Brihtric, brother of Alderman Edric, bewrayed Wulnoth, the South-Saxon knight, father of Earl Godwin, to the king; and he went into exile, and enticed the navy, till he had with him twenty ships; with which he plundered everywhere by the south coast, and wrought every kind of mischief. When it was told the navy that they might easily seize him, if they would look about them, then took Brihtric with him eighty ships; and thought that he should acquire for himself much reputation, by getting Wulnoth into his hands alive or dead. But, whilst they were proceeding thitherward, there came such a wind against them, as no man remembered before; which beat and tossed the ships, and drove them aground; whereupon Wulnoth soon came, and burned them. When this was known to the remaining ships, where the king was, how the others fared, it was then as if all were lost. The king went home, with the aldermen and the nobility; and thus lightly did they forsake the ships; whilst the men that were in them rowed them back to London. Thus lightly did they suffer the labour of all the people to be in vain; nor was the terror lessened, as all England hoped. When this naval expedition was thus ended, then came, soon after Lammas, the formidable army of the enemy, called Thurkill's army, to Sandwich; and soon they bent their march to Canterbury; which city they would quickly have stormed, had they not rather desired peace; and all the men of East-Kent made peace

---

it is difficult to ascertain the exact proportion of ships and armour which each person was to furnish.
"Vid. Flor." an. 1008.

with the army, and gave them 3,000 pounds for security. The army soon after that went about till they came to the Isle of Wight; and everywhere in Sussex, and in Hampshire, and also in Berkshire, they plundered and burned, as THEIR CUSTOM IS.[53] Then ordered the king to summon out all the population, that men might hold firm against them on every side; but nevertheless they marched as they pleased. On one occasion the king had begun his march before them, as they proceeded to their ships, and all the people were ready to fall upon them; but the plan was then frustrated through Alderman Edric, AS IT EVER IS STILL. Then after Martinmas they went back again to Kent, and chose their winter-quarters on the Thames; obtaining their provisions from Essex, and from the shires that were next, on both sides of the Thames. And oft they fought against the city of London; but glory be to God, that it yet standeth firm: and they ever there met with ill fare. Then after midwinter took they an excursion up through Chiltern,[54] and so to Oxford; which city they burned, and plundered on both sides of the Thames to their ships. Being fore-warned that there was an army gathered against them at London, they went over at Staines; and thus were they in motion all the winter, and in spring, appeared again in Kent, and repaired their ships.

A.D. 1010. This year came the aforesaid army, after Easter, into East Anglia; and went up at Ipswich, marching continually till they came where they understood Ulfcytel was with his army. This was on the day called the first of the Ascension of our Lord. The East-Angles soon fled. Cambridgeshire stood firm against them. There was slain Athelstan, the king's relative, and Oswy, and his son, and Wulfric, son of Leofwin, and Edwy, brother of Efy, and many other good

---

53 *These expressions in the present tense afford a strong proof that the original records of these transactions are nearly coeval with the transactions themselves. Later MSS. use the past tense.*

54 *i.e. the Chiltern Hills; from which the south-eastern part of Oxfordshire is called the Chiltern district.*

thanes, and a multitude of the people. Thurkytel Myrehead first began the flight; and the Danes remained masters of the field of slaughter. There were they horsed; and afterwards took possession of East-Anglia, where they plundered and burned three months; and then proceeded further into the wild fens, slaying both men and cattle, and burning throughout the fens. Thetford also they burned, and Cambridge; and afterwards went back southward into the Thames; and the horsemen rode towards the ships. Then went they west-ward into Oxfordshire, and thence to Buckinghamshire, and so along the Ouse till they came to Bedford, and so forth to Temsford, always burning as they went. Then returned they to their ships with their spoil, which they apportioned to the ships. When the king's army should have gone out to meet them as they went up, then went they home; and when they were in the east, then was the army detained in the west; and when they were in the south, then was the army in the north. Then all the privy council were summoned before the king, to consult how they might defend this country. But, whatever was advised, it stood not a month; and at length there was not a chief that would collect an army, but each fled as he could: no shire, moreover, would stand by another. Before the feast-day of St. Andrew came the enemy to Northampton, and soon burned the town, and took as much spoil thereabout as they would; and then returned over the Thames into Wessex, and so by Cannings-marsh, burning all the way. When they had gone as far as they would, then came they by midwinter to their ships.

A.D. 1011. This year sent the king and his council to the army, and desired peace; promising them both tribute and provisions, on condition that they ceased from plunder. They had now overrun East-Anglia [1], and Essex [2], and Middlesex [3], and Oxfordshire [4], and Cambridgeshire [5], and Hertfordshire [6], and Buckinghamshire [7], and Bedfordshire [8], and half of Huntingdonshire [9], and much of Northamptonshire [10]; and, to the south of the Thames, all Kent, and Sussex, and Hastings, and Surrey, and Berkshire, and Hampshire, and much of Wiltshire. All these disasters befel us through bad counsels; that they would not offer tribute in time, or fight with them; but, when they had done most mischief, then entered they into peace and amity with them. And not the less for all this peace, and amity, and tribute, they went everywhere in troops; plundering, and spoiling, and slaying our miserable people. In this year, between the Nativity of St. Mary and Michaelmas, they beset Canterbury, and entered therein through treachery; for Elfmar delivered the city to them, whose life Archbishop Elfeah formerly saved. And there they seized Archbishop Elfeah, and Elfward the king's steward, and Abbess Leofruna,[55] and Bishop Godwin; and Abbot Elfmar they suffered to go away. And they took therein all the men, and husbands, and wives; and it was impossible for any man to say how many they were; and in the city they continued afterwards as long as they would. And, when they had surveyed all the city, they then returned to their ships, and led the archbishop with them. Then was a captive he who before was of England head and Christendom;— there might be seen great wretchedness, where oft before great bliss was seen, in the fated city, whence first to us came Christendom, and bliss 'fore God and 'fore the world.And the archbishop they kept with them until the time when they martyred him.

A.D. 1012. This year came Alderman Edric, and all the oldest counsellors of England, clerk and laity, to London before Easter, which was then on the ides of April; and there they abode, over Easter, until all the tribute was paid, which was 48,000 pounds. Then on the Saturday was the army much

---

55 "*Leofruna abbatissa*".—*Flor. The insertion of this quotation from Florence of Worcester is important, as it confirms the reading adopted in the text. The abbreviation "abbt", instead of "abb", seems to mark the abbess. She was the last abbess of St. Mildred's in the Isle of Thanet; not Canterbury, as Harpsfield and Lambard say.*

A VIctorial depiction of King Sweyn and the Jomsvikings at the funeral ale of his father Harald Bluetooth. A funeral ale was a ritual drink and feast held a week after the person's death.

stirred against the bishop; because he would not promise them any fee, and forbade that any man should give anything for him. They were also much drunken; for there was wine brought them from the south. Then took they the bishop, and led him to their hustings, on the eve of the Sunday after Easter, which was the thirteenth before the calends of May; and there they then shamefully killed him. They overwhelmed him with bones and horns of oxen; and one of them smote him with an axe-iron on the head; so that he sunk downwards with the blow; and his holy blood fell on the earth, whilst his sacred soul was sent to the realm of God. The corpse in the morning was carried to London; and the bishops, Ednoth and Elfhun, and the citizens, received him with all honour, and buried him in St. Paul's minster; where God now showeth this holy martyr's miracles. When the tribute was paid, and the peace-oaths were sworn, then dispersed the army as widely as it was before collected. Then submitted to the king five and forty of the ships of the enemy; and promised him, that they would defend this land, and he should feed and clothe them.

A.D. 1013. The year after that Archbishop Elfeah was martyred, the king appointed Lifing to the archiepiscopal see of Canterbury. And in the same year, before the month August, came King Sweyne with his fleet to Sandwich; and very soon went about East-Anglia into the Humber-mouth, and so upward along the Trent, until he came to Gainsborough. Then soon submitted to him Earl Utred, and all the Northumbrians, and all the people of Lindsey, and afterwards the people of the Five Boroughs, and soon after all the army to the north of Watling-street; and hostages were given him from each shire. When he understood that all the people were subject to him, then ordered he that his army should have provision and horses; and he then went southward with his main army, committing his ships and the hostages to his son Knute. And after he came over Watling-street, they wrought the greatest mischief that any army could do. Then he went to Oxford; and the population soon submitted, and gave hostages; thence to Winchester, where they did the same. Thence went they eastward to London; and many of the party sunk in the Thames, because they kept not to any bridge. When he came to the city, the population would not submit; but held their ground in full fight against him, because therein was King Ethelred, and Thurkill with him. Then went King Sweyne thence to Wallingford; and so over Thames westward to Bath, where he abode with his army. Thither came Alderman Ethelmar, and all the western thanes with him, and all submitted to Sweyne, and gave hostages. When he had thus settled all, then went he northward to his ships; and all the population fully received him, and considered him full king. The population of London also after this submitted to him, and gave hostages; because they dreaded that he would undo them. Then bade Sweyne full tribute and forage for his army during the winter; and Thurkill bade the same for the army that lay at Greenwich: besides this, they plundered as oft as they would. And when this nation could neither resist in the south nor in the north, King Ethelred abode some while with the fleet that lay in the Thames; and the lady[56] went afterwards over sea to her brother Richard, accompanied by Elfsy, Abbot of Peterborough. The king sent Bishop Elfun with the ethelings, Edward and Alfred, over sea; that he might instruct them. Then went the king from the fleet, about midwinter, to the Isle of Wight; and there abode for the season; after which he went over sea to Richard, with whom he abode till the time when Sweyne died. Whilst the lady was with her brother beyond sea, Elfsy, Abbot of Peterborough, who was there with her, went to the abbey called Boneval, where St. Florentine's body lay; and there found a miserable place, a miserable abbot, and miserable monks: because they had been plundered. There he bought of the abbot, and of the monks, the body of St. Florentine, all but the head, for 500 pounds; which, on his return home, he offered to Christ and St. Peter.

A.D. 1014. This year King Sweyne ended his days at Candlemas, the third day before the nones of February; and the same year Elfwy, Bishop of York, was consecrated in London, on the festival of St. Juliana. The fleet all chose Knute for king; whereupon advised all the counsellors of England, clergy and laity, that they should send after King Ethelred; saying, that no sovereign was dearer to them than their natural lord, if he would govern them better than he did before. Then sent the king hither his son Edward, with his messengers; who had orders to greet all his people, saying that he would be their faithful lord—would better each of those things that they disliked—and that each of the things should be

---

56 *This was a title bestowed on the queen.*

forgiven which had been either done or said against him; provided they all unanimously, without treachery, turned to him. Then was full friendship established, in word and in deed and in compact, on either side. And every Danish king they proclaimed an outlaw for ever from England. Then came King Ethelred home, in Lent, to his own people; and he was gladly received by them all. Meanwhile, after the death of Sweyne, sat Knute with his army in Gainsborough until Easter; and it was agreed between him and the people of Lindsey, that they should supply him with horses, and afterwards go out all together and plunder. But King Ethelred with his full force came to Lindsey before they were ready; and they plundered and burned, and slew all the men that they could reach. Knute, the son of Sweyne, went out with his fleet (so were the wretched people deluded by him), and proceeded southward until he came to Sandwich. There he landed the hostages that were given to his father, and cut off their hands and ears and their noses. Besides all these evils, the king ordered a tribute to the army that lay at Greenwich, of 21,000 pounds. This year, on the eve of St. Michael's day, came the great sea-flood, which spread wide over this land, and ran so far up as it never did before, overwhelming many towns, and an innumerable multitude of people.

A.D. 1015. This year was the great council at Oxford; where Alderman Edric betrayed Sigferth and Morcar, the eldest thanes belonging to the Seven Towns. He allured them into his bower, where they were shamefully slain. Then the king took all their possessions, and ordered the widow of Sigferth to be secured, and brought within Malmsbury. After a little interval, Edmund Etheling went and seized her, against the king's will, and had her to wife. Then, before the Nativity of St. Mary, went the etheling west-north into the Five Towns,[57]

---

57 *The "seven" towns mentioned above are reduced here to "five"; probably because two had already submitted to the king on the death of the two thanes, Sigferth and Morcar. These five were, as originally, Leicester, Lincoln, Stamford, Nottingham, and Derby. Vid. an. 942, 1013.*

and soon plundered all the property of Sigferth and Morcar; and all the people submitted to him. At the same time came King Knute to Sandwich, and went soon all about Kent into Wessex, until he came to the mouth of the Frome; and then plundered in Dorset, and in Wiltshire, and in Somerset. King Ethelred, meanwhile, lay sick at Corsham; and Alderman Edric collected an army there, and Edmund the etheling in the north. When they came together, the alderman designed to betray Edmund the etheling, but he could not; whereupon they separated without an engagement, and sheered off from their enemies. Alderman Edric then seduced forty ships from the king, and submitted to Knute. The West-Saxons also submitted, and gave hostages, and horsed the army. And he continued there until midwinter.

A.D. 1016. This year came King Knute with a marine force of one hundred and sixty ships, and Alderman Edric with him, over the Thames into Mercia at Cricklade; whence they proceeded to Warwickshire, during the middle of the winter, and plundered therein, and burned, and slew all they met. Then began Edmund the etheling to gather an army, which, when it was collected, could avail him nothing, unless the king were there and they had the assistance of the citizens of London. The expedition therefore was frustrated, and each man betook himself home. After this, an army was again ordered, under full penalties, that every person, however distant, should go forth; and they sent to the king in London, and besought him to come to meet the army with the aid that he could collect. When they were all assembled, it succeeded nothing better than it often did before; and, when it was told the king, that those persons would betray him who ought to assist him, then forsook he the army, and returned again to London. Then rode Edmund the etheling to Earl Utred in Northumbria; and every man supposed that they would collect an army King Knute; but they went into Stafforddhire, and to Shrewsbury, and to Chester; and they plundered on their parts, and Knute on his. He went out through Buckinghamshire to Bedfordshire; thence to Huntingdonshire, and so into Northamptonshire along the fens to Stamford. Thence into Lincolnshire. Thence to Nottinghamshire; and so into Northumbria toward York. When Utred understood this, he ceased from plundering, and hastened northward, and submitted for need, and all the Northumbrians with him; but, though he gave hostages, he was nevertheless slain by the advice of Alderman Edric, and Thurkytel, the son of Nafan, with him. After this, King Knute appointed Eric earl over Northumbria, as Utred was; and then went southward another way, all by west, till the whole army came, before Easter, to the ships. Meantime Edmund Etheling went to London to his father: and after Easter went King Knute with all his ships toward London; but it happened that King Ethelred died ere the ships came. He ended his days on St. George's day; having held his kingdom in much tribulation and difficulty as long as his life continued. After his decease, all the peers that were in London, and the citizens, chose Edmund king; who bravely defended his kingdom while his time was. Then came the ships to Greenwich, about the gang-days, and within a short interval went to London; where they sunk a deep ditch on the south side, and dragged their ships to the west side of the bridge. Afterwards they trenched the city without, so that no man could go in or out, and often fought against it: but the citizens bravely withstood them. King Edmund had ere this gone out, and invaded the West-Saxons, who all submitted to him; and soon afterward he fought with the enemy at Pen near Gillingham. A second battle he fought, after midsummer, at Sherston; where much slaughter was made on either side, and the leaders themselves came together in the fight. Alderman Edric and Aylmer the darling were assisting the army against

King Edmund. Then collected he his force the third time, and went to London, all by north of the Thames, and so out through Clayhanger, and relieved the citizens, driving the enemy to their ships. It was within two nights after that the king went over at Brentford; where he fought with the enemy, and put them to flight: but there many of the English were drowned, from their own carelessness; who went before the main army with a design to plunder. After this the king went into Wessex, and collected his army; but the enemy soon returned to London, and beset the city without, and fought strongly against it both by water and land. But the almighty God delivered them. The enemy went afterward from London with their ships into the Orwell; where they went up and proceeded into Mercia, slaying and burning whatsoever they overtook, as their custom is; and, having provided themselves with meat, they drove their ships and their herds into the Medway. Then assembled King Edmund the fourth time all the English nation, and forded over the Thames at Brentford; whence he proceeded into Kent. The enemy fled before him with their horses into the Isle of Shepey; and the king slew as many of them as he could overtake. Alderman Edric then went to meet the king at Aylesford; than which no measure could be more ill-advised. The enemy, meanwhile, returned into Essex, and advanced into Mercia, destroying all that he overtook. When the king understood that the army was up, then collected he the fifth time all the English nation, and went behind them, and overtook them in Essex, on the down called Assingdon; where they fiercely came together. Then did Alderman Edric as he often did before—he first began the flight with the Maisevethians, and so betrayed his natural lord and all the people of England. There had Knute the victory, though all England fought against him! There was then slain Bishop Ednoth, and Abbot Wulsy, and Alderman Elfric, and Alderman Godwin of Lindsey, and

Ulfkytel of East-Anglia, and Ethelward, the son of Alderman Ethelsy.[58] And all the nobility of the English nation was there undone! After this fight went King Knute up with his army into Glocestershire, where he heard say that King Edmund was. Then advised Alderman Edric, and the counsellors that were there assembled, that the kings should make peace with each other, and produce hostages. Then both the kings met together at Olney, south of Deerhurst, and became allies and sworn brothers. There they confirmed their friendship both with pledges and with oaths, and settled the pay of the army. With this covenant they parted: King Edmund took to Wessex, and Knute to Mercia and the northern district. The army then went to their ships with the things they had taken; and the people of London made peace with them, and purchased their security, whereupon they brought their ships to London, and provided themselves winter-quarters therein. On the feast of St. Andrew died King Edmund; and he is buried with his grandfather Edgar at Gastonbury. In the same year died Wulfgar, Abbot of Abingdon; and Ethelsy took to the abbacy.

A.D. 1017. This year King Knute took to the whole government of England, and divided it into four parts: Wessex for himself, East-Anglia for Thurkyll, Mercia for Edric, Northumbria for Eric. This year also was Alderman Edric slain at London, and Norman, son of Alderman Leofwin, and Ethelward, son of Ethelmar the Great, and Britric, son of Elfege of Devonshire. King Knute also banished Edwy etheling, whom he afterwards ordered to be slain, and Edwy, king of the churls; and before the calends of August the king gave an order to fetch him the widow of the other king, Ethelred, the daughter of Richard, to wife.

---

58 *There is a marked difference respecting the name of this alderman in MSS. Some have Ethelsy, as above; others, Elfwine, and Ethelwine. The two last may be reconciled, as the name in either case would now be Elwin; but Ethelsy, and Elsy are widely different. Florence of Worcester not only supports the authority of Ethelwine, but explains it "Dei amici."*

[A.D. 1017. This year Canute was chosen king.]

A.D. 1018. This year was the payment of the tribute over all England; that was, altogether, two and seventy thousand pounds, besides that which the citizens of London paid; and that was ten thousand five hundred pounds. The army then went partly to Denmark; and forty ships were left with King Knute. The Danes and Angles were united at Oxford under Edgar's law; and this year died Abbot Ethelsy at Abingdon, to whom Ethelwine succeeded.

A.D. 1019. This year went King Knute with nine ships to Denmark, where he abode all the winter; and Archbishop Elfstan died this year, who was also named Lifing. He was a very upright man both before God and before the world.

[A.D. 1019. And this winter died Archbishop Elfstan [of Canterbury]: he was named Living; and he was a very provident man, both as to God and as to the world.]

A.D. 1020. This year came King Knute back to England; and there was at Easter a great council at Cirencester, where Alderman Ethelward was outlawed, and Edwy, king of the churls. This year went the king to Assingdon; with Earl Thurkyll, and Archbishop Wulfstan, and other bishops, and also abbots, and many monks with them; and he ordered to be built there a minster of stone and lime, for the souls of the men who were there slain, and gave it to his own priest, whose name was Stigand; and they consecrated the minster at Assingdon. And Ethelnoth the monk, who had been dean at Christ's church, was the same year on the ides of November consecrated Bishop of Christ's church by Archbishop Wulfstan.

[A.D. 1020. And caused to be built there [Canterbury] a minster of stone and lime, for the souls of the men who there were slain, and gave it to one of his priests, whose name was Stigand.]

A.D. 1021. This year King Knute, at Martinmas, outlawed Earl Thurkyll; and Bishop Elfgar, the abundant giver of alms, died in the morning of Christmas day.

A.D. 1022. This year went King Knute out with his ships to the Isle of Wight. And Bishop Ethelnoth went to Rome; where he was received with much honour by Benedict the magnificent pope, who with his own hand placed the pall upon him, and with great pomp consecrated him archbishop, and blessed him, on the nones of October. The archbishop on the self-same day with the same pall performed mass, as the pope directed him, after which he was magnificently entertained by the pope himself; and afterwards with a full blessing proceeded homewards. Abbot Leofwine, who had been unjustly expelled from Ely, was his companion; and he cleared himself of everything, which, as the pope informed him, had been laid to his charge, on the testimony of the archbishop and of all the company that were with him.

[A.D. 1022. And afterwards with the pall he there [at Rome] performed mass as the pope instructed him: and he feasted after that with the pope; and afterwards went home with a full blessing.]

A.D. 1023. This year returned King Knute to England; and Thurkyll and he were reconciled. He committed Denmark and his son to the care of Thurkyll, whilst he took Thurkyll's son with him to England. This year died Archbishop Wulfstan; and Elfric succeeded him; and Archbishop Egelnoth blessed him in Canterbury. This year King Knute in London, in St. Paul's minster, gave full leave[59] to Archbishop Ethelnoth, Bishop Britwine, and all God's servants that were with them, that they might take up from the grave the archbishop, Saint Elphege. And they did so, on the sixth day before the ides of June; and the illustrious king, and the archbishop, and the diocesan bishops, and the earls, and very many others,

59 *Matthew of Westminster says the king took up the body with his own hands.*

both clergy and laity, carried by ship his holy corpse over the Thames to Southwark. And there they committed the holy martyr to the archbishop and his companions; and they with worthy pomp and sprightly joy carried him to Rochester. There on the third day came the Lady Emma with her royal son Hardacnute; and they all with much majesty, and bliss, and songs of praise, carried the holy archbishop into Canterbury, and so brought him gloriously into the church, on the third day before the ides of June. Afterwards, on the eighth day, the seventeenth before the calends of July, Archbishop Ethelnoth, and Bishop Elfsy, and Bishop Britwine, and all they that were with them, lodged the holy corpse of Saint Elphege on the north side of the altar of Christ; to the praise of God, and to the glory of the holy archbishop, and to the everlasting salvation of all those who there his holy body daily seek with earnest heart and all humility. May God Almighty have mercy on all Christian men through the holy intercession of Elphege!

[A.D. 1023. And he caused St. Elphege's remains to be borne from London to Canterbury.]

A.D. 1025. This year went King Knute to Denmark with a fleet to the holm by the holy river; where against him came Ulf and Eglaf, with a very large force both by land and sea, from Sweden. There were very many men lost on the side of King Knute, both of Danish and English; and the Swedes had possession of the field of battle.

A.D. 1026. This year went Bishop Elfric to Rome, and received the pall of Pope John on the second day before the ides of November.

A.D. 1028. This year went King Knute from England to Norway with fifty ships manned with English thanes, and drove King Olave from the land, which he entirely secured to himself.

A.D. 1029. This year King Knute returned home to England.

Edmund Ironside fighting with King Knute

A.D. 1030. This year returned King Olave into Norway; but the people gathered together against him, and fought against him; and he was there slain, in Norway, by his own people, and was afterwards canonised. Before this, in the same year, died Hacon the doughty earl, at sea.

[A.D. 1030. This year came King Olave again into Norway, and the people gathered against him, and fought against him; and he was there slain.]

A.D. 1031. This year returned King Knute; and as soon as he came to England he gave to Christ's church in Canterbury the haven of Sandwich, and all the rights that arise therefrom, on either side of the haven; so that when the tide is highest and fullest, and there be a ship floating as near the land as possible, and there be a man standing upon the ship with a taper-axe in his hand, whithersoever the large taper-axe might be thrown out of the ship, throughout all that land the ministers of Christ's church should enjoy their rights. This year went King Knute to Rome; and the same year, as soon as he returned home, he went to Scotland; and Malcolm, king of the Scots, submitted to him, and became his man, with two other kings, Macbeth and Jehmar; but he held his allegiance a little while only. Robert, Earl of Normandy, went this year to Jerusalem, where he died; and William, who was afterwards

King of England, succeeded to the earldom, though he was a child.

A.D. 1032. This year appeared that wild fire, such as no man ever remembered before, which did great damage in many places. The same year died Elfsy, Bishop of Winchester; and Elfwin, the king's priest, succeeded him.

A.D. 1033. This year died Bishop Merewhite in Somersetshire, who is buried at Glastonbury; and Bishop Leofsy, whose body resteth at Worcester, and to whose see Brihteh was promoted.

A.D. 1034. This year died Bishop Etheric, who lies at Ramsey.

A.D. 1035. This year died King Knute at Shaftesbury, on the second day before the ides of November; and he is buried at Winchester in the old minster. He was king over all England very near twenty winters. Soon after his decease, there was a council of all the nobles at Oxford; wherein Earl Leofric, and almost all the thanes north of the Thames, and the naval men in London, chose Harold to be governor of all England, for himself and his brother Hardacnute, who was in Denmark. Earl Godwin, and all the eldest men in Wessex, withstood it as long as they could; but they could do nothing against it. It was then resolved that Elfgiva, the mother of Hardacnute, should remain at Winchester with the household of the king her son. They held all Wessex in hand, and Earl Godwin was their chief man. Some men said of Harold, that he was the son of King Knute and of Elfgive the daughter of Alderman Elfelm; but it was thought very incredible by many men. He was, nevertheless, full king over all England. Harold himself said that he was the son of Knute and of Elfgive the Hampshire lady; though it was not true; but he sent and ordered to be taken from her all the best treasure that she could not hold, which King Knute possessed; and she nevertheless abode there continually within the city as long

*Angels crown King Canute and his wife Emma of Normandy as they
present a large gold cross to Hyde Abbey*

as she could.

A.D. 1036. This year came hither Alfred the innocent etheling, son of King Ethelred, and wished to visit his mother, who abode at Winchester: but Earl Godwin, and other men who had much power in this land, did not suffer it; because such conduct was very agreeable to Harold, though it was unjust. Him did Godwin let, and in prison set. His friends, who did not fly, they slew promiscuously. And those they did not sell, like slaughter'd cattle fell! Whilst some they spared to bind, only to wander blind! Some ham-strung, helpless stood, whilst others they pursued. A deed more dreary none in this our land was done, since Englishmen gave place to hordes of Danish race. But repose we must in God our trust, that blithe as day with Christ live they, who guiltless died — their country's pride! The prince with courage met each cruel evil yet; till 'twas decreed, they should him lead, all bound, as he was then, to Ely-bury fen. But soon their royal prize bereft they of his eyes! Then to the monks they brought their captive; where he sought a refuge from his foes till life's sad evening close. His body ordered then these good and holy men, according to his worth, low in the sacred earth, to the steeple full-nigh, in the south aile to lie of the transept west — his soul with Christ doth rest.

[A.D. 1036. This year died King Canute at Shaftesbury, and he is buried at Winchester in the Old-minster: and he was king over all England very nigh twenty years. And soon after his decease there was a meeting of all the witan at Oxford; and Leofric, the earl, and almost all the thanes north of the Thames, and the "lithsmen" at London, chose Harold for chief of all England, him and his brother Hardecanute who was in Denmark. And Godwin the earl and all the chief men of Wessex withstood it as long as they could; but they were unable to effect anything in opposition to it. And then it was decreed that Elfgive, Hardecanute's mother, should dwell at

Winchester with the king's, her son's, household, and hold all Wessex in his power; and Godwin the earl was their man. Some men said of Harold that he was son of King Canute and of Elfgive, daughter of Elfelm the ealdorman, but it seemed quite incredible to many men; and he was nevertheless full king over all England.]

A.D. 1037. This year men chose Harold king over all; and forsook Hardacnute, because he was too long in Denmark; and then drove out his mother Elgiva, the relict of King Knute, without any pity, against the raging winter! She, who was the mother of Edward as well as of King Hardacnute, sought then the peace of Baldwin by the south sea. Then came she to Bruges, beyond sea; and Earl Baldwin well received her there; and he gave her a habitation at Bruges, and protected her, and entertained her there as long as she had need. Ere this in the same year died Eafy, the excellent Dean of Evesham.

[A.D. 1037. This year was driven out Elfgive, King Canute's relict; she was King Hardecanute's mother; and she then sought the protection of Baldwin south of the sea, and he gave her a dwelling in Bruges, and protected and kept her, the while that she there was.]

A.D. 1038. This year died Ethelnoth, the good archbishop, on the calends of November; and, within a little of this time, Bishop Ethelric in Sussex, who prayed to God that he would not let him live any time after his dear father Ethelnoth; and within seven nights of this he also departed. Then, before Christmas, died Bishop Brihteh in Worcestershire; and soon after this, Bishop Elfric in East Anglia. Then succeeded Bishop Edsy to the archbishopric, Grimkytel to the see of Sussex, and Bishop Lifing to that of Worcester shire and Gloucestershire.

[A.D. 1038. This year died Ethelnoth, the good archbishop, on the kalends of November, and a little after, Ethelric, bishop in Sussex, and then before Christmas, Briteagus, Bishop in Worcestershire, and soon after, Elfric, bishop in East-Anglia.]

A.D. 1039. This year happened the terrible wind; and Bishop Britmar died at Lichfield. The Welsh slew Edwin, brother of Earl Leofric, and Thurkil, and Elfget, and many good men with them. This year also came Hardacnute to Bruges, where his mother was.

[A.D. 1039. This year King Harold died at Oxford, on the sixteenth before the kalends of April, and he was buried at Westminster. And he ruled England four years and sixteen weeks; and in his days sixteen ships were retained in pay, at the rate of eight marks for each rower, in like manner as had been before done in the days of King Canute. And in this same year came King Hardecanute to Sandwich, seven days before midsummer. And he was soon acknowledged as well by English as by Danes; though his advisers afterwards grievously requited it, when they decreed that seventy-two ships should be retained in pay, at the rate of eight marks for each rower. And in this same year the sester of wheat went up to fifty-five pence, and even further.]

A.D. 1040. This year died King Harold at Oxford, on the sixteenth before the calends of April; and he was buried at Westminster. He governed England four years and sixteen weeks; and in his days tribute was paid to sixteen ships, at the rate of eight marks for each steersman, as was done before in King Knute's days. The same year they sent after Hardacnute to Bruges, supposing they did well; and he came hither to Sandwich with sixty ships, seven nights before midsummer. He was soon received both by the Angles and Danes, though his advisers afterwards severely paid for it. They ordered a tribute for sixty-two ships, at the rate of eight marks for each steersman. Then were alienated from him all that before desired him; for he framed nothing royal during his whole reign. He ordered the dead Harold to be dragged up and thrown into a ditch. This year rose the sester of wheat to fifty-five pence, and even further. This year Archbishop Edsy went to Rome.

[A.D. 1040. This year was the tribute paid; that twenty-one thousand pounds and ninety-nine pounds. And after that they paid to thirty-two ships, eleven thousand and forty-eight pounds. And, in this same year, came Edward, son of King Ethelred, hither to land, from Weal-land; he was brother of King Hardecanute: they were both sons of Elfgive; Emma, who was daughter of Earl Richard.]

A.D. 1041. This year was the tribute paid to the army; that was, 21,099 pounds; and afterwards to thirty-two ships, 11,048 pounds. This year also ordered Hardacnute to lay waste all Worcestershire, on account of the two servants of his household, who exacted the heavy tribute. That people slew them in the town within the minster. Early in this same year came Edward, the son of King Ethelred, hither to land, from Weal-land to Madron. He was the brother of King Hardacnute, and had been driven from this land for many years: but he was nevertheless sworn as king, and abode in his brother's court while he lived. They were both sons of Elfgive Emma, who was the daughter o[oe] Earl Richard. In this year also Hardacnute betrayed Eadulf, under the mask of friendship. He was also allied to him by marriage. This year was Egelric consecrated Bishop of York, on the third day before the ides of January.

[A.D. 1041. This year died King Hardecanute at Lambeth, on the sixth before the ides of June: and he was king over all England two years wanting ten days; and he is buried in the Old-minster at Winchester with King Canute his father. And his mother, for his soul, gave to the New-minster the head of St. Valentine the martyr. And before he was buried, all people chose Edward for king at London: may he hold it the while that God shall grant it to him! And all that year was a very heavy time, in many things and divers, as well in respect to ill seasons as to the fruits of the earth. And so much cattle perished in the year as no man before remembered, as well through various diseases as through tempests. And in this same time died Elsinus, Abbot of Peterborough; and then Arnwius the monk was chosen abbot, because he was a very good man, and of great simplicity.]

A.D. 1042. This year died King Hardacnute at Lambeth, as he stood drinking: he fell suddenly to the earth with a tremendous struggle; but those who were nigh at hand took him up; and he spoke not a word afterwards, but expired on the sixth day before the ides of June. He was king over all England two years wanting ten nights; and he is buried in the old minster at Winchester with King Knute his father. And his mother for his soul gave to the new minster the head of St. Valentine the Martyr: and ere he was buried all people chose Edward for king in London. And they received him as their king, as was natural; and he reigned as long as God granted him. All that year was the season very severe in many and various respects: both from the inclemency of the weather, and the loss of the fruits of the earth. More cattle died this year than any man ever remembered, either from various diseases, or from the severity of the weather. At this same time died Elfsinus, Abbot of Peterborough; and they chose Arnwy, a monk, for their abbot; because he was a very good and benevolent man.

A.D. 1043. This year was Edward consecrated king at Winchester, early on Easter-day, with much pomp. Then was Easter on the third day before the nones of April. Archbishop Edsy consecrated him, and before all people well admonished him. And Stigand the priest was consecrated bishop over the East Angles. And this year, fourteen nights before the mass of St. Andrew, it was advised the king, that he and Earl

Edward the Confessor as shown in the Bayeux Tapestry

Leofric and Earl Godwin and Earl Siward with their retinue, should ride from Gloucester to Winchester unawares upon the lady; and they deprived her of all the treasures that she had; which were immense; because she was formerly very hard upon the king her son, and did less for him than he wished before he was king, and also since: but they suffered her to remain there afterwards. And soon after this the king determined to invest all the land that his mother had in her hands, and took from her all that she had in gold and in silver and in numberless things; because she formerly held it too fast against him. Soon after this Stigand was deprived of his bishopric; and they took all that he had into their hands for the king, because he was nighest the counsel of his mother;

and she acted as he advised, as men supposed.

[A.D. 1043. This year was Edward consecrated king at Winchester on the first day of Easter. And this year, fourteen days before Andrew's-mass, the king was advised to ride from Gloucester, and Leofric the earl, and Godwin the earl, and Sigwarth [Siward] the earl, with their followers, to Winchester, unawares upon the lady [Emma]; and they bereaved her of all the treasures which she possessed, they were not to be told, because before that she had been very hard with the king her son; inasmuch as she had done less for him than he would, before he was king, and also since: and they suffered her after that to remain therein. This year King Edward took the daughter [Edgitha] of Godwin the earl for his wife. And in this same year died Bishop Brithwin, and he held the bishopric thirty-eight years, that was the bishopric of Sherborne, and Herman the king's priest succeeded to the bishopric. And in this year Wulfric was hallowed Abbot of St. Augustine's at Christmas, on Stephen's mass-day, by leave of the king, and, on account of his great infirmity, of Abbot Elfstun.]

A.D. 1044. This year Archbishop Edsy resigned his see from infirmity, and consecrated Siward, Abbot of Abingdon, bishop thereto, with the permission and advice of the king and Earl Godwin. It was known to few men else before it was done; because the archbishop feared that some other man would either beg or buy it, whom he might worse trust and oblige than him, if it were known to many men. This year there was very great hunger over all England, and corn so dear as no man remembered before; so that the sester of wheat rose to sixty pence, and even further. And this same year the king went out to Sandwich with thirty-five ships; and Athelstan, the churchwarden, succeeded to the abbacy of Abingdon, and Stigand returned to his bishopric. In the same year also King Edward took to wife Edgitha, the daughter of Earl Godwin, ten nights before Candlemas. And in the same year died Britwold, Bishop of Wiltshire, on the tenth day before the calends of May; which bishopric he held thirty-eight winters; that was, the bishopric of Sherborn. And Herman, the king's priest, succeeded to the bishopric. This year Wulfric was consecrated Abbot of St. Augustine's, at Christmas, on the mass-day of St. Stephen, by the king's leave and that of Abbot Elfstan, by reason of his great infirmity.

[A.D. 1044. This year died Living, Bishop in Devonshire, and Leoftic succeeded thereto; he was the king's priest. And in this same year died Elfstan, Abbot of St. Augustine's, on the third before the nones of July. And in this same year was outlawed Osgod Clapa.]

A.D. 1045. This year died Elfward, Bishop of London, on the eighth day before the calends of August. He was formerly Abbot of Evesham, and well furthered that monastery the while that he was there. He went then to Ramsey, and there resigned his life: and Mannie was chosen abbot, being consecrated on the fourth day before the ides of August. This year Gunnilda, a woman of rank, a relative of King Knute, was driven out, and resided afterwards at Bruges a long while, and then went to Denmark. King Edward during the year collected a large fleet at Sandwich, through the threatening of Magnus of Norway; but his contests with Sweyne in Denmark prevented him from coming hither.

[A.D. 1045. This year died Grimkytel, Bishop in Sussex, and Heca, the king's priest, succeeded thereto. And in this year died Alwyn, Bishop of Winchester, on the fourth before the kalends of September; and Stigand, bishop to the north [Flanders], succeeded thereto. And in the same year Sweyn the earl went out to Baldwin's land [Of Elmham] to Bruges and abode there all the winter; and then in summer he went out.]

A.D. 1046. This year died Lifting, the eloquent bishop, on the tenth day before the calends of April. He had three bishoprics; one in Devonshire, one in Cornwall, and another in Worcestershire. Then succeeded Leofric, who was the king's priest, to Devonshire and to Cornwall, and Bishop Aldred to Worcestershire. This year died Elfwine, Bishop of Winchester, on the fourth day before the calends of September; and Stigand, Bishop of Norfolk, was raised to his see. Ere this, in the same year, died Grimkytel, Bishop of Sussex; and he lies at Christ-church, in Canterbury. And Heca, the' king's priest, succeeded to the bishopric. Sweyne also sent hither, and requested the aid of fifty ships against Magnus, king of the Norwegians; but it was thought unwise by all the people, and it was prevented, because that Magnus had a large navy: and he drove Sweyne out, and with much slaughter won the land. The Danes then gave him much money, and received him as king. The same year Magnus died. The same year also Earl Sweyne went out to Baldwin's land, to Bruges; and remained there all the winter. In the summer he departed.

A.D. 1046. This year went Earl Sweyne into Wales; and Griffin, king of the northern men with him; and hostages were delivered to him. As he returned homeward, he ordered the Abbess of Leominster to be fetched him; and he had her as long as he list, after which he let her go home. In this same year was outlawed Osgod Clapa, the master of horse, before midwinter. And in the same year, after Candlemas, came the strong winter, with frost and with snow, and with all kinds of bad weather; so that there was no man then alive who could remember so severe a winter as this was, both through loss of men and through loss of cattle; yea, fowls and fishes through much cold and hunger perished.

[A.D. 1046. This year died Brithwin, bishop in Wiltshire, and Herman was appointed to his see. In that year King Edward gathered a large ship-force at Sandwich, on account of the threatening of Magnus in Norway: but his and Sweyn's contention in Denmark hindered his coming here. This year died Athelstan, Abbot of Abingdon, and Sparhawk, monk of St. Edmund's-bury, succeeded him. And in this same year died bishop Siward, and Archbishop Eadsine again obtained the whole bishopric. And in this same year Lothen and Irling came with twenty-five ships to Sandwich, and there took unspeakable booty, in men, and in gold, and in silver, so that no man knew how much it all was. And they then went about Thanet, and would there do the like; but the land's-folk strenuously withstood them, and denied them as well landing as water; and thence utterly put them to flight. And they betook themselves then into Essex, and there they ravaged, and took men, and property, and whatsoever they might find. And they betook themselves then east to Baldwine's land, and there they sold what they had plundered; and after that went their way east, whence they before had come. In this year was the great synod at St. Remi's [Rheins]. Thereat was Leo the pope, and the Archbishop of Burgundy [Lyons], and the Archbishop of Besancon, and the Archbishop of Treves, and the Archbishop of Rheims; and many men besides, both clergy and laity. And King Edward sent thither Bishop Dudoc [Of Wells], and Wulfric, Abbot of St. Augustine's, and Abbot Elfwin [Of Ramsey], that they might make known to the king what should be there resolved on for Christendom. And in this same year King Edward went out to Sandwich with a great fleet. And Sweyn the earl, son of Godwin the earl, came in to Bosham with seven ships; and he obtained the king's protection, and he was promised that he should be held worthy of everything which he before possessed. Then Harold the earl, his brother, and Beorn the earl contended that he should not be held worthy of any of the things which the king had granted to them: but a protection of four days was appointed him to go to his ships. Then befell it during this, that word came to the king that hostile ships lay westward, and were ravaging. Then went Godwin the earl west about with two of the king's ships; the one commanded Harold the earl, and the other Tosty his brother; and forty-two of the people's ships. Then Harold the earl was removed from the king's ship which Harold the earl before had commanded. Then went they west to Pevensey, and lay there weather-bound. Upon this, after two days, then came Sweyn the earl thither, and spoke with his father, and with Beorn the earl, and begged of Beorn that he would go with him to the king at Sandwich, and help him to the king's friendship: and he granted it. Then went they as if they would go to the king. Then whilst they were riding, then begged Sweyn of him that he would go with him to his ships: saying that his seamen would depart from him unless he should at the soonest come thither. Then went they both where his ships lay. When they came thither, then begged Sweyn the earl of him that he would go with him on ship-board. He strenuously refused, so long as until his seamen seized him, and threw him into the boat, and bound him, and rowed to the ship, and put him there aboard. Then they hoisted up their sails and ran west to Exmouth, and had him with them until they slew him: and they took the body and buried it in a church. And then his friends and litsmen came from London, and took him up, and bore him to Winchester to the Old-minster, and he is there buried with King Canute his uncle. And Sweyn went then east to Baldwin's land, and sat down there all the winter at Bruges, with his full protection. And in the same year died Eadnoth [II.] bishop [Of Dorchester] of the north and Ulf was made bishop.]

A.D. 1047. This year died Athelstan, Abbot of Abingdon, on the fourth day before the calends of April; and Sparhawk, monk of St. Edmundsbury, succeeded him. Easter day was then on the third day before the nones of April; and there was over all England very great loss of men this year also. The same year came to Sandwich Lothen and Irling, with twenty-five ships, and plundered and took incalculable spoil, in men, and in gold, and in silver, so that no man wist what it all was; and went then about Thanet, and would there have done the same; but the land-folk firmly withstood, and resisted them both by land and sea, and thence put them to flight withal. They betook themselves thence into Essex, where they plundered and took men, and whatsoever they could find, whence they departed eastward to Baldwin's land, and having deposited the booty they had gained, they returned east to the place whence they had come before.

[A.D. 1047. This year died Living the eloquent bishop, on the tenth before the kalends of April, and he had three bishoprics; one in Devonshire, and in Cornwall, and in Worcester. Then Leofric[60] succeeded to Devonshire and to Cornwall, and Bishop Aldred to Worcester. And in this year Osgod, the master of the horse, was outlawed: and Magnus [King of Norway] won Denmark. In this year there was a great council in London at mid-Lent, and nine ships of lightermen were discharged, and five remained behind. In this same year came Sweyn the earl into England. And in this same year was the great synod at Rome, and King Edward sent thither Bishop Heroman and Bishop Aldred; and they came thither on Easter eve. And afterwards the pope held a synod at Vercelli, and Bishop Ulf came thereto; and well nigh would they have broken his staff, if he had not given very great gifts; because he knew not how to do his duty so well as he should. And in this year died Archbishop Eadsine, on the fourth before the kalends of November.]

A.D. 1048. This year came Sweyne back to Denmark; and Harold, the uncle of Magnus, went to Norway on the death

---

60 *Leofric removed the see to Exeter.*

of Magnus, and the Northmen submitted to him. He sent an embassy of peace to this land, as did also Sweyne from Denmark, requesting of King Edward naval assistance to the amount at least of fifty ships; but all the people resisted it. This year also there was an earthquake, on the calends of May, in many places; at Worcester, at Wick, and at Derby, and elsewhere wide throughout England; with very great loss by disease of men and of cattle over all England; and the wild fire in Derbyshire and elsewhere did much harm. In the same year the enemy plundered Sandwich, and the Isle of Wight, and slew the best men that were there; and King Edward and the earls went out after them with their ships. The same year Bishop Siward resigned his bishopric from infirmity, and retired to Abingdon; upon which Archbishop Edsy resumed the bishopric; and he died within eight weeks of this, on the tenth day before the calends of November.

[A.D. 1048. This year was the severe winter: and this year died Alwyn, Bishop of Winchester, and Bishop Stigand was raised to his see. And before that, in the same year, died Grinketel, Bishop in Sussex, and Heca the priest succeeded to the bishopric. And Sweyn also sent hither, begging assistance against Magnus, King of Norway; that fifty ships should be sent to his aid. But it seemed unadvisable to all people: and it was then hindered by reason that Magnus had a great ship-force. And he then drove out Sweyn, and with much man-slaying won the land: and the Danes paid him much money and acknowledged him as king. And that same year Magnus died. In this year King Edward appointed Robert, of London, Archbishop of Canterbury, during Lent. And in the same Lent he went to Rome after his pall: and the king gave the bishopric of London to Sparhafoc, Abbot of Abingdon; and the king gave the abbacy of Abingdon to Bishop Rodulf, his kinsman. Then came the archbishop from Rome one day before St. Peter's mass-eve, and entered on his archiepiscopal see at Christ's Church on St. Peter's mass-day; and soon after went to the king. Then came Abbot Sparhafoc to him with the king's writ and seal, in order that he should consecrate him Bishop of London. Then the archbishop refused, and said that the pope had forbidden it him. Then went the abbot to the archbishop again for that purpose, and there desired episcopal ordination; and the archbishop constantly refused him, and said that the pope had forbidden it him. Then went the abbot to London, and occupied the bishopric which the king before had granted him, with his full leave, all the summer and the harvest. And then came Eustace [Earl of Boulogne] from beyond sea soon after the bishop, and went to the king, and spoke with him that which he then would, and went then homeward. When he came to Canterbury, east, then took he refreshment there, and his men, and went to Dover. When he was some mile or more, on this side of Dover, then he put on his breast-plate, and so did all his companions, and went to Dover. When they came thither, then would they lodge themselves where they chose. Then came one of his men, and would abide in the house of a householder against his will, and wounded the householder; and the householder slew the other. Then Eustace got upon his horse, and his companions upon theirs; and they went to the householder, and slew him within his own dwelling; and they went up towards the town, and slew, as well within as without, more than twenty men. And the townsmen slew nineteen men on the other side, and wounded they knew not how many. And Eustace escaped with a few men, and went again to the king, and made known to him, in part, how they had fared. And the king became very wroth with the townsmen. And the king sent off Godwin the earl, and bade him go into Kent in a hostile manner to Dover: for Eustace had made it appear to the king, that it had been more the fault of the townsmen than his: but it was not so. And the earl would not consent to the inroad, because he was loth to injure his own people. Then the king sent after all his council, and bade them come to Gloucester, nigh the aftermass of St. Mary. Then had the Welshmen erected a castle in Herefordshire among the people of Sweyn the earl, and wrought every kind of harm and disgrace to the king's men there about which they could. Then came Godwin the earl, and Sweyn the earl, and Harold the earl, together at Beverstone, and many men with them, in order that they might go to their royal lord, and to all the peers who were assembled with him, in order that they might have the advice of the king and his aid, and of all this council, how they might avenge the king's disgrace, and the whole nation's. Then were the Welshmen with the king beforehand, and accused the earls, so that they might not come within his eyes' sight; because they said that they were coming thither in order to betray the king. Thither had come Siward the earl [Of Northumbria] and Leofric the earl [Of Mercia], and much people with them, from the north, to the king; and it was made known to the Earl Godwin and his sons, that the king and the men who were with him, were taking counsel concerning them: and they arrayed themselves on the other hand resolutely, though it were loathful to them that they should stand against their royal lord. Then the peers on either side decreed that every kind of evil should cease: and the king gave the peace of God and his full friendship to either side. Then the king and his peers decreed that a council of all the nobles should be held for the second time in London at the harvest equinox; and the king directed the army to be called out, as well south of the Thames as north, all that was in any way most eminent. Then declared they Sweyn the earl an outlaw, and summoned Godwin the earl and Harold the earl, to the council, as quickly as they could effect it. When they had come thither, then were they summoned into the council. Then required he safe conduct and hostages, so that he might come, unbetrayed, into the council and out of the council. Then the king demanded all the thanes whom the earls before had: and they granted them all into his hands. Then the king sent again to them, and commanded them that they should come with twelve men to the king's council. Then the earl again required safe conduct and hostages, that he might defend himself against each of those things which were laid to him. Then were the hostages refused him; and he was allowed a safe conduct for five nights to go out of the land. And then Godwin the earl and Sweyn the earl went to Bosham, and shoved out their ships, and betook themselves beyond sea, and sought Baldwin's protection, and abode there all the winter. And Harold the earl went west to Ireland, and was there all the winter within the king's protection. And soon after this happened, then put away the king the lady who had been consecrated his queen [Editha], and caused to be taken from her all which she possessed, in land, and in gold, and in silver, and in all things, and delivered her to his sister at Wherwell. And Abbot Sparhafoc was then driven out of the bishopric of London, and William the king's priest was ordained thereto. And then Odda was appointed earl over Devonshire, and over Somerset, and over Dorset, and over the Welsh. And Algar, the son of Leofric the earl, was appointed to the earldom which Harold before held.]

A.D. 1049.[61] This year the emperor gathered an innumerable army against Baldwin of Bruges, because he had destroyed the palace of Nimeguen, and because of many other ungracious acts that he did against him. The army was immense that he had collected together. There was Leo, the Pope of Rome, and the patriarch, and many other great men of several provinces. He sent also to King Edward, and requested of him naval aid, that he might not permit him to escape from him by water. Whereupon he went to Sandwich, and lay

---

61 *i.e. The ships of Sweyne, who had retired thither, as before described.*

there with a large naval armament, until the emperor had all that he wished of Baldwin. Thither also came back again Earl Sweyne, who had gone from this land to Denmark, and there ruined his cause with the Danes. He came hither with a pretence, saying that he would again submit to the king, and be his man; and he requested Earl Beorn to be of assistance to him, and give him land to feed him on. But Harold, his brother, and Earl Beorn resisted, and would give him nothing of that which the king had given them. The king also refused him everything. Whereupon Swevne retired to his ships at Bosham. Then, after the settlement between the emperor and Baldwin, many ships went home, and the king remained behind Sandwich with a few ships. Earl Godwin also sailed forty-two ships from Sandwich to Pevensey, and Earl Beorn went with him. Then the king gave leave to all the Mercians to return home, and they did so. Then it was told the king that Osgod lay at Ulps with thirty-nine ships; whereupon the king sent after the ships that he might dispatch, which before had gone homewards, but still lay at the Nore. Then Osgod fetched his wife from Bruges; and they went back again with six ships; but the rest went towards Essex, to Eadulf's-ness, and there plundered, and then returned to their ships. But there came upon them a strong wind, so that they were all lost but four persons, who were afterwards slain beyond sea. Whilst Earl Godwin and Earl Beorn lay at Pevensey with their ships, came Earl Sweyne, and with a pretence requested of Earl Beorn, who was his uncle's son, that he would be his companion to the king at Sandwich, and better his condition with him; adding, that he would swear oaths to him, and be faithful to him. Whereupon Beorn concluded, that he would not for their relationship betray him. He therefore took three companions with him, and they rode to Bosham, where his[62] ships lay, as though they should proceed to Sandwich; but

62 *So Florence of Worcester, whose authority we here follow for the sake of perspicuity, though some of these events are placed in the MSS. to very different years; as the story of Beorn.*

they suddenly bound him, and led him to the ships, and went thence with him to Dartmouth, where they ordered him to be slain and buried deep. He was afterwards found, and Harold his cousin fetched him thence, and led him to Winchester, to the old minster, where he buried him with King Knute, his uncle. Then the king and all the army proclaimed Sweyne an outlaw. A little before this the men of Hastings and thereabout fought his two ships with their ships, and slew all the men, and brought the ships to Sandwich to the king. Eight ships had he, ere he betrayed Beorn; afterwards they all forsook him except two; whereupon he went eastward to the land of Baldwin, and sat there all the winter at Bruges, in full security. In the same year came up from Ireland thirty-six ships on the Welsh coast, and thereabout committed outrages, with the aid of Griffin, the Welsh king. The people were soon gathered against them, and there was also with them Bishop Eldred, but they had too little assistance, and the enemy came unawares on them very early in the morning, and slew on the spot many good men; but the others burst forth with the bishop. This was done on the fourth day before the calends of August. This year died the good Bishop Ednoth in Oxfordshire; and Oswy, Abbot of Thomey; and Wulfnoth, Abbot of Westminster; and King Edward gave the bishopric which Ednoth had to Ulf his priest, but it ill betided him; and he was driven from it, because he did nought like a bishop therein, so that it shameth us now to say more. Bishop Siward also died who lies at Abingdon. In this same year King Edward put nine ships out of pay; and the crews departed, and went away with the ships withal, leaving five ships only behind, for whom the king ordered twelve months pay. The same year went Bishops Hereman and Aldred to the pope at Rome on the king's errand. This year was also consecrated the great minster at Rheims, in the presence of Pope Leo and the emperor. There was also a great synod at St. Remy;[63] at which was present Pope Leo, with the Archbishops of Burgundy, of Besancon, of Treves, and of Rheims; and many wise men besides, both clergy and laity. A great synod there held they respecting the service of God, at the instance of St. Leo the pope. It is difficult to recognise all the bishops that came thither, and also abbots. King Edward sent thither Bishop Dudoc, and Abbot Wulfric, of St. Augustine's, and Elfwin, Abbot of Ramsey, with the intent that they should report to the king what was determined there concerning Christendom. This same year came Earl Sweyne into England.

[A.D. 1049. This year Sweyn came again to Denmark, and Harold. uncle of Magnus, went to Norway after Magnus was dead; and the Normans acknowledged him: and he sent hither to land concerning peace. And Sweyn also sent from Denmark, and begged of King Edward the aid of his ships. They were to be at least fifty ships: but all people opposed it. And this year also there was an earthquake, on the kalends of May, in many places in Worcester, and in Wick, and in Derby, and elsewhere; and also there was a great mortality among men, and murrain among cattle: and moreover, the wild-fire did much evil in Derbyshire and elsewhere.]

A.D. 1050. This year returned the bishops home from Rome;[64] and Earl Sweyne had his sentence of outlawry reversed. The same year died Edsy, Archbishop of Canterbury, on the fourth day before the calends of November; and also in the same year Elfric, Archbishop of York, on the eleventh before

63 "Vid. Flor." A.D. 1049, and verbatim from him in the same year, Sim. Dunelm. "inter X. Script. p. 184, I, 10. See also Ordericus Vitalis, A.D. 1050. This dedication of the church of St. Remi, a structure well worth the attention of the architectural antiquary, is still commemorated by an annual loire, or fair, on the first of October, at which the editor was present in the year 1815, and purchased at a stall a valuable and scarce history of Rheims, from which he extracts the following account of the synod mentioned above:—

"Il fut assemble a l'occasion de la dedicace de la nouvelle eglise qu' Herimar, abbe de ce monastere, avoit fait batir, seconde par les liberalites des citoyens, etc." ("Hist. de Reims", p. 226.) But, according to our Chronicle, the pope took occasion from this synod to make some general regulations which concerned all Christendom.

64 Hereman and Aldred, who went on a mission to the pope from King Edward, as stated in the preceding year.

the calends of February, a very venerable man and wise, and his body lies at Peterborough. Then had King Edward a meeting of the great council in London, in mid-lent, at which he appointed Robert the Frank, who was before Bishop of London, Archbishop of Canterbury; and he, during the same Lent, went to Rome after his pall. The king meanwhile gave the see of London to Sparhawk, Abbot of Abingdon, but it was taken from him again before he was consecrated. The king also gave the abbacy of Abingdon to Bishop Rodulph his cousin. The same year he put all the lightermen out of pay.[65] The pope held a council again, at Vercelli; and Bishop Ulf came thither, where he nearly had his staff broken, had he not paid more money, because he could not perform his duties so well as he should do. The same year King Edward abolished the Danegeld which King Ethelred imposed. That was in the thirty-ninth year after it had begun. That tribute harassed all the people of England so long as is above written; and it was always paid before other imposts, which were levied indiscriminately, and vexed men variously.

[A.D. 1050. Thither also came Sweyn the earl, who before had gone from this land to Denmark, and who there had ruined himself with the Danes. He came thither with false pretences; saying that he would again be obedient to the king. And Beorn the earl promised him that he would be of assistance to him. Then, after the reconciliation of the emperor and of Baldwin, many of the ships went home, and the king remained behind at Sandwich with a few ships; and Godwin the earl also went with forty-two ships from Sandwich to Pevensey, and Beorn the earl went with him. Then was it made known to the king that Osgood lay at Ulps with thirty-nine ships; and the king then sent after the ships which before had gone home, that he might send after him. And Osgod fetched his wife from

---

65 *Nine ships were put out of commission the year before; but five being left on the pay-list for a twelvemonth, they were also now laid up.*

Bruges, and they went back again with six ships. And the others landed in Sussex [Essex] at Eadulf-ness, and there did harm, and went again to their ships: and then a strong wind came against them, so that they were all destroyed, except four, whose crews were slain beyond sea. While Godwin the earl and Beorn the earl lay at Pevensey, then came Sweyn the earl, and begged Beorn the earl, with fraud, who was his uncle's son, that he would be his companion to the king at Sandwich, and better his affairs with him. He went then, on account of the relationship, with three companions, with him; and he led him then towards Bosham, where his ships lay: and then they bound him, and led him on ship-board. Then went he thence with him to Dartmouth, and there ordered him to be slain, and deeply buried. Afterwards he was found, and borne to Winchester, and buried with king Canute his uncle. A little before that, the men of Hastings and thereabout, fought two of his ships with their ships; and slew all the men, and brought the ships to Sandwich to the king. Eight ships he had before he betrayed Beorn; after that all forsook him except two. In the same year arrived in the Welsh Axa, from Ireland, thirty-six ships, and thereabout did harm, with the help of Griffin the Welsh king. The people were gathered together against them; Bishop Aldred [Of Worchester] was also there with them; but they had too little power. And they came unawares upon them at very early morn; and there they slew many good men, and the others escaped with the bishop: this was done on the fourth before the kalends of August. This year died, in Oxfordshire, Oswy, Abbot of Thorney, and Wulfnoth, Abbot of Westminster; and Ulf the priest was appointed as pastor to the bishopric which Eadnoth had held; but he was after that driven away; because he did nothing bishop-like therein: so that it shameth us now to tell more about it. And Bishop Siward died: he lieth at Abingdon. And this year was consecrated the great minster at Rheims: there was Pope Leo [IX.] and the emperor [Henry III]; and there they held a great synod concerning God's service. St. Leo the pope presided at the synod: it is difficult to have a knowledge of the bishops who came there, and how many abbots: and hence, from this land were sent two—from St. Augustine's and from Ramsey.]

A.D. 1051. This year came Archbishop Robert hither over sea with his pall from Rome, one day before St. Peter's eve: and he took his archiepiscopal seat at Christ-church on St. Peter's day, and soon after this went to the king. Then came Abbot Sparhawk to him with the king's writ and seal, to the intent that he should consecrate him Bishop o[oe] London; but the archbishop refused, saying that the pope had forbidden him. Then went the abbot to the archbishop again for the same purpose, and there demanded episcopal consecration; but the archbishop obstinately refused, repeating that the pope had forbidden him. Then went the abbot to London, and sat at the bishopric which the king had before given him, with his full leave, all the summer and the autumn. Then during the same year came Eustace, who had the sister of King Edward to wife, from beyond sea, soon after the bishop, and went to the king; and having spoken with him whatever he chose, he then went homeward. When he came to Canterbury eastward, there took he a repast, and his men; whence he proceeded to Dover. When he was about a mile or more on this side Dover, he put on his breast-plate; and so did all his companions: and they proceeded to Dover. When they came thither, they resolved to quarter themselves wherever they lived. Then came one of his men, and would lodge at the house of a master of a family against his will; but having wounded the master of the house, he was slain by the other. Then was Eustace quickly upon his horse, and his companions upon theirs; and having gone to the master of the family, they slew him on his own hearth; then going up to the boroughward, they slew both within and without more than twenty men. The townsmen slew nineteen men on the other side, and wounded more, but they knew not how many. Eustace escaped with a few men, and went again to the king, telling him partially how they had fared. The king was very wroth with the townsmen, and sent off Earl Godwin, bidding him go into Kent with hostility to Dover. For Eustace had told the king that the guilt of the townsmen was greater than his. But it was not so: and the earl would not consent to the expedition, because he was loth to destroy his own people. Then sent the king after all his council, and bade them come to Gloucester nigh the after-mass of St. Mary. Meanwhile Godwin took it much to heart, that in his earldom such a thing should happen. Whereupon be began to gather forces over all his earldom, and Earl Sweyne, his son, over his; and Harold, his other son, over his earldom: and they assembled all in Gloucestershire, at Langtree, a large and innumerable army, all ready for battle against the king; unless Eustace and his men were delivered to them handcuffed, and also the Frenchmen that were in the castle. This was done seven nights before the latter mass of St. Mary, when King Edward was sitting at Gloucester. Whereupon he sent after Earl Leofric, and north after Earl Siward, and summoned their retinues. At first they came to him with moderate aid; but when they found how it was in the south, then sent they north over all their earldom, and ordered a large force to the help of their lord. So did Ralph also over his earldom. Then came they all to Gloucester to the aid of the king, though it was late. So unanimous were they all in defence of the king, that they would seek Godwin's army if the king desired it. But some prevented that; because it was very unwise that they should come together; for in the two armies was there almost all that was noblest in England. They therefore prevented this, that they might not leave the land at the mercy of our foes, whilst engaged in a destructive conflict betwixt ourselves. Then it was advised that they should exchange hostages between them. And they issued proclamations throughout to London, whither all the people were summoned over all this north end in Siward's earldom, and in Leofric's, and also elsewhere; and Earl Godwin was to come thither with his sons to a conference; They came as far as Southwark, and very many with them from Wessex; but his army continually diminished more and more; for they bound over to the king all the thanes that belonged to Earl Harold his son, and outlawed Earl Sweyne his other son. When therefore it could not serve his purpose to come to a conference against the king and against the army that was with him, he went in the night away. In the morning the king held a council, and proclaimed him an outlaw, with his whole army; himself and his wife, and all his three sons—Sweyne and Tosty and Grith. And he went south to Thorney,[66] with his wife, and Sweyne his son, and Tosty and his wife, a cousin of Baldwin of Bruges, and his son Grith. Earl Harold with Leofwine went to Bristol in the ship that Earl Sweyne had before prepared and provisioned for himself; and the king sent Bishop Aldred from London with his retinue, with orders to overtake him ere he came to ship. But they either could not or would not: and he then went out from the mouth of the Avon; but he encountered such adverse weather, that he got off with difficulty, and suffered great loss. He then went forth to Ireland, as soon as the weather permitted. In the meantime the Welshmen had wrought a castle in Herefordshire, in the territory of Earl Sweyne, and brought as much injury and disgrace on the king's men thereabout as they could. Then came Earl Godwin, and Earl Sweyne, and Earl Harold, together at Beverstone, and many men with them; to the intent that they might go to their natural lord, and to all the peers that were assembled with him; to have the

66 *The ancient name of Westminster; which came into disuse because there was another Thorney in Cambridgeshire.*

king's counsel and assistance, and that of all the peers, how they might avenge the insult offered to the king, and to all the nation. But the Welshmen were before with the king, and bewrayed the earls, so that they were not permitted to come within the sight of his eyes; for they declared that they intended to come thither to betray the king. There was now assembled before the king[67] Earl Siward, and Earl Leofric, and much people with them from the north: and it was told Earl Godwin and his sons, that the king and the men who were with him would take counsel against them; but they prepared themselves firmly to resist, though they were loth to proceed against their natural lord. Then advised the peers on either side, that they should abstain from all hostility: and the king gave God's peace and his full friendship to each party. Then advised the king and his council, that there should be a second time a general assembly of all the nobles in London, at the autumnal equinox: and the king ordered out an army both south and north of the Thames, the best that ever was. Then was Earl Sweyne proclaimed an outlaw; and Earl Godwin and Earl Harold were summoned to the council as early as they could come. When they came thither and were cited to the council, then required they security and hostages, that they might come into the council and go out without treachery. The king then demanded all the thanes that the earls had; and they put them all into his hands. Then sent the king again to them, and commanded them to come with twelve men to the king's council. Then desired the earl again security and hostages, that he might answer singly to each of the things that were laid to his charge. But the hostages were refused; and a truce of five nights was allowed him to depart from the land. Then went Earl Godwin and Earl Sweyne to Bosham, and drew out their ships, and went beyond sea, seeking the protection of Baldwin; and there

67 i.e. at Gloucester, according to the printed Chronicle; which omits all that took place in the meantime at London and Southwark.

they abode all the winter. Earl Harold went westward to Ireland, and was there all the winter on the king's security. It was from Thorney[68] that Godwin and those that were with him went to Bruges, to Baldwin's land, in one ship, with as much treasure as they could lodge therein for each man. Wonderful would it have been thought by every man that was then in England, if any person had said before this that it would end thus! For he was before raised to such a height, that he ruled the king and all England; his sons were earls, and the king's darlings; and his daughter wedded and united to the king. Soon after this took place, the king dismissed the lady who had been consecrated his queen, and ordered to be taken from her all that she had in land, and in gold, and in silver, and in all things; and committed her to the care of his sister at Wherwell. Soon after came Earl William from beyond sea with a large retinue of Frenchmen; and the king entertained him and as many of his companions as were convenient to him, and let him depart again. Then was Abbot Sparhawk driven from his bishopric at London; and William the king's priest was invested therewith. Then was Oddy appointed earl over Devonshire, and over Somerset, and over Dorset, and over Wales; and Algar, the son of Earl Leofric, was promoted to the earldom which Harold before possessed.

[A.D. 1051. In this year died Eadsine, Archbishop of Canterbury; and the king gave to Robert the Frenchman, who before had been Bishop of London, the archbishopric. And Sparhafoc, Abbot of Abingdon, succeeded to the bishopric of London; and it was afterwards taken from him before he was consecrated. And Bishop Heroman and Bishop Aldred went to Rome.]

A.D. 1052. This year, on the second day before the nones of March, died the aged Lady Elfgiva Emma, the mother of King Edward and of King Hardacnute, the relict of King

---

68 *Now Westminster.*

Ethelred and of King Knute; and her body lies in the old minster with King Knute. At this time Griffin, the Welsh king, plundered in Herefordshire till he came very nigh to Leominster; and they gathered against him both the landsmen and the Frenchmen from the castle; and there were slain very many good men of the English, and also of the French. This was on the same day thirteen years after that Edwin was slain with his companions. In the same year advised the king and his council, that ships should be sent out to Sandwich, and that Earl Ralph and Earl Odda should be appointed headmen thereto. Then went Earl Godwin out from Bruges with his ships to Ysendyck; and sailed forth one day before midsummer-eve, till he came to the Ness that is to the south of Romney. When it came to the knowledge of the earls out at Sandwich, they went out after the other ships; and a land-force was also ordered out against the ships. Meanwhile Earl Godwin had warning, and betook himself into Pevensey: and the weather was so boisterous, that the earls could not learn what had become of Earl Godwin. But Earl Godwin then went out again until he came back to Bruges; and the other ships returned back again to Sandwich. Then it was advised that the ships should go back again to London, and that other earls and other pilots should be appointed over them. But it was delayed so long that the marine army all deserted; and they all betook themselves home. When Earl Godwin understood that, he drew up his sail and his ship: and they[69] went west at once to the Isle of Wight; and landing there, they plundered so long that the people gave them as much as they required of them. Then proceeded they westward until they came to Portland, where they landed and did as much harm as they could possibly do. Meanwhile Harold had gone out from Ireland with nine ships, and came up at Potlock with his ships to the mouth of the Severn, near the boundaries

---

69 *i.e. Earl Godwin and his crew.*

of Somerset and Devonshire, and there plundered much. The land-folk collected against him, both from Somerset and from Devonshire: but he put them to flight, and slew there more than thirty good thanes, besides others; and went soon after about Penwithstert, where was much people gathered against him; but he spared not to provide himself with meat, and went up and slew on the spot a great number of the people — seizing in cattle, in men, and in money, whatever he could. Then went he eastward to his father; and they went both together eastward[70] until they came to the Isle of Wight, where they seized whatever had been left them before. Thence they went to Pevensey, and got out with them as many ships as had gone in there, and so proceeded forth till they came to the Ness;[71] getting all the ships that were at Romney, and at Hithe, and at Folkstone. Then ordered King Edward to fit out forty smacks that lay at Sandwich many weeks, to watch Earl Godwin, who was at Bruges during the winter; but he nevertheless came hither first to land, so as to escape their notice. And whilst he abode in this land, he enticed to him all the Kentish men, and all the boatmen from Hastings, and everywhere thereabout by the sea-coast, and all the men of Essex and Sussex and Surrey, and many others besides. Then said they all that they would with him live or die. When the fleet that lay at Sandwich had intelligence about Godwin's expedition, they set sail after him; but he escaped them, and betook himself wherever he might: and the fleet returned to Sandwich, and so homeward to London. When Godwin understood that the fleet that lay at Sandwich was gone home, then went he back again to the Isle of Wight, and lay thereabout by the sea-coast so long that they came together — he and his son Earl Harold. But they did no great harm after they came together; save that they took meat, and

70 i.e. from the Isle of Portland; where Godwin had landed after the plunder of the Isle of Wight.

71 i.e. Dungeness; where they collected all the ships stationed in the great bay formed by the ports of Romney, Hithe, and Folkstone.

enticed to them all the land-folk by the sea-coast and also upward in the land. And they proceeded toward Sandwich, ever alluring forth with them all the boatmen that they met; and to Sandwich they came with an increasing army. They then steered eastward round to Dover, and landing there, took as many ships and hostages as they chose, and so returned to Sandwich, where they did the same; and men everywhere gave them hostages and provisions, wherever they required them. Then proceeded they to the Nore, and so toward London; but some of the ships landed on the Isle of Shepey, and did much harm there; whence they steered to Milton Regis, and burned it all, and then proceeded toward London after the earls. When they came to London, there lay the king and all his earls to meet them, with fifty ships. The earls[72] then sent to the king, praying that they might be each possessed of those things which had been unjustly taken from them. But the king resisted some while; so long that the people who were with the earl were very much stirred against the king and against his people, so that the earl himself with difficulty appeased them. When King Edward understood that, then sent he upward after more aid; but they came very late. And Godwin stationed himself continually before London with his fleet, till he came to Southwark; where he abode some time, until the flood[73] came up. On this occasion he also contrived with the burgesses that they should do almost all that he would. When he had arranged his whole expedition, then came the flood; and they soon weighed anchor, and steered through the bridge by the south side. The land-force meanwhile came above, and arranged themselves by the Strand; and they formed an angle with the ships against the north side, as if they wished to surround the king's ships. The king had also a great land-force on his side, to add to his

72 i.e. Godwin and his son Harold.
73 i.e. the tide of the river.

205

shipmen: but they were most of them loth to fight with their own kinsmen—for there was little else of any great importance but Englishmen on either side; and they were also unwilling that this land should be the more exposed to outlandish people, because they destroyed each other. Then it was determined that wise men should be sent between them, who should settle peace on either side. Godwin went up, and Harold his son, and their navy, as many as they then thought proper. Then advanced Bishop Stigand with God's assistance, and the wise men both within the town and without; who determined that hostages should be given on either side. And so they did. When Archbishop Robert and the Frenchmen knew that, they took horse; and went some west to Pentecost Castle, some north to Robert's castle. Archbishop Robert and Bishop Ulf, with their companions, went out at Eastgate, slaying or else maiming many young men, and betook themselves at once to Eadulf's-ness; where he put himself on board a crazy ship, and went at once over sea, leaving his pall and all Christendom here on land, as God ordained, because he had obtained an honour which God disclaimed. Then was proclaimed a general council without London; and all the earls and the best men in the land were at the council. There took up Earl Godwin his burthen, and cleared himself there before his lord King Edward, and before all the nation; proving that he was innocent of the crime laid to his charge, and to his son Harold and all his children. And the king gave the earl and his children, and all the men that were with him, his full friendship, and the full earldom, and all that he possessed before; and he gave the lady all that she had before. Archbishop Robert was fully proclaimed an outlaw, with all the Frenchmen; because they chiefly made the discord between Earl Godwin and the king: and Bishop Stigand succeeded to the archbishopric at Canterbury. At the council therefore they gave Godwin fairly his earldom, so full and so free as he at first possessed it; and his sons also all that they formerly had; and his wife and his daughter so full and so free as they formerly had. And they fastened full friendship between them, and ordained good laws to all people. Then they outlawed all Frenchmen—who before instituted bad laws, and judged unrighteous judgment, and brought bad counsels into this land—except so many as they concluded it was agreeable to the king to have with him, who were true to him and to all his people. It was with difficulty that Bishop Robert, and Bishop William, and Bishop Ulf, escaped with the Frenchmen that were with them, and so went over sea. Earl Godwin, and Harold, and the queen, sat in their stations. Sweyne had before gone to Jerusalem from Bruges, and died on his way home at Constantinople, at Michaelmas. It was on the Monday after the festival of St. Mary, that Godwin came with his ships to Southwark: and on the morning afterwards, on the Tuesday, they were reconciled as it stands here before recorded. Godwin then sickened soon after he came up, and returned back. But he made altogether too little restitution of God's property, which he acquired from many places. At the same time Arnwy, Abbot of Peterborough, resigned his abbacy in full health; and gave it to the monk Leofric, with the king's leave and that of the monks; and the Abbot Arnwy lived afterwards eight winters. The Abbot Leofric gilded the minster, so that it was called Gildenborough; and it then waxed very much in land, and in gold, and in silver.

[A.D. 1052. This year died Alfric, Archbishop of York, a very pious man, and wise. And in the same year King Edward abolished the tribute, which King Ethelred had before imposed: that was in the nine-and-thirtieth year after he had begun it. That tax distressed all the English nation during so long a time, as it has been written; that was ever before other taxes which were variously paid, and wherewith the people were manifestly distressed. In the same year Eustace [Earl of Boulougne] landed at Dover: he had King Edward's sister to wife. Then went his men inconsiderately after quarters, and a certain man of the town they slew; and another man of the town their companion; so that there lay seven of his companions. And much harm was there done on either side, by horse and also by weapons, until the people gathered together: and then they fled away until they came to the king at Gloucester; and he gave them protection. When Godwin, the earl, understood that such things should have happened in his earldom, then began he to gather together people over all his earldom,[74] and Sweyn, the earl, his son, over his, and Harold, his other son, over his earldom; and they all drew together in Gloucestershire, at Langtree, a great force and countless, all ready for battle against the king, unless Eustace were given up, and his men placed in their hands, and also the Frenchmen who were in the castle. This was done seven days before the latter mass of St. Mary. Then was King Edward sitting at Gloucester. Then sent he after Leofric the earl [Of Mercia] and north after Siward the earl [Of Northumbria] and begged their forces. And then they came to him; first with a moderate aid, but after they knew how it was there, in the south, then sent they north over all their earldoms, and caused to be ordered out a large force for the help of their lord; and Ralph, also, over his earldom: and then came they all to Gloucester to help the king, though it might be late. Then were they all so united in opinion with the king that they would have sought out Godwin's forces if the king had so willed. Then thought some of them that it would be a great folly that they should join battle; because there was nearly all that was most noble in England in the two

74 *Godwin's earldom consisted of Wessex, Sussex, and Kent: Sweyn's of Oxford, Gloucester, Hereford, Somerset, and Berkshire: and Harold's of Essex, East-Anglia, Huntingdon, and Cambridgeshire.*

armies, and they thought that they should expose the land to our foes, and cause great destruction among ourselves. Then counselled they that hostages should be given mutually; and they appointed a term at London, and thither the people were ordered out over all this north end, in Siward's earldom, and in Leofric's, and also elsewhere; and Godwin, the earl, and his sons were to come there with their defence. Then came they to Southwark, and a great multitude with them, from Wessex; but his band continually diminished the longer he stayed. And they exacted pledges for the king from all the thanes who were under Harold, the earl, his son; and then they outlawed Sweyn, the earl, his other son. Then did it not suit him to come with a defence to meet the king, and to meet the army which was with him. Then went he by night away; and the king on the morrow held a council, and, together with all the army, declared him an outlaw, him and all his sons. And he went south to Thorney, and his wife, and Sweyn his son, and Tosty and his wife, Baldwin's relation of Bruges, and Grith his son. And Harold, the earl, and Leofwine, went to Bristol in the ship which Sweyn, the earl, had before got ready for himself, and provisioned. And the king sent Bishop Aldred [Of Worcester] to London with a force; and they were to overtake him ere he came on ship-board: but they could not or they would not. And he went out from Avonmouth, and met with such heavy weather that he with difficulty got away; and there he sustained much damage. Then went he forth to Ireland when fit weather came. And Godwin, and those who were with him, went from Thorney to Bruges, to Baldwin's land, in one ship, with as much treasure as they might therein best stow for each man. It would have seemed wondrous to every man who was in England if any one before that had said that it should end thus; for he had been erewhile to that degree exalted, as if he ruled the king and all England; and his sons were earls and the king's darlings, and his daughter wedded and united to the king: she was brought to Wherwell, and they delivered her to the abbess. Then, soon, came William, the earl [Of Normandy], from beyond seas with a great band of Frenchmen; and the king received him, and as many of his companions as it pleased him; and let him away again. This same year was given to William, the priest, the bishopric of London, which before had been given to Sparhafoc.]

[A.D. 1052. This year died Elfgive, the lady, relict of King Ethelred and of King Canute, on the second before the nones of March. In the same year Griffin, the Welsh king, plundered in Herefordshire, until he came very nigh to Leominster; and they gathered against him, as well the landsmen as the Frenchmen of the castle, and there were slain of the English very many good men, and also of the Frenchmen; that was on the same day, on which, thirteen years before, Eadwine had been slain by his companions.]

[A.D. 1052. In this year died Elgive Emma, King Edward's mother and King Hardecanute's. And in this same year, the king decreed, and his council, that ships should proceed to Sandwich; and they set Ralph, the earl, and Odda, the earl [Of Devon], as headmen thereto. Then Godwin, the earl, went out from Bruges with his ships to Ysendyck, and left it one day before Midsummer's-mass eve, so that he came to Ness, which is south of Romney. Then came it to the knowledge of the earls out at Sandwich; and they then went out after the other ships, and a land-force was ordered out against the ships. Then during this, Godwin, the earl, was warned, and then he went to Pevensey; and the weather was very severe, so that the earls could not learn what was become of Godwin, the earl. And then Godwin, the earl, went out again, until he came once more to Bruges; and the other ships returned again to Sandwich. And then it was decreed that the ships should return once more to London, and that other earls and commanders should be appointed to the ships. Then was it delayed so long that the ship-force all departed, and all of them went home. When Godwin, the earl, learned that, then drew he up his sail, and his fleet, and then went west direct to the Isle of Wight, and there landed and ravaged so long there, until the people yielded them so much as they laid on them. And then they went westward until they came to Portland, and there they landed, and did whatsoever harm they were able to do. Then was Harold come out from Ireland with nine ships; and then landed at Porlock, and there much people was gathered against him; but he failed not to procure himself provisions. He proceeded further, and slew there a great number of the people, and took of cattle, and of men, and of property as it suited him. He then went eastward to his father; and then they both went eastward until they came to the Isle of Wight, and there took that which was yet remaining for them. And then they went thence to Pevensey and got away thence as many ships as were there fit for service, and so onwards until he came to Ness, and got all the ships which were in Romney, and in Hythe, and in Folkstone. And then they went east to Dover, and there landed, and there took ships and hostages, as many as they would, and so went to Sandwich and did "hand" the same; and everywhere hostages were given them, and provisions wherever they desired. And then they went to North-mouth, and so toward London; and some of the ships went within Sheppey, and there did much harm, and went their way to King's Milton, and that they all burned, and betook themselves then toward London after the earls. When they came to London, there lay the king and all the earls there against them, with fifty ships. Then the earls sent to the king, and required of him, that they might be held worthy of each of those things which had been unjustly taken from them. Then the king, however, resisted some while; so long as until the people who were with the earl were much stirred against the king and against his people, so that the earl himself with difficulty stilled the people. Then Bishop Stigand interposed with God's help, and the wise men as well within the town as without; and they decreed that hostages should be set forth on either side: and thus was it done. When Archbishop Robert and the Frenchmen learned that, they took their horses and went, some west to Pentecost's castle, some north to Robert's castle. And Archbishop Robert and Bishop Ulf went out at East-gate, and their companions, and slew and otherwise injured many young men, and went their way to direct Eadulf's-ness; and he there put himself in a crazy ship, and went direct over sea, and left his pall and all Christendom here on land, so as God would have it, inasmuch as he had before obtained the dignity so as God would not have it. Then there was a great council proclaimed without London: and all the earls and the chief men who were in this land were at the council. There Godwin bore forth his defence, and justified himself, before King Edward his lord, and before all people of the land, that he was guiltless of that which was laid against him, and against Harold his son, and all his children. And the king gave to the earl and his children his full friendship, and full earldom, and all that he before possessed, and to all the men who were with him. And the king gave to the lady [Editha] all that she before possessed. And they declared Archbishop Robert utterly an outlaw, and all the Frenchmen, because they had made most of the difference between Godwin, the earl, and the king. And Bishop Stigand obtained the Archbishopric of Canterbury. In this same time Arnwy, Abbot of Peterborough, left the abbacy, in sound health, and gave it to Leofric the monk, by leave of the king and of the monks; and Abbot Arnwy lived afterwards eight years. And Abbot Leofric then (enriched) the minster, so that it was called the Golden-borough. Then it waxed greatly, in land, and in gold, and in silver.]

Archbishop Stigand from the Bayeux Tapestry

[A.D. 1052. And went so to the Isle of Wight, and there took all the ships which could be of any service, and hostages, and betook himself so eastward. And Harold had landed with nine ships at Porlock, and slew there much people, and took cattle, and men, and property, and went his way eastward to his father, and they both went to Romney, to Hythe, to Folkstone, to Dover, to Sandwich, and ever they took all the ships which they found, which could be of any service, and hostages, all as they proceeded; and went then to London.]

A.D. 1053. About this time was the great wind, on the mass-night of St. Thomas; which did much harm everywhere. And all the midwinter also was much wind. It was this year resolved to slay Rees, the Welsh king's brother, because he did harm; and they brought his head to Gloucester on the eve of Twelfth-day. In this same year, before Allhallowmas, died Wulfsy, Bishop of Lichfield; and Godwin, Abbot of Winchcomb; and Aylward, Abbot of Glastonbury; all within one month. And Leofwine, Abbot of Coventry, took to the bishopric at Lichfield; Bishop Aldred to the abbacy at Winchcomb; and Aylnoth took to the abbacy at Glastonbury. The same year died Elfric, brother of Odda, at Deerhurst; and his body resteth at Pershore. In this year was the king at Winchester, at Easter; and Earl Godwin with him, and Earl Harold his son, and Tosty. On the day after Easter sat he with the king at table; when he suddenly sunk beneath against the foot-rail, deprived of speech and of all his strength. He was brought into the king's chamber; and they supposed that it would pass over: but it was not so. He continued thus speechless and helpless till the Thursday; when he resigned his life, on the seventeenth before the calends of May; and he was buried at Winchester in the old minster. Earl Harold, his son, took to the earldom that his father had before, and to all that his father possessed; whilst Earl Elgar took to the earldom that Harold had before. The Welshmen this year slew a great many of the warders of the English people at Westbury. This year there was no archbishop in this land: but Bishop Stigand held the see of Canterbury at Christ church, and Kinsey that of York. Leofwine and Wulfwy went over sea, and had themselves consecrated bishops there. Wulfwy took to the bishopric which Ulf had whilst he was living and in exile.

[A.D. 1053. This year was the great wind on Thomas's-mass-night, and also the whole midwinter there was much wind; and it was decreed that Rees, the Welsh king's brother, should be slain, because he had done harm; and his head was brought to Gloucester on Twelfth-day eve. And the same year, before All Hallows-mass, died Wulfsy, Bishop of Lichfield, and Godwin, Abbot of Winchcomb, and Egelward, Abbot of Clastonbury, all within one month, and Leofwine succeeded to the Bishopric of Lichfield, and Bishop Aidred [Of Worcester] took the abbacy at Winchcomb, and Egelnoth succeeded to the abbacy at Glastonbury. And the same year died Elfric, Odda's brother at Deorhurst; and his body resteth at Pershore. And the same year died Godwin the earl; and he fell ill as he sat with the king at Winchester. And Harold his son succeeded to the earldom which his father before held; and Elgar, the earl, succeeded to the earldom which Harold before held.]

[A.D. 1053. In this year died Godwin, the earl, on the seventeenth before the kalends of May, and he is buried at Winchester, in the Old-minster; and Harold, the earl, his son, succeeded to the earldom, and to all that which his father had held: and Elgar, the earl, succeeded to the earldom which Harold before held.]

A.D. 1054. This year died Leo the holy pope, at Rome: and Victor was chosen pope in his stead. And in this year was so great loss of cattle as was not remembered for many winters before. This year went Earl Siward with a large army against Scotland, consisting both of marines and landforces; and engaging with the Scots, he put to flight the King Macbeth; slew all the best in the land; and led thence much spoil, such as no man before obtained. Many fell also on his side, both Danish and English; even his own son, Osborn, and his sister's son, Sihward: and many of his house-carls, and also of the king's, were there slain that day, which was that of the Seven Sleepers. This same year went Bishop Aldred south over sea into Saxony, to Cologne, on the king's errand; where he was entertained with great respect by the emperor, abode there well-nigh a year, and received presents not only from the court, but from the Bishop of Cologne and the emperor. He commissioned Bishop Leofwine to consecrate the minster at Evesham; and it was consecrated in the same year, on the sixth before the ides of October. This year also died Osgod Clapa suddenly in his bed, as he lay at rest.

[A.D. 1054. This year went Siward the earl with a great army into Scotland, both with a ship-force and with a landforce, and fought against the Scots, and put to flight King Macbeth, and slew all who were the chief men in the land, and led thence much booty, such as no man before had obtained. But his son Osborn, and his sister's son Siward, and some of his house-carls, and also of the king's, were there slain, on the day of the Seven Sleepers. The same year went Bishop Aldred to Cologne, over sea, on the king's errand; and he was there received with much worship by the emperor [Henry III], and there he dwelt well nigh a year; and either gave him entertainment, both the Bishop of Cologne and the emperor. And he gave leave to Bishop Leofwine [Of Lichfield] to consecrate the minster at Evesham on the sixth before the ides of October. In this year died Osgod suddenly in his bed. And this year died St. Leo the pope; and Victor was chosen pope in his stead.]

A.D. 1055. This year died Earl Siward at York; and his body lies within the minster at Galmanho,[75] which he had himself ordered to be built and consecrated, in the name of God and St. Olave, to the honour of God and to all his saints. Archbishop Kinsey fetched his pall from Pope Victor. Then, within a little time after, a general council was summoned in London, seven nights before mid-Lent; at which Earl Elgar, son of Earl Leofric, was outlawed almost without any guilt; because it was said against him that he was the betrayer of the king and of all the people of the land. And he was arraigned thereof before all that were there assembled, though the crime laid to his charge was unintentional. The king, however, gave the earldom, which Earl Siward formerly had, to Tosty, son

75 *The church, dedicated to St. Olave, was given by Alan Earl of Richmond, about thirty-three years afterwards, to the first abbot of St. Mary's in York, to assist him in the construction of the new abbey. It appears from a MS. quoted by Leland, that Bootham-bar was formerly called "Galman-hithe", not Galmanlith, as printed by Tanner and others.*

of Earl Godwin. Whereupon Earl Elgar sought Griffin's territory in North-Wales; whence he went to Ireland, and there gave him a fleet of eighteen ships, besides his own; and then returned to Wales to King Griffin with the armament, who received him on terms of amity. And they gathered a great force with the Irishmen and the Welsh: and Earl Ralph collected a great army against them at the town of Hereford; where they met; but ere there was a spear thrown the English people fled, because they were on horses. The enemy then made a great slaughter there—about four hundred or five hundred men; they on the other side none. They went then to the town, and burned it utterly; and the large minster[76] also which the worthy Bishop Athelstan had caused to be built, that they plundered and bereft of relic and of reef, and of all things whatever; and the people they slew, and led some away. Then an army from all parts of England was gathered very nigh;[77] and they came to Gloucester: whence they sallied not far out against the Welsh, and there lay some time. And Earl Harold caused the dike to be dug about the town the while. Meantime men began to speak of peace; and Earl Harold and those who were with him came to Bilsley, where amity and friendship were established between them. The sentence of outlawry against Earl Elgar was reversed; and they gave him all that was taken from him before. The fleet returned to Chester, and there awaited their pay, which Elgar promised them. The slaughter was on the ninth before the calends of November. In the same year died Tremerig, the Welsh bishop, soon after the plundering; who was Bishop Athelstan's substitute, after he became infirm.

[A.D. 1055. In this year died Siward the earl at York, and he

76 Called St. Ethelbert's minster; because the relics of the holy King Ethelbert were there deposited and preserved.

77 The place where this army was assembled, though said to be very nigh to Hereford, was only so with reference to the great distance from which some part of the forces came; as they were gathered from all England. They met, I conjecture, on the memorable spot called "Harold's Cross", near Cheltenham, and thence proceeded, as here stated, to Gloucester.

lies at Galmanho, in the minster which himself caused to be built, and consecrated in God's and Olave's name. And Tosty succeeded to the earldom which he had held. And Archbishop Kynsey [Of York], fetched his pall from Pope Victor. And soon thereafter was outlawed Elgar the earl, son of Leofric the earl, well-nigh without guilt. But he went to Ireland and to Wales, and procured himself there a great force, and so went to Hereford: but there came against him Ralph the earl, with a large army, and with a slight conflict he put them to flight, and much people slew in the flight: and they went then into Hereford-port, and that they ravaged, and burned the great minster which Bishop Athelstan had built, and slew the priests within the minster, and many in addition thereto, and took all the treasures therein, and carried them away with them. And when they had done the utmost evil, this counsel was counselled: that Elgar the earl should be inlawed, and be given his earldom, and all that had been taken from him. This ravaging happened on the 9th before the Kalends of November. In the same year died Tremerin the Welsh bishop [Of St. David's] soon after that ravaging: and he was Bishop Athelstan's coadjutor from the time that he had become infirm.]

[A.D. 1055. In this year died Siward the earl: and then was summoned a general council, seven days before Mid-lent; and they outlawed Elgar the earl, because it was cast upon him that he was a traitor to the king and to all the people of the land. And he made a confession of it before all the men who were there gathered; though the word escaped him unintentionally. And the king gave the earldom to Tosty, son of Earl Godwin, which Siward the earl before held. And Elgar the earl sought Griffin's protection in North-Wales. And in this year Griffin and Elgar burned St. Ethelbert's minster, and all the town of Hereford.]

A.D. 1056. This year Bishop Egelric resigned his bishopric at

Durham, and retired to Peterborough minster; and his brother Egelwine succeeded him. The worthy Bishop Athelstan died on the fourth before the ides of February; and his body lies at Hereford. To him succeeded Leofgar, who was Earl Harold's mass-priest. He wore his knapsack in his priesthood, until he was a bishop. He abandoned his chrism and his rood—his ghostly weapons—and took to his spear and to his sword, after his bishophood; and so marched to the field against Griffin the Welsh king.[78] But he was there slain, and his priests with him, and Elnoth the sheriff, and many other good men with them; and the rest fled. This was eight nights before midsummer. Difficult is it to relate all the vexation and the journeying, the marching and the fatigue, the fall of men, and of horses also, which the whole army of the English suffered, until Earl Leofric, and Earl Harold, and Bishop Eldred, came together and made peace between them; so that Griffin swore oaths, that he would be a firm and faithful viceroy to King Edward. Then Bishop Eldred took to the bishopric which Leofgar had before eleven weeks and four days. The same year died Cona the emperor; and Earl Odda, whose body lies at Pershore, and who was admitted a monk before his end; which was on the second before the calends of September; a good man and virtuous and truly noble.

A.D. 1057. This year came Edward Etheling, son of King Edmund, to this land, and soon after died. His body is buried within St. Paul's minster at London. He was brother's son to King Edward. King Edmund was called Ironside for his valour. This etheling King Knute had sent into Hungary, to betray him; but he there grew in favour with good men, as God granted him, and it well became him; so that he obtained the emperor's cousin in marriage, and by her had a fair offspring. Her name was Agatha. We know not for

---

78   *This was no uncommon thing among the Saxon clergy, bishops and all. The tone of elevated diction in which the writer describes the military enterprise of Leofgar and his companions, testifies his admiration.*

what reason it was done, that he should see his relation, King Edward. Alas! that was a rueful time, and injurious to all this nation—that he ended his life so soon after he came to England, to the misfortune of this miserable people. The same year died Earl Leofric, on the second before the calends of October; who was very wise before God, and also before the world; and who benefited all this nation.[79] He lies at Coventry[80]: and his son Elgar took to his territory. This year died Earl Ralph, on the twelfth before the calends of January; and lies at Peterborough. Also died Bishop Heca, in Sussex; and Egelric was elevated to his see. This year also died Pope Victor; and Stephen was chosen pope, who was Abbot of Monut Cassino.

[A.D. 1057. In this year Edward Etheling, King Edmund's son, came hither to land, and soon after died, and his body is buried within St. Paul's minster at London. And Pope Victor died, and Stephen [IX.] was chosen pope: he was Abbot of Mont-Cassino. And Leofric the earl died, and Elgar his son succeeded to the earldom which the father before held.]

A.D. 1058. This year was Earl Elgar banished: but he soon came in again by force, through Griffin's assistance: and a naval armament came from Norway. It is tedious to tell how it all fell out. In this same year Bishop Aldred consecrated the minster church at Gloucester, which he himself had raised[81] to the honour of God and St. Peter; and then went to Jerusalem[82] with such dignity as no other man did before him, and betook himself there to God. A worthy gift he also offered to our Lord's sepulchre; which was a golden chalice of the value of five marks, of very wonderful workmanship. In the same year died Pope Stephen; and Benedict was appointed pope.

79 *See more concerning him in Florence of Worcester. His lady, Godiva, is better known at Coventry. See her story at large in Bromton and Matthew of Westminster.*

80 *He died at his villa at Bromleage (Bromley in Staffordshire).—Flor.*

81 *He built a new church from the foundation, on a larger plan. The monastery existed from the earliest times.*

82 *Florence of Worcester says, that he went through Hungary to Jerusalem.*

He sent hither the pall to Bishop Stigand; who as archbishop consecrated Egelric a monk at Christ church, Bishop of Sussex; and Abbot Siward Bishop of Rochester.

[A.D. 1058. This year died Pope Stephen, and Benedict was consecrated pope: the same sent hither to land a pall to Archbishop Stigand. And in this year died Heca, Bishop of Sussex; and Archbishop Stigand ordained Algeric, a monk at Christchurch, Bishop of Sussex, and Abbot Siward Bishop of Rochester.]

A.D. 1059. This year was Nicholas chosen pope, who had been Bishop of Florence; and Benedict was expelled, who was pope before. This year also was consecrated the steeple[83] at Peterborough, on the sixteenth before the calends of November.

A.D. 1060. This year was a great earthquake on the Translation of St. Martin, and King Henry died in France. Kinsey, Archbishop of York, died on the eleventh before the calends of January; and he lies at Peterborough. Bishop Aldred succeeded to the see, and Walter to that of Herefordshire. Dudoc also died, who was Bishop of Somersetshire; and Gisa the priest was appointed in his stead.

A.D. 1061. This year went Bishop Aldred to Rome after his pall; which he received at the hands of Pope Nicholas. Earl Tosty and his wife also went to Rome; and the bishop and the earl met with great difficulty as they returned home. In the same year died Bishop Godwin at St. Martin's,[84] on the seventh before the ides of March; and in the self-same year died Wulfric, Abbot of St. Augustine's, in the Easterweek, on the fourteenth before the calends of May. Pope Nicholas also died; and Alexander was chosen pope, who was Bishop of

---

83 *This must not be confounded with a spire-steeple. The expression was used to denote a tower, long before spires were invented.*

84 *Lye interprets it erroneously the "festival" of St. Martin — "ad S. Martini festum:" whereas the expression relates to the place, not to the time of his death, which is mentioned immediately afterwards.*

Lucca. When word came to the king that the Abbot Wulfric was dead, then chose he Ethelsy, a monk of the old minster, to succeed; who followed Archbishop Stigand, and was consecrated abbot at Windsor on St. Augustine's mass-day.

[A.D. 1061. In this year died Dudoc, Bishop of Somerset, and Giso succeeded. And in the same year died Godwin, Bishop of St. Martin's, on the seventh before the ides of March. And in the self-same year died Wulfric, Abbot of St. Augustine's, within the Easter week, on the fourteenth before the kalends of May. When word came to the king that Abbot Wulfric was departed, then chose he Ethelsy the monk thereto, from the Old-Minster, who then followed Archbishop Stigand, and was consecrated abbot at Windsor, on St. Augustine's mass-day.]

A.D. 1063. This year went Earl Harold, after mid-winter, from Gloucester to Rhyddlan; which belonged to Griffin: and that habitation he burned, with his ships and all the rigging belonging thereto; and put him to flight. Then in the gang-days went Harold with his ships from Bristol about Wales; where he made a truce with the people, and they gave him hostages. Tosty meanwhile advanced with a land-force against them, and plundered the land. But in the harvest of the same year was King Griffin slain, on the nones of August, by his own men, through the war that he waged with Earl Harold. He was king over all the Welsh nation. And his head was brought to Earl Harold; who sent it to the king, with his ship's head, and the rigging therewith. King Edward committed the land to his two brothers, Blethgent and Rigwatle; who swore oaths, and gave hostages to the king and to the earl, that they would be faithful to him in all things, ready to aid him everywhere by water and land, and would pay him such tribute from the land as was paid long before to other kings.

[A.D. 1063. This year went Harold the earl, and his brother Tosty the earl, as well with a land-force as a shipforce, into

Wales, and they subdued the land; and the people delivered hostages to them, and submitted; and went afterwards and slew their King Griffin, and brought to Harold his head: and he appointed another king thereto.]

A.D. 1065. This year, before Lammas, ordered Earl Harold his men to build at Portskeweth in Wales. But when he had begun, and collected many materials, and thought to have King Edward there for the purpose of hunting, even when it was all ready, came Caradoc, son of Griffin, with all the gang that he could get, and slew almost all that were building there; and they seized the materials that were there got ready. Wist we not who first advised the wicked deed. This was done on the mass-day of St. Bartholomew. Soon after this all the thanes in Yorkshire and in Northumberland gathered themselves together at York, and outlawed their Earl Tosty; slaying all the men of his clan that they could reach, both Danish and English; and took all his weapons in York, with gold and silver, and all his money that they could anywhere there find. They then sent after Morkar, son of Earl Elgar, and chose him for their earl. He went south with all the shire, and with Nottinghamshire and Derbyshire and Lincolnshire, till he came to Northampton; where his brother Edwin came to meet him with the men that were in his earldom. Many Britons also came with him. Harold also there met them; on whom they imposed an errand to King Edward, sending also messengers with him, and requesting that they might have Morcar for their earl. This the king granted; and sent back Harold to them, to Northampton, on the eve of St. Simon and St. Jude; and announced to them the same, and confirmed it by hand, and renewed there the laws of Knute. But the Northern men did much harm about Northampton, whilst he went on their errand: either that they slew men, and burned houses and corn; or took all the cattle that they could come at; which amounted to many thousands. Many hundred men also they took, and led northward with them; so that not only that shire, but others near it were the worse for many winters. Then Earl Tosty and his wife, and all they who acted with him, went south over sea with him to Earl Baldwin; who received them all: and they were there all the winter. About midwinter King Edward came to Westminster, and had the minster there consecrated, which he had himself built to the honour of God, and St. Peter, and all God's saints. This church-hallowing was on Childermas-day. He died on the eve of twelfth-day; and he was buried on twelfth-day in the same minster; as it is hereafter said. Here Edward king,[85] of Angles lord, sent his stedfast soul to Christ. In the kingdom of God a holy spirit! He in the world here abode awhile, in the kingly throng of council sage. Four and twenty winters wielding the sceptre freely, wealth he dispensed. In the tide of health, the youthful monarch, offspring of Ethelred! ruled well his subjects; the Welsh and the Scots, and the Britons also, Angles and Saxons relations of old. So apprehend the first in rank, that to Edward all the noble king were firmly held high-seated men. Blithe-minded aye was the harmless king; though he long ere, of land bereft, abode in exile wide on the earth; when Knute o'ercame the kin of Ethelred, and the Danes wielded the dear kingdom of Engle-land. Eight and twenty winters' rounds they wealth dispensed. Then came forth free in his chambers, in royal array, good, pure, and mild, Edward the noble; by his country defended— by land and people. Until suddenly came the bitter Death and this king so dear snatched from the earth. Angels carried his soul sincere into the light of heaven. But the prudent king had settled the realm on high-born men— on Harold himself, the noble earl; who in every season faithfully heard and obeyed his lord, in word and deed; nor gave to any what might be wanted by the nation's king. This year also was Earl Harold

85 *This threnodia on the death of Edward the Confessor will be found to correspond, both in metre and expression, with the poetical paraphrase of Genesis ascribed to Caedmon.*

hallowed to king; but he enjoyed little tranquillity therein the while that he wielded the kingdom.

[A.D. 1065. And the man-slaying was on St. Bartholomew's mass-day. And then, after Michael's-mass, all the thanes in Yorkshire went to York, and there slew all Earl Tosty's household servants whom they might hear of, and took his treasures: and Tosty was then at Britford with the king. And then, very soon thereafter, was a great council at Northampton; and then at Oxford on the day of Simon and Jude. And there was Harold the earl, and would work their reconciliation if he might, but he could not: but all his earldom him unanimously forsook and outlawed, and all who with him lawlessness upheld, because he robbed God first, and all those bereaved over whom he had power of life and of land. And they then took to themselves Morkar for earl; and Tosty went then over sea, and his wife with him, to Baldwin's land, and they took up their winter residence at St. Omer's.]

A.D. 1066. This year came King Harold from York to Westminster, on the Easter succeeding the midwinter when the king (Edward) died. Easter was then on the sixteenth day before the calends of May. Then was over all England such a token seen as no man ever saw before. Some men said that it was the comet-star, which others denominate the long-hair'd star. It appeared first on the eve called "Litania major", that is, on the eighth before the calends off May; and so shone all the week. Soon after this came in Earl Tosty from beyond sea into the Isle of Wight, with as large a fleet as he could get; and he was there supplied with money and provisions. Thence he proceeded, and committed outrages everywhere by the sea-coast where he could land, until he came to Sandwich. When it was told King Harold, who was in London, that his brother Tosty was come to Sandwich, he gathered so large a force, naval and military, as no king before collected in this land; for it was credibly reported that

225

The battle of Stamford Bridge, depicting King Harald Hardrada hit in the neck by an arrow.

Earl William from Normandy, King Edward's cousin, would come hither and gain this land; just as it afterwards happened. When Tosty understood that King Harold was on the way to Sandwich, he departed thence, and took some of the boatmen with him, willing and unwilling, and went north into the Humber with sixty skips; whence he plundered in Lindsey, and there slew many good men. When the Earls Edwin and Morkar understood that, they came hither, and drove him from the land. And the boatmen forsook him. Then he went to Scotland with twelve smacks; and the king of the Scots entertained him, and aided him with provisions; and he abode there all the summer. There met him Harold, King of Norway, with three hundred ships. And Tosty submitted to him, and became his man.[86] Then came King Harold[87] to Sandwich, where he awaited his fleet; for it was long ere it could be collected: but when it was assembled, he went into the Isle of Wight, and there lay all the summer and the autumn. There

---

86 *These facts, though stated in one MS. only, prove the early cooperation of Tosty with the King of Norway. It is remarkable that this statement is confirmed by Snorre, who says that Tosty was with Harald, the King of Norway, in all these expeditions. Vid "Antiq. Celto-Scand." p. 204.*

87 *i.e. Harold, King of England; "our" king, as we find him Afterwards called in B iv., to distinguish him from Harald, King of Norway.*

was also a land-force every where by the sea, though it availed nought in the end. It was now the nativity of St. Mary, when the provisioning of the men began; and no man could keep them there any longer. They therefore had leave to go home: and the king rode up, and the ships were driven to London; but many perished ere they came thither. When the ships were come home, then came Harald, King of Norway, north into the Tine, unawares, with a very great sea-force— no small one; that might be, with three hundred ships or more; and Earl Tosty came to him with all those that he had got; just as they had before said: and they both then went up with all the fleet along the Ouse toward York.[88] When it was told King Harold in the south, after he had come from the ships, that Harald, King of Norway, and Earl Tosty were come up near York, then went he northward by day and night, as soon as he could collect his army. But, ere King Harold could come thither, the Earls Edwin and Morkar had gathered from their earldoms as great a force as they could get, and fought with the enemy.[89] They made a great slaughter too; but there was a good number of the English people slain, and drowned, and put to flight: and the Northmen had possession of the field of battle. It was then told Harold, king of the English, that this had thus happened. And this fight was on the eve of St. Matthew the apostle, which was Wednesday. Then after the fight went Harold, King of Norway, and Earl Tosty into York with as many followers as they thought fit; and having procured hostages and provisions from the city, they proceeded to their ships, and proclaimed full friendship, on condition that all would go southward with them, and gain this land. In the midst of this came Harold, king of the English, with all his army, on the Sunday, to Tadcaster; where

88 *Not only the twelve smacks with which he went into Scotland during the summer, as before stated, but an accession of force from all quarters.*

89 *On the north bank of the Ouse, according to Florence of Worcester; the enemy having landed at Richale (now "Riccal"). Simeon of Durham names the spot "Apud Fulford," i.e. Fulford-water, south of the city of York.*

he collected his fleet. Thence he proceeded on Monday throughout York. But Harald, King of Norway, and Earl Tosty, with their forces, were gone from their ships beyond York to Stanfordbridge; for that it was given them to understand, that hostages would be brought to them there from all the shire. Thither came Harold, king of the English, unawares against them beyond the bridge; and they closed together there, and continued long in the day fighting very severely. There was slain Harald the Fair-hair'd, King of Norway, and Earl Tosty, and a multitude of people with them, both of Normans and English;[90] and the Normans that were left fled from the English, who slew them hotly behind; until some came to their ships, some were drowned, some burned to death, and thus variously destroyed; so that there was little left: and the English gained possession of the field. But there was one of the Norwegians who withstood the English folk, so that they could not pass over the bridge, nor complete the victory. An Englishman aimed at him with a javelin, but it availed nothing. Then came another under the bridge, who pierced him terribly inwards under the coat of mail. And Harold, king of the English, then came over the bridge, followed by his army; and there they made a great slaughter, both of the Norwegians and of the Flemings. But Harold let the king's son, Edmund, go home to Norway with all the ships. He also gave quarter to Olave, the Norwegian king's son, and to their bishop, and to the earl of the Orkneys, and to all those that were left in the ships; who then went up to our king, and took oaths that they would ever maintain faith and friendship unto this land. Whereupon the King let them go home with twenty-four ships. These two general battles were fought within five nights. Meantime Earl William came

90 *It is scarcely necessary to observe that the term "English" begins about this time to be substituted for "Angles"; and that the Normans are not merely the Norwegians, but the Danes and other adventurers from the north, joined with the forces of France and Flanders; who, we shall presently see, overwhelmed by their numbers the expiring, liberties of England. The Franks begin also to assume the name of Frencyscan or "Frenchmen".*

up from Normandy into Pevensey on the eve of St. Michael's mass; and soon after his landing was effected, they constructed a castle at the port of Hastings. This was then told to King Harold; and he gathered a large force, and came to meet him at the estuary of Appledore. William, however, came against him unawares, ere his army was collected; but the king, nevertheless, very hardly encountered him with the men that would support him: and there was a great slaughter made on either side. There was slain King Harold, and Leofwin his brother, and Earl Girth his brother, with many good men: and the Frenchmen gained the field of battle, as God granted them for the sins of the nation. Archbishop Aldred and the corporation of London were then desirous of having child Edgar to king, as he was quite natural to them; and Edwin and Morkar promised them that they would fight with them. But the more prompt the business should ever be, so was it from day to day the later and worse; as in the end it all fared. This battle was fought on the day of Pope Calixtus: and Earl William returned to Hastings, and waited there to know whether the people would submit to him. But when he found that they would not come to him, he went up with all his force that was left and that came since to him from over sea, and ravaged all the country that he overran, until he came to Berkhampstead; where Archbishop Aldred came to meet him, with child Edgar, and Earls Edwin and Morkar, and all the best men from London; who submitted then for need, when the most harm was done. It was very ill-advised that they did not so before, seeing that God would not better things for our sins. And they gave him hostages and took oaths: and he promised them that he would be a faithful lord to them; though in the midst of this they plundered wherever they went. Then on midwinter's day Archbishop Aldred hallowed him to king at Westminster, and gave him possession with the books of Christ, and also swore him, ere that he would set the crown on his head, that he would so well govern this nation as any before him best did, if they would be faithful to him. Neverrhetess he laid very heavy tribute on men, and in Lent went over sea to Normandy, taking with him Archbishop Stigand, and Abbot Aylnoth of Glastonbury, and the child Edgar, and the Earls Edwin, Morkar, and Waltheof, and many other good men of England. Bishop Odo and Earl William lived here afterwards, and wrought castles widely through this country, and harassed the miserable people; and ever since has evil increased very much. May the end be good, when God will! In that same expedition[91] was Leofric, Abbot of Peterborough; who sickened there, and came home, and died soon after, on the night of Allhallow-mass. God honour his soul! In his day was all bliss and all good at Peterborough. He was beloved by all; so that the king gave to St. Peter and him the abbey at Burton, and that at Coventry, which the Earl Leofric, who was his uncle, had formerly made; with that of Croyland, and that of Thorney. He did so much good to the minster of Peterborough, in gold, and in silver, and in shroud, and in land, as no other ever did before him, nor any one after him. But now was Gilden-borough become a wretched borough. The monks then chose for abbot Provost Brand, because he was a very good man, and very wise; and sent him to Edgar Etheling, for that the land-folk supposed that he should be king: and the etheling received him gladly. When King William heard say that, he was very wroth, and said that the abbot had renounced him: but good men went between them, and reconciled them; because the abbot was a good man. He gave the king forty marks of gold for his reconciliation; and he lived but a little while after—only three years. Afterwards came all wretchedness and all evil to the minster. God have mercy on it!

91   i.e. in the expedition against the usurper William.

William the Conqueror invading England. Painted c. 1400- 1410, Paris

[A.D. 1066. This year died King Edward, and Harold the earl succeeded to the kingdom, and held it forty weeks and one day. And this year came William, and won England. And in this year Christ-Church [Canterbury] was burned. And this year appeared a comet on the fourteenth before the kalends of May.]

[A.D. 1066. ...And then he [Tosty] went thence, and did harm everywhere by the sea-coast where he could land, as far as Sandwich. Then was it made known to King Harold, who was in London, that Tosty his brother was come to Sandwich. Then gathered he so great a ship-force, and also a land force, as no king here in the land had before gathered, because it had been soothly said unto him, that William the earl from Normandy, King Edward's kinsman, would come hither and subdue this land: all as it afterwards happened. When Tosty learned that King Harold was on his way to Sandwich, then went he from Sandwich, and took some of the boatmen with him, some willingly and some unwillingly; and went then north into Humber, and there ravaged in Lindsey, and there slew many good men. When Edwin the earl and Morcar the earl understood that, then came they thither, and drove him out of the land. And he went then to Scotland: and the king of Scots protected him, and assisted him with provisions; and he there abode all the summer. Then came King Harold to Sandwich, and there awaited his fleet, because it was long before it could be gathered together. And when his fleet was gathered together, then went he into the Isle of Wight, and there lay all the summer and the harvest; and a land-force was kept everywhere by the sea, though in the end it was of no benefit. When it was the Nativity of St. Mary, then were the men's provisions gone, and no man could any longer keep them there. Then were the men allowed to go home, and the king rode up, and the ships were dispatched to London; and many perished before they came thither. When the ships had reached home, then came King Harald from Norway, north into Tyne, and unawares, with a very large ship-force, and no small one; that might be, or more. And Tosty the earl came to him with all that he had gotten, all as they had before agreed; and then they went both, with all the fleet, along the Ouse, up towards York. Then was it made known to King Harold in the south, as he was come from on ship-board, that Harald King of Norway and Tosty the earl were landed near York. Then went he northward, day and night, as quickly as he could gather his forces. Then, before that King Harold could come thither, then gathered Edwin the earl and Morcar the earl from their earldom as great a force as they could get together; and they fought against the army, and made great slaughter: and there was much of the English people slain, and drowned, and driven away in flight; and the Northmen had possession of the place of carnage. And this fight was on the vigil of St. Matthew the apostle, and it was Wednesday. And then, after the fight, went Harald, King of Norway, and Tosty the earl, into York, with as much people as seemed meet to them. And they delivered hostages to them from the city, and also assisted them with provisions; and so they went thence to their ships, and they agreed upon a full peace, so that they should all go with him south, and this land subdue. Then, during this, came Harold, king of the Angles, with all his forces, on the Sunday, to Tadcaster, and there drew up his force, and went then on Monday throughout York; and Harald, King of Norway, and Tosty the earl, and their forces, were gone from their ships beyond York to Stanfordbridge, because it had been promised them for a certainty, that there, from all the shire, hostages should be brought to meet them. Then came Harold, king of the English, against them, unawares, beyond the bridge, and they there joined battle, and very strenuously, for a long time of the day, continued fighting: and there was Harald, King of Norway, and Tosty the earl slain, and numberless of the people with them, as well of the Northmen as of the English: and the Northmen fled from the English. Then was there one of the Norwegians who withstood the English people, so that they might not pass over the bridge, nor obtain the victory. Then an Englishman aimed at him with a javelin, but availed nothing; and then came another under the bridge, and pierced him terribly inwards under the coat of mail. Then came Harold, king of the English, over the bridge, and his forces onward with him, and there made great slaughter, as well of Norwegians as of Flemings. And the King's son, Edmund, Harold let go home to Norway, with all the ships.]

[A.D. 1066. In this year was consecrated the minster at Westminster, on Childer-mass-day. And King Edward died

A Victorian depiction of the death of King Harold II in 1066.

on the eve of Twelfth-day; and he was buried on Twelfth-day within the newly consecrated church at Westminster. And Harold the earl succeeded to the kingdom of England, even as the king had granted it to him, and men also had chosen him thereto; and he was crowned as king on Twelfth-day. And that same year that he became king, he went out with a fleet against William [Earl of Normandy]; and the while, came Tosty the earl into Humber with sixty ships. Edwin the earl came with a land-force and drove him out; and the boatmen forsook him. And he went to Scotland with twelve vessels; and Harald, the King of Norway, met him with three hundred ships, and Tosty submitted to him; and they both went into Humber, until they came to York. And Morcar the earl, and Edwin the earl, fought against them; and the king of the Norwegians had the victory. And it was made known to King Harold how it there was done, and had happened; and he came there with a great army of English men, and met him at Stanfordbridge, and slew him and the earl Tosty, and boldly overcame all the army. And the while, William the earl landed at Hastings, on St. Michael's-day: and Harold came from the north, and fought against him before all his army had come up: and there he fell, and his two brothers, Girth and Leofwin; and William subdued this land. And he came to Westminster, and Archbishop Aldred consecrated him king, and men paid him tribute, delivered him hostages, and afterwards bought their land. And then was Leofric, Abbot of Peterborough, in that same expedition; and there he sickened, and came home, and was dead soon thereafter, on All-hallows-mass-night; God be merciful to his soul! In his day was all bliss and all good in Peterborough; and he was dear to all people, so that the king gave to St. Peter and to him the abbacy at Burton, and that of Coventry, which Leofric the earl, who was his uncle, before had made, and that of Crowland, and that of Thorney. And he conferred so much of good upon the minster of Peterborough, in gold, and in silver, and in vestments, and in land, as never any other did before him, nor any after him. After, Golden-borough became a wretched borough. Then chose the monks for abbot Brand the provost, by reason that he was a very good man, and very wise, and sent him then to Edgar the etheling, by reason that the people of the land supposed that he should become king: and the etheling granted it him then gladly. When King William heard say that, then was he very wroth,

The death of King Harold II as depicted in the Bayeux Tapestry

and said that the abbot had despised him. Then went good men between them, and reconciled them, by reason that the abbot was a good man. Then gave he the king forty marks of gold for a reconciliation; and then thereafter, lived he a little while, but three years. After that came every tribulation and every evil to the minster. God have mercy on it!]

A.D. 1067. This year came the king back again to England on St. Nicholas's day; and the same day was burned the church of Christ at Canterbury. Bishop Wulfwy also died, and is buried at his see in Dorchester. The child Edric and the Britons were unsettled this year, and fought with the castlemen at Hereford, and did them much harm. The king this year imposed a heavy guild on the wretched people; but, notwithstanding, let his men always plunder all the country that they went over; and then he marched to Devonshire, and beset the city of Exeter eighteen days. There were many of his army slain; out he had promised them well, and performed ill; and the citizens surrendered the city because the thanes had betrayed them. This summer the child Edgar departed, with his mother Agatha, and his two sisters, Margaret and Christina, and Merle-Sweyne, and many good men with them; and came to Scotland under the protection of King Malcolm, who entertained them all. Then began

King Malcolm to yearn after the child's sister, Margaret, to wife; but he and all his men long refused; and she also herself was averse, and said that she would neither have him nor any one else, if the Supreme Power would grant, that she in her maidenhood might please the mighty Lord with a carnal heart, in this short life, in pure continence. The king, however, earnestly urged her brother, until he answered Yea. And indeed he durst not otherwise; for they were come into his kingdom. So that then it was fulfilled, as God had long ere foreshowed; and else it could not be; as he himself saith in his gospel: that "not even a sparrow on the ground may fall, without his foreshowing." The prescient Creator wist long before what he of her would have done; for that she should increase the glory of God in this land, lead the king aright from the path of error, bend him and his people together to a better way, and suppress the bad customs which the nation formerly followed: all which she afterwards did. The king therefore received her, though it was against her will, and was pleased with her manners, and thanked God, who in his might had given him such a match. He wisely bethought himself, as he was a prudent man, and turned himself to God, and renounced all impurity; accordingly, as the apostle Paul, the teacher of all the gentries, saith: "Salvabitur vir infidelis per mulierem fidelem; sic et mulier infidelis per virum fidelem," etc.: that is in our language, "Full oft the unbelieving husband is sanctified and healed through the believing wife, and so belike the wife through the believing husband." This queen aforesaid performed afterwards many useful deeds in this land to the glory of God, and also in her royal estate she well conducted herself, as her nature was. Of a faithful and noble kin was she sprung. Her father was Edward Etheling, son of King Edmund. Edmund was the son of Ethelred; Ethelred the son of Edgar; Edgar the son of Edred; and so forth in that royal line: and her maternal kindred goeth to the Emperor

Edith Swan-neck discovering the body of Harold Godwinson.

Henry, who had the sovereignty over Rome. This year went out Githa, Harold's mother, and the wives of many good men with her, to the Flat-Holm, and there abode some time; and so departed thence over sea to St. Omer's. This Easter came the king to Winchester; and Easter was then on the tenth before the calends of April. Soon after this came the Lady Matilda hither to this land; and Archbishop Eldred hallowed her to queen at Westminster on Whit Sunday. Then it was told the king, that the people in the North had gathered themselves together, and would stand against him if he came. Whereupon he went to Nottingham, and wrought there a castle; and so advanced to York, and there wrought two castles; and the same at Lincoln, and everywhere in that quarter. Then Earl Gospatric and the best men went into Scotland. Amidst this came one of Harold's sons from Ireland with a naval force into the mouth of the Avon unawares, and plundered soon over all that quarter; whence they went to Bristol, and would have stormed the town; but the people bravely withstood them. When they could gain nothing from the town, they went to their ships with the booty which they had acquired by plunder; and then they advanced upon Somersetshire, and there went up; and Ednoth, master of the horse, fought with them; but he was there slain, and many good men on either side; and those that were left departed thence.

A.D. 1068. This year King William gave Earl Robert the earldom over Northumberland; but the landsmen attacked him in the town of Durham, and slew him, and nine hundred men with him. Soon afterwards Edgar Etheling came with all the Northumbrians to York; and the townsmen made a treaty with him: but King William came from the South unawares on them with a large army, and put them to flight, and slew on the spot those who could not escape; which were many hundred men; and plundered the town. St. Peter's minster he made a profanation, and all other places also he despoiled and trampled upon; and the etheling went back again to Scotland. After this came Harold's sons from Ireland, about midsummer, with sixty-four ships into the mouth of the Taft, where they unwarily landed: and Earl Breon came unawares against them with a large army, and fought with them, and slew there all the best men that were in the fleet; and the others, being small forces, escaped to the ships: and Harold's sons went back to Ireland again.

A.D. 1069. This year died Aldred, Archbishop of York; and he is there buried, at his see. He died on the day of Protus and Hyacinthus, having held the see with much dignity ten years wanting only fifteen weeks. Soon after this came from Denmark three of the sons of King Sweyne with two hundred and forty ships, together with Earl Esborn and Earl Thurkill, into the Humber; where they were met by the child Edgar, and Earl Waltheof, and Merle-Sweyne, and Earl Gospatric with the Northumbrians, and all the landsmen; riding and marching full merrily with an immense army: and so all unanimously advanced to York; where they stormed and demolished the castle, and won innumerable treasures therein; slew there many hundreds of Frenchmen, and led many with them to the ships; but, ere that the shipmen came thither, the Frenchmen had burned the city, and also the holy minster of St. Peter had they entirely plundered, and destroyed with fire. When the king heard this, then went he northward with all the force that he could collect, despoiling and laying waste the shire withal; whilst the fleet lay all the winter in the Humber, where the king could not come at them. The king was in York on Christmas Day, and so all the winter on land, and came to Winchester at Easter. Bishop Egelric, who was at Peterborough, was this year betrayed, and led to Westminster; and his brother Egelwine was outlawed. This year also died Brand, Abbot of Peterborough, on the fifth before the calends of December.

A.D. 1070. This year Landfranc, who was Abbot of Caen, came to England; and after a few days he became Archbishop of Canterbury. He was invested on the fourth before the calends of September in his own see by eight bishops, his suffragans. The others, who were not there, by messengers and by letter declared why they could not be there. The same year Thomas, who was chosen Bishop of York, came to Canterbury, to be invested there after the ancient custom. But when Landfranc craved confirmation of his obedience with an oath, he refused; and said, that he ought not to do it. Whereupon Archbishop Landfranc was wroth, and bade the bishops, who were come thither by Archbishop Landfranc's command to do the service, and all the monks to unrobe themselves. And they by his order so did. Thomas, therefore, for the time, departed without consecration. Soon after this, it happened that the Archbishop Landfranc went to Rome, and Thomas with him. When they came thither, and had spoken about other things concerning which they wished to speak, then began Thomas his speech: how he came to Canterbury, and how the archbishop required obedience of him with an oath; but he declined it. Then began the Archbishop Landfranc to show with clear distinction, that what he craved he craved by right; and with strong arguments he confirmed the same before the Pope Alexander, and before all the council that was collected there; and so they went home. After this came Thomas to Canterbury; and all that the archbishop required of him he humbly fulfilled, and afterwards received consecration. This year Earl Waltheof agreed with the king; but in the Lent of the same year the king ordered all the monasteries in England to be plundered. In the same year came King Sweyne from Denmark into the Humber; and the landsmen came to meet him, and made a treaty with him; thinking that he would overrun the land. Then came into Ely Christien, the Danish bishop, and Earl Osbern, and the Danish domestics with them; and the English people from all the fen-lands came to them; supposing that they should win all that land. Then the monks of Peterborough heard say, that their own men would plunder the minster; namely Hereward and his gang: because they understood that the king had given the abbacy to a French abbot, whose name was Thorold;—that he was a very stern man, and was then come into Stamford with all his Frenchmen. Now there was a churchwarden, whose name was Yware; who took away by night all that he could, testaments, mass-hackles, cantel-copes, and reefs, and such other small things, whatsoever he could; and went early, before day, to the Abbot Thorold; telling him that he sought his protection, and informing him how the outlaws were coming to Peterborough, and that he did all by advice of the monks. Early in the morning came all the outlaws with many ships, resolving to enter the minster; but the monks withstood, so that they could not come in. Then they laid on fire, and burned all the houses of the monks, and all the town except one house. Then came they in through fire at the Bull-hithe gate; where the monks met them, and besought peace of them. But they regarded nothing. They went into the minster, climbed up to the holy rood, took away the diadem from our Lord's head, all of pure gold, and seized the bracket that was underneath his feet, which was all of red gold. They climbed up to the steeple, brought down the table that was hid there, which was all of gold and silver, seized two golden shrines, and nine of silver, and took away fifteen large crucifixes, of gold and of silver; in short, they seized there so much gold and silver, and so many treasures, in money, in raiment, and in books, as no man could tell another; and said, that they did it from their attachment to the minster. Afterwards they went to their ships, proceeded to Ely, and deposited there all the treasure. The Danes, believing that they should overcome the Frenchmen, drove out all the monks; leaving there only one, whose name was Leofwine Lang, who lay sick in the infirmary. Then came Abbot Thorold and eight times twenty Frenchmen with him, all full-armed. When he came thither, he found all within and without consumed by fire, except the church alone; but the outlaws were all with the fleet, knowing that he would come thither. This was done on the fourth day before the nones of June. The two kings, William and Sweyne, were now reconciled; and the Danes went out of Ely with all the aforesaid treasure, and carried it away with them. But when they came into the middle of the sea, there came a violent storm, and dispersed all the ships wherein the treasures were. Some went to Norway, some to Ireland, some to Denmark. All that reached the latter, consisted of the table, and some shrines, and some crucifixes, and many of the other treasures; which they brought to a king's town, called — —, and deposited it all there in the church. Afterwards through their own carelessness, and through their drunkenness, in one night the church and all that was therein was consumed by fire. Thus was the minster of Peterborough burned and plundered. Almighty God have mercy on it through his great goodness. Thus came the Abbot Thorold to Peterborough; and the monks too returned, and performed the service of Christ in the church, which had before stood a full week without any kind of rite. When Bishop Aylric heard it, he excommunicated all the men who that evil deed had done. There was a great famine this year: and in the summer came the fleet in the north from the Humber into the Thames, and lay there two nights, and made afterwards for Denmark. Earl Baldwin also died, and his son Arnulf succeeded to the earldom. Earl William, in conjunction with the king of the Franks, was to be his guardian; but Earl Robert came and slew his kinsman Arnulf and the earl, put the king to flight, and slew many thousands of his men.

A.D. 1071. This year Earl Edwin and Earl Morkar fled out,[92] and roamed at random in woods and in fields. Then went Earl Morkar to Ely by ship; but Earl Edwin was treacherously slain by his own men. Then came Bishop Aylwine, and Siward Barn, and many hundred men with them, into Ely. When King William heard that, then ordered he out a naval force and land force, and beset the land all about, and wrought a bridge, and went in; and the naval force at the same time on the sea-side. And the outlaws then all surrendered; that was, Bishop Aylwine, and Earl Morkar, and all that were with them; except Hereward[93] alone, and all those that would join him, whom he led out triumphantly. And the king took their ships, and weapons, and many treasures;[94] and all the men he disposed of as he thought proper. Bishop Aylwine he sent to Abingdon, where he died in the beginning of the winter.

A.D. 1072. This year King William led a naval force and a land force to Scotland, and beset that land on the sea-side with ships, whilst he led his land-force in at the Tweed;[95] but he found nothing there of any value. King Malcolm, however, came, and made peace with King William, and gave hostages, and became his man; whereupon the king returned home with all his force. This year died Bishop Aylric. He had been invested Bishop of York; but that see was unjustly taken from him, and he then had the bishopric of Durham given him; which he held as long as he chose, but resigned it afterwards, and retired to Peterborough minster; where he abode twelve years. After that King William won England, then took he him from Peterborough, and sent him to Westminster; where

92 i.e.—threw off their allegiance to the Norman usurper, and became voluntary outlaws. The habits of these outlaws, or, at least, of their imitators and descendants in the next century, are well described in the romance of "Ivanhoe".

93 The author of the Gallo-Norman poem printed by Sparke elevates his diction to a higher tone, when describing the feasts of this same Hereward, whom he calls "le uthlage hardi."

94 Or much "coin"; many "scaettae"; such being the denomination of the silver money of the Saxons.

95 Florence of Worcester and those who follow him say that William proceeded as far as Abernethy; where Malcolm met him, and surrendered to him.

he died on the ides of October, and he is there buried, within the minster, in the porch of St. Nicholas.

A.D. 1073. This year led King William an army, English and French, over sea, and won the district of Maine; which the English very much injured by destroying the vineyards, burning the towns, and spoiling the land. But they subdued it all into the hand of King William, and afterwards returned home to England.

A.D. 1074. This year King William went over sea to Normandy; and child Edgar came from Flanders into Scotland on St. Grimbald's mass-day; where King Malcolm and his sister Margaret received him with much pomp. At the same time sent Philip, the King of France, a letter to him, bidding him to come to him, and he would give him the castle of Montreuil; that he might afterwards daily annoy his enemies. What then? King Malcolm and his sister Margaret gave him and his men great presents, and many treasures; in skins ornamented with purple, in pelisses made of martin-skins, of grey-skins, and of ermine-skins, in palls, and in vessels of gold and silver; and conducted him and his crew with great pomp from his territory. But in their voyage evil befel them; for when they were out at sea, there came upon them such rough weather, and the stormy sea and the strong wind drove them so violently on the shore, that all their ships burst, and they also themselves came with difficulty to the land. Their treasure was nearly all lost, and some of his men also were taken by the French; but he himself and his best men returned again to Scotland, some roughly travelling on foot, and some miserably mounted. Then King Malcolm advised him to send to King William over sea, to request his friendship, which he did; and the king gave it him, and sent after him. Again, therefore, King Malcolm and his sister gave him and all his men numberless treasures, and again conducted him very magnificently from their territory. The sheriff of York came to meet him at Durham, and went all the way with him; ordering meat and fodder to be found for him at every castle to which they came, until they came over sea to the king. Then King William received him with much pomp; and he was there afterwards in his court, enjoying such rights as he confirmed to him by law.

A.D. 1075. This year King William gave Earl Ralph the daughter of William Fitz-Osborne to wife. This same Ralph was British on his mother's side; but his father, whose name was also Ralph, was English; and born in Norfolk. The king therefore gave his son the earldom of Norfolk and Suffolk; and he then led the bride to Norwich. There was that bride-ale The source of man's bale. There was Earl Roger, and Earl Waltheof, and bishops, and abbots; who there resolved, that they would drive the king out of the realm of England. But it was soon told the king in Normandy how it was determined. It was Earl Roger and Earl Ralph who were the authors of that plot; and who enticed the Britons to them, and sent eastward to Denmark after a fleet to assist them. Roger went westward to his earldom, and collected his people there, to the king's annoyance, as he thought; but it was to the great disadvantage of himself. He was however prevented. Ralph also in his earldom would go forth with his people; but the castlemen that were in England and also the people of the land, came against him, and prevented him from doing anything. He escaped however to the ships at Norwich.[96] And his wife was in the castle; which she held until peace was made with her; when she went out of England, with all her men who wished to join her. The king afterwards came to England, and seized Earl Roger, his relative, and put him in prison. And Earl Waltheof went over sea, and bewrayed himself; but he asked forgiveness, and proffered gifts of

---

96 *Whence he sailed to Bretagne, according to Flor. S. Dunelm, etc.; but according to Henry of Huntingdon he fled directly to Denmark, returning afterwards with Cnute and Hacco, who invaded England With a fleet of 200 sail.*

ransom. The king, however, let him off lightly, until he[97] came to England; when he had him seized. Soon after that came east from Denmark two hundred ships; wherein were two captains, Cnute Swainson, and Earl Hacco; but they durst not maintain a fight with King William. They went rather to York, and broke into St. Peter's minster, and took therein much treasure, and so went away. They made for Flanders over sea; but they all perished who were privy to that design; that was, the son of Earl Hacco, and many others with him. This year died the Lady Edgitha, who was the relict of King Edward, seven nights before Christmas, at Winchester; and the king caused her to be brought to Westminster with great pomp; and he laid her with King Edward, her lord. And the king was then at Westminster, at midwinter; where all the Britons were condemned who were at the bride-ale at Norwich. Some were punished with blindness; some were driven from the land; and some were towed to Scandinavia. So were the traitors of King William subdued.

A.D. 1076. This year died Sweyne, King of Denmark; and Harold his son took to the kingdom. And the king gave the abbacy of Westminster to Abbot Vitalis, who had been Abbot of Bernay. This year also was Earl Waltheof beheaded at Winchester, on the mass-day of St. Petronilla;[98] and his body was carried to Croyland, where he lies buried. King William now went over sea, and led his army to Brittany, and beset the castle of Dol; but the Bretons defended it, until the king came from France; whereupon William departed thence, having lost there both men and horses, and many of his treasures.

A.D. 1077. This year were reconciled the king of the Franks

---

97   *i.e. Earl Waltheof.*

98   *This notice of St. Petronilla, whose name and existence seem scarcely to have been known to the Latin historians, we owe exclusively to the valuable MS. "Cotton Tiberius" B lv. Yet if ever female saint deserved to be commemorated as a conspicuous example of early piety and christian zeal, it must be Petronilla.*

and William, King of England. But it continued only a little while. This year was London burned, one night before the Assumption of St. Mary, so terribly as it never was before, since it was built. This year the moon was eclipsed three nights before Candlemas; and in the same year died Aylwy, the prudent Abbot of Evesham, on the fourteenth day before the calends of March, on the mass-day of St. Juliana; and Walter was appointed abbot in his stead; and Bishop Herman also died, on the tenth day before the calends of March, who was Bishop in Berkshire, and in Wiltshire, and in Dorsetshire. This year also King Malcolm won the mother of Malslaythe.... and all his best men, and all his treasures, and his cattle; and he himself not easily escaped.... This year also was the dry summer; and wild fire came upon many shires, and burned many towns; and also many cities were ruined thereby.

A.D. 1079. This year Robert, the son of King William, deserted from his father to his uncle Robert in Flanders; because his father would not let him govern his earldom in Normandy; which he himself, and also King Philip with his permission, had given him. The best men that were in the land also had sworn oaths of allegiance to him, and taken him for their lord. This year, therefore, Robert fought with his father, without Normandy, by a castle called Gerberoy; and wounded him in the hand; and his horse, that he sat upon, was killed under him; and he that brought him another was killed there right with a dart. That was Tookie Wiggodson. Many were there slain, and also taken. His son William too was there wounded; but Robert returned to Flanders. We will not here, however, record any more injury that he did his father. This year came King Malcolm from Scotland into England, betwixt the two festivals of St. Mary, with a large army, which plundered Northumberland till it came to the Tine, and slew many hundreds of men, and carried home much coin, and treasure, and men in captivity.

A.D. 1080. This year was Bishop Walker slain in Durham, at a council; and an hundred men with him, French and Flemish. He himself was born in Lorrain. This did the Northumbrians in the month of May.[99]

A.D. 1081. This year the king led an army into Wales, and there freed many hundreds of men.

A.D. 1082. This year the king seized Bishop Odo; and this year also was a great famine.

A.D. 1083. This year arose the tumult at Glastonbury betwixt the Abbot Thurstan and his monks. It proceeded first from the abbot's want of wisdom, that he misgoverned his monks in many things. But the monks meant well to him; and told him that he should govern them rightly, and love them, and they would be faithful and obedient to him. The abbot, however, would hear nothing of this; but evil entreated them, and threatened them worse. One day the abbot went into the chapter-house, and spoke against the monks, and attempted to mislead them;[100] and sent after some laymen, and they came full-armed into the chapter-house upon the monks. Then were the monks very much afraid[101] of them, and wist not what they were to do, but they shot forward, and some ran into the church, and locked the doors after them. But they followed them into the minster, and resolved to drag them out, so that they durst not go out. A rueful thing happened on that day. The Frenchmen broke into the choir, and hurled their weapons toward the altar, where the monks were; and some of the knights went upon the upper floor,[102] and shot

---

99 *The brevity of our Chronicle here, and in the two following years, in consequence of the termination of "Cotton Tiberius" B iv., is remarkable. From the year 1083 it assumes a character more decidedly Anglo-Norman.*

100 *i.e. In the service; by teaching them a new-fangled chant, brought from Feschamp in Normandy, instead of that to which they had been accustomed, and which is called the Gregorian chant.*

101 *Literally, "afeared of them"—i.e. terrified by them.*

102 *Probably along the open galleries in the upper story of the choir.*

their arrows downward incessantly toward the sanctuary; so that on the crucifix that stood above the altar they stuck many arrows. And the wretched monks lay about the altar, and some crept under, and earnestly called upon God, imploring his mercy, since they could not obtain any at the hands of men. What can we say, but that they continued to shoot their arrows; whilst the others broke down the doors, and came in, and slew[103] some of the monks to death, and wounded many therein; so that the blood came from the altar upon the steps, and from the steps on the floor. Three there were slain to death, and eighteen wounded. And in this same year departed Matilda, queen of King William, on the day after All-Hallow-mass. And in the same year also, after mid-winter, the king ordained a large and heavy contribution[104] over all England; that was, upon each hide of land, two and seventy pence.

A.D. 1084. In this year died Wulfwold, Abbot of Chertsey, on the thirteenth day before the calends of May.

A.D. 1085. In this year men reported, and of a truth asserted, that Cnute, King of Denmark, son of King Sweyne, was coming hitherward, and was resolved to win this land, with the assistance of Robert, Earl of Flanders;[105] for Cnute had Robert's daughter. When William, King of England, who was then resident in Normandy (for he had both England and Normandy), understood this, he went into England with so large an army of horse and foot, from France and Brittany, as never before sought this land; so that men wondered how this land could feed all that force. But the king left the army to shift for themselves through all this land amongst his subjects, who fed them, each according to his quota of land. Men suffered much distress this year; and the king caused the

---

103 *"Slaegan", in its first sense, signifies "to strike violently"; whence the term "sledge-hammer". This consideration will remove the supposed pleonasm in the Saxon phrase, which is here literally translated.*

104 *"Gild," Sax.; which in this instance was a land-tax of one shilling to a yardland.*

105 *—and of Clave Kyrre, King of Norway. Vid. "Antiq. Celto-Scand".*

land to be laid waste about the sea coast; that, if his foes came up, they might not have anything on which they could very readily seize. But when the king understood of a truth that his foes were impeded, and could not further their expedition,[106] then let he some of the army go to their own land; but some he held in this land over the winter. Then, at the midwinter, was the king in Gloucester with his council, and held there his court five days. And afterwards the archbishop and clergy had a synod three days. There was Mauritius chosen Bishop of London, William of Norfolk, and Robert of Cheshire. These were all the king's clerks. After this had the king a large meeting, and very deep consultation with his council, about this land; how it was occupied, and by what sort of men. Then sent he his men over all England into each shire; commissioning them to find out "How many hundreds of hides were in the shire, what land the king himself had, and what stock upon the land; or, what dues he ought to have by the year from the shire." Also he commissioned them to record in writing, "How much land his archbishops had, and his diocesan bishops, and his abbots, and his earls;" and though I may be prolix and tedious, "What, or how much, each man had, who was an occupier of land in England, either in land or in stock, and how much money it were worth." So very narrowly, indeed, did he commission them to trace it out, that there was not one single hide, nor a yard[107] of land, nay, moreover (it is shameful to tell, though he thought it no shame to do it), not even an ox, nor a cow, nor a swine was there left, that was not set down in his writ. And all the recorded particulars were afterwards brought to him.[108]

---

106 *Because there was a mutiny in the Danish fleet; which was carried to such a height, that the king, after his return to Denmark, was slain by his own subjects. Vid. "Antiq. Celto-Scand", also our "Chronicle" A.D. 1087.*

107 *i.e. a fourth part of an acre.*

108 *At Winchester; where the king held his court at Easter in the following year; and the survey was accordingly deposited there; whence it was called "Rotulus Wintoniae", and "Liber Wintoniae".*

A page from the Domesday Book for Warwickshire (showing Birmingham). This was the great survey commissioned by William the Conqueror and completed in 1086.

A.D. 1086. This year the king bare his crown, and held his court, in Winchester at Easter; and he so arranged, that he was by the Pentecost at Westminster, and dubbed his son Henry a knight there. Afterwards he moved about so that he came by Lammas to Sarum; where he was met by his councillors; and all the landsmen that were of any account over all England became this man's vassals as they were; and they all bowed themselves before him, and became his men, and swore him oaths of allegiance that they would against all other men be faithful to him. Thence he proceeded into the Isle of Wight; because he wished to go into Normandy, and so he afterwards did; though he first did according to his custom; he collected a very large sum from his people, wherever he could make any demand, whether with justice or otherwise. Then he went into Normandy; and Edgar Etheling, the relation of King Edward, revolted from him, for he received not much honour from him; but may the Almighty God give him honour hereafter. And Christina, the sister of the etheling, went into the monastery of Rumsey, and received the holy veil. And the same year there was a very heavy season, and a swinkful and sorrowful year in England, in murrain of cattle, and corn and fruits were at a stand, and so much untowardness in the weather, as a man may not easily think; so tremendous was the thunder and lightning, that it killed many men; and it continually grew worse and worse with men. May God Almighty better it whenever it be his will.

A.D. 1087. After the birth of our Lord and Saviour Christ, one thousand and eighty-seven winters; in the one and twentieth year after William began to govern and direct England, as God granted him, was a very heavy and pestilent season in this land. Such a sickness came on men, that full nigh every other man was in the worst disorder, that is, in the diarrhoea; and that so dreadfully, that many men died in the disorder. Afterwards came, through the badness of the weather as we before mentioned, so great a famine over all England, that many hundreds of men died a miserable death through hunger. Alas! how wretched and how rueful a time was there! When the poor wretches lay full nigh driven to death prematurely, and afterwards came sharp hunger, and dispatched them withall! Who will not be penetrated with grief at such a season? or who is so hardhearted as not to weep at such misfortune? Yet such things happen for folks' sins, that they will not love God and righteousness. So it was in those days, that little righteousness was in this land with any men but with the monks alone, wherever they fared well. The king and the head men loved much, and overmuch, covetousness in gold and in silver; and recked not how sinfully it was got, provided it came to them. The king let his land at as high a rate as he possibly could; then came some other person, and bade more than the former one gave, and the king let it to the men that bade him more. Then came the third, and bade yet more; and the king let it to hand to the men that bade him most of all: and he recked not how very sinfully the stewards got it of wretched men, nor how many unlawful deeds they did; but the more men spake about right law, the more unlawfully they acted. They erected unjust tolls, and many other unjust things they did, that are difficult to reckon. Also in the same year, before harvest, the holy minster of St. Paul, the episcopal see in London, was completely burned, with many other minsters, and the greatest part, and the richest of the whole city. So also, about the same time, full nigh each head-port in all England was entirely burned. Alas! rueful and woeful was the fate of the year that brought forth so many misfortunes. In the same year also, before the Assumption of St. Mary, King William went from Normandy into France with an army, and made war upon his own lord Philip, the king, and slew many of his men, and burned the town of Mante, and all the holy minsters that were in the town; and two holy men that served God, leading the life of anachorets, were burned therein. This being thus done, King William returned to Normandy. Rueful was the thing he did; but a more rueful him befel. How more rueful? He fell sick, and it dreadfully ailed him. What shall I say? Sharp death, that passes by neither rich men nor poor, seized him also. He died in Normandy, on the next day after the Nativity of St. Mary, and he was buried at Caen in St. Stephen's minster, which he had formerly reared, and afterwards endowed with manifold gifts. Alas! how false and how uncertain is this world's weal! He that was before a rich king, and lord of many lands, had not then of all his land more than a space of seven feet! and he that was whilom enshrouded in gold and gems, lay there covered with mould! He left behind him three sons; the eldest, called Robert, who was earl in Normandy after him; the second, called William, who wore the crown after him in England; and the third, called Henry, to whom his father bequeathed immense treasure. If any person wishes to know what kind of man he was, or what honour he had, or of how many lands he was lord, then will we write about him as well as we understand him: we who often looked upon him, and lived sometime in his court. This King William then that we speak about was a very wise man, and very rich; more splendid and powerful than any of his predecessors were. He was mild to the good men that loved God, and beyond all measure severe to the men that gainsayed his will. On that same spot where God granted him that he should gain England, he reared a mighty minster, and set monks therein, and well endowed it. In his days was the great monastery in Canterbury built, and also very many others over all England. This land was moreover well filled with monks, who modelled their lives after the rule of St. Benedict. But such was the state of Christianity in his time, that each man followed what belonged to his profession—he that would. He was also very dignified. Thrice he bare his crown each year, as oft as he was in England. At Easter he bare it in Winchester, at Pentecost in Westminster, at midwinter in Glocester. And then were with him all the rich men over all England; archbishops and diocesan bishops, abbots and earls, thanes and knights. So very stern was he also and hot, that no man durst do anything against his will. He had earls in his custody, who acted against his will. Bishops he hurled from their bishoprics, and abbots from their abbacies, and thanes into prison. At length he spared not his own brother Odo, who was a very rich bishop in Normandy. At Baieux was his episcopal stall; and he was the foremost man of all to aggrandise the king. He had an earldom in England; and when the king was in Normandy, then was he the mightiest man in this land. Him he confined in prison. But amongst other things is not to be forgotten that good peace that he made in this land; so that a man of any account might go over his kingdom unhurt with his bosom full of gold. No man durst slay another, had he never so much evil done to the other; and if any churl lay with a woman against her will, he soon lost the limb that he played with. He truly reigned over England; and by his capacity so thoroughly surveyed it, that there was not a hide of land in England that he wist not who had it, or what it was worth, and afterwards set it down in his book.[109] The land of the Britons was in his power; and he wrought castles therein; and ruled Anglesey withal. So also he subdued Scotland by his great strength. As to Normandy, that was his native land; but he reigned also over the earldom called Maine; and if he might have yet lived two years more, he would have won Ireland by his valour, and without any weapons. Assuredly in his time had men much distress, and very many sorrows. Castles he let men build, and miserably swink the poor. The king himself was so very rigid; and extorted from his subjects many marks of gold, and many hundred pounds of silver; which he took of his people, for little need, by right and by unright. He was fallen into covetousness, and greediness he loved withal. He made many deer-parks; and he established laws therewith; so that whosoever slew a hart, or a hind,

---

109 *An evident allusion to the compilation of Doomsday book, already described in A.D. 1085.*

should be deprived of his eyesight. As he forbade men to kill the harts, so also the boars; and he loved the tall deer as if he were their father. Likewise he decreed by the hares, that they should go free. His rich men bemoaned it, and the poor men shuddered at it. But he was so stern, that he recked not the hatred of them all; for they must follow withal the king's will, if they would live, or have land, or possessions, or even his peace. Alas! that any man should presume so to puff himself up, and boast o'er all men. May the Almighty God show mercy to his soul, and grant him forgiveness of his sins! These things have we written concerning him, both good and evil; that men may choose the good after their goodness, and flee from the evil withal, and go in the way that leadeth us to the kingdom of heaven. Many things may we write that were done in this same year. So it was in Denmark, that the Danes, a nation that was formerly accounted the truest of all, were turned aside to the greatest untruth, and to the greatest treachery that ever could be. They chose and bowed to King Cnute, and swore him oaths, and afterwards dastardly slew him in a church. It happened also in Spain, that the heathens went and made inroads upon the Christians, and reduced much of the country to their dominion. But the king of the Christians, Alphonzo by name, sent everywhere into each land, and desired assistance. And they came to his support from every land that was Christian; and they went and slew or drove away all the heathen folk, and won their land again, through God's assistance. In this land also, in the same year, died many rich men; Stigand, Bishop of Chichester, and the Abbot of St. Augustine, and the Abbot of Bath, and the Abbot of Pershore, and the lord of them all, William, King of England, that we spoke of before. After his death his son, called William also as the father, took to the kingdom, and was blessed to king by Archbishop Landfranc at Westminster three days ere Michaelmas day.

William II, also known as Wiliam Rufus, began his reign in 1087.

And all the men in England submitted to him, and swore oaths to him. This being thus done, the king went to Winchester, and opened the treasure house, and the treasures that his father had gathered, in gold, and in silver, and in vases, and in palls, and in gems, and in many other valuable things that are difficult to enumerate. Then the king did as his father bade him ere he was dead; he there distributed treasures for his father's soul to each monastery that was in England; to some ten marks of gold, to some six, to each upland[110] church sixty pence. And into each shire were sent a hundred pounds of money to distribute amongst poor men for his soul. And ere he departed, he bade that they should release all the men that were in prison under his power. And the king was on the midwinter in London.

A.D. 1088. In this year was this land much stirred, and filled with great treachery; so that the richest Frenchmen that were in this land would betray their lord the king, and would have his brother Robert king, who was earl in Normandy. In this design was engaged first Bishop Odo, and Bishop Gosfrith, and William, Bishop of Durham. So well did the king by the bishop [Odo] that all England fared according to his counsel, and as he would. And the bishop thought to do by him as Judas Iscariot did by our Lord. And Earl Roger was also of this faction; and much people was with him all Frenchmen. This conspiracy was formed in Lent. As soon as Easter came, then went they forth, and harrowed, and burned, and wasted the king's farms; and they despoiled the lands of all the men that were in the king's service. And they each of them went to his castle, and manned it, and provisioned it as well as they could. Bishop Gosfrith, and Robert the peace-breaker, went to Bristol, and plundered it, and brought the spoil to the castle. Afterwards they went out of the castle, and plundered Bath, and all the land thereabout; and all the

110 *Uppe-land, Sax.—i.e. village-church.*

honor[111] of Berkeley they laid waste. And the men that eldest were of Hereford, and all the shire forthwith, and the men of Shropshire, with much people of Wales, came and plundered and burned in Worcestershire, until they came to the city itself, which it was their design to set on fire, and then to rifle the minster, and win the king's castle to their hands. The worthy Bishop Wulfstan, seeing these things, was much agitated in his mind, because to him was betaken the custody of the castle. Nevertheless his hired men went out of the castle with few attendants, and, through God's mercy and the bishop's merits, slew or took five hundred men, and put all the others to flight. The Bishop of Durham did all the harm that he could over all by the north. Roger was the name of one of them;[112] who leaped into the castle at Norwich, and did yet the worst of all over all that land. Hugh also was one, who did nothing better either in Leicestershire or in Northamptonshire. The Bishop Odo being one, though of the same family from which the king himself was descended, went into Kent to his earldom, and greatly despoiled it; and having laid waste the lands of the king and of the archbishop withal, he brought the booty into his castle at Rochester. When the king understood all these things, and what treachery they were employing against him, then was he in his mind much agitated. He then sent after Englishmen, described to them his need, earnestly requested their support, and promised them the best laws that ever before were in this land; each unright guild he forbade, and restored to the men their woods and chaces. But it stood no while. The Englishmen however went to the assistance of the king their lord. They advanced toward Rochester, with a view to get possession of the Bishop Odo; for they thought, if they had him who was at first the head of the conspiracy, they might the better get

---

111 *i.e. jurisdiction. We have adopted the modern title of the district; but the Saxon term occurs in many of the ancient evidences of Berkeley Castle.*

112 *i.e. of the conspirators.*

possession of all the others. They came then to the castle at Tunbridge; and there were in the castle the knights of Bishop Odo, and many others who were resolved to hold it against the king. But the Englishmen advanced, and broke into the castle, and the men that were therein agreed with the king. The king with his army went toward Rochester. And they supposed that the bishop was therein; but it was made known to the king that the bishop was gone to the castle at Pevensea. And the king with his army went after, and beset the castle about with a very large force full six weeks. During this time the Earl of Normandy, Robert, the king's brother, gathered a very considerable force, and thought to win England with the support of those men that were in this land against the king. And he sent some of his men to this land, intending to come himself after. But the Englishmen that guarded the sea lighted upon some of the men, and slew them, and drowned more than any man could tell. When provisions afterwards failed those within the castle, they earnestly besought peace, and gave themselves up to the king; and the bishop swore that he would depart out of England, and no more come on this land, unless the king sent after him, and that he would give up the castle at Rochester. Just as the bishop was going with an intention to give up the castle, and the king had sent his men with him, then arose the men that were in the castle, and took the bishop and the king's men, and put them into prison. In the castle were some very good knights; Eustace the Young, and the three sons of Earl Roger, and all the best born men that were in this land or in Normandy. When the king understood this thing, then went he after with the army that he had there, and sent over all England. and bade that each man that was faithful should come to him, French and English, from sea-port and from upland. Then came to him much people; and he went to Rochester, and beset the castle, until they that were therein agreed, and gave up the castle.

The Bishop Odo with the men that were in the castle went over sea, and the bishop thus abandoned the dignity that he had in this land. The king afterwards sent an army to Durham, and allowed it to beset the castle, and the bishop agreed, and gave up the castle, and relinquished his bishopric, and went to Normandy. Many Frenchmen also abandoned their lands, and went over sea; and the king gave their lands to the men that were faithful to him.

A.D. 1089. In this year the venerable father and favourer of monks, Archbishop Landfranc, departed this life; but we hope that he is gone to the heavenly kingdom. There was also over all England much earth-stirring on the third day before the ides of August, and it was a very late year in corn, and in every kind of fruits, so that many men reaped their corn about Martinmas, and yet later.

A.D. 1090. Indiction XIII. These things thus done, just as we have already said above, by the king, and by his brother and by this men, the king was considering how he might wreak his vengeance on his brother Robert, harass him most, and win Normandy of him. And indeed through his craft, or through bribery, he got possession of the castle at St. Valeri, and the haven; and so he got possession of that at Albemarle. And therein he set his knights; and they did harm to the land in harrowing and burning. After this he got possession of more castles in the land; and therein lodged his horsemen. When the Earl of Normandy, Robert, understood that his sworn men deceived him, and gave up their castles to do him harm, then sent he to his lord, Philip, king of the Franks; and he came to Normandy with a large army, and the king and the earl with an immense force beset the castle about, wherein were the men of the King of England. But the King William of England sent to Philip, king of the Franks; and he for his love, or for his great treasure, abandoned thus his subject the Earl Robert and his land; and returned again to France, and let them so remain. And in the midst of these things this land was much oppressed by unlawful exactions and by many other misfortunes.

A.D. 1091. In this year the King William held his court at Christmas in Westminster, and thereafter at Candlemas he went, for the annoyance of his brother, out of England into Normandy. Whilst he was there, their reconciliation took place, on the condition, that the earl put into his hands Feschamp, and the earldom of Ou, and Cherbourg; and in addition to this, that the king's men should be secure in the castles that they had won against the will of the earl. And the king in return promised him those many [castles] that their father had formerly won, and also to reduce those that had revolted from the earl, also all that his father had there beyond, except those that he had then given the king, and that all those, that in England before for the earl had lost their land, should have it again by this treaty, and that the earl should have in England just so much as was specified in this agreement. And if the earl died without a son by lawful wedlock, the king should be heir of all Normandy; and by virtue of this same treaty, if the king died, the earl should be heir of all England. To this treaty swore twelve of the best men of the king's side, and twelve of the earl's, though it stood but a little while afterwards. In the midst of this treaty was Edgar Etheling deprived of the land that the earl had before permitted him to keep in hand; and he went out of Normandy to the king, his sister's husband, in Scotland, and to his sister. Whilst the King William was out of England, the King Malcolm of Scotland came hither into England, and overran a great deal of it, until the good men that governed this land sent an army against him and repulsed him. When the King William in Normandy heard this, then prepared he his departure, and came to England, and his brother, the Earl Robert, with him; and he soon issued an order to collect a force both naval and military; but the naval force, ere it could come to Scotland, perished almost miserably, a few days before St. Michael's mass. And the king and his brother proceeded with the land-force; but when the King Malcolm heard that they were resolved to seek him with an army, he went with his force out of Scotland into Lothaine in England, and there abode. When the King William came near with his army, then interceded between them Earl Robert, and Edgar Etheling, and so made the peace of the kings, that the King Malcolm came to our king, and did homage,[113] promising all such obedience as he formerly paid to his father; and that he confirmed with an oath. And the King William promised him in land and in all things whatever he formerly had under his father. In this settlement was also Edgar Etheling united with the king. And the kings then with much satisfaction departed; yet that stood but a little while. And the Earl Robert tarried here full nigh until Christmas with the king, and during this time found but little of the truth of their agreement; and two days before that tide he took ship in the Isle of Wight, and went into Normandy, and Edgar Etheling with him.

A.D. 1092. In this year the King William with a large army went north to Carlisle, and restored the town, and reared the castle, and drove out Dolphin that before governed the land, and set his own men in the castle, and then returned hither southward. And a vast number of rustic people with wives and with cattle he sent thither, to dwell there in order to till the land.

A.D. 1093. In this year, during Lent, was the King William at Glocester so sick, that he was by all reported dead. And in his illness he made many good promises to lead his own life aright; to grant peace and protection to the churches of God, and never more again with fee to sell; to have none but righteous laws amongst his people. The archbishopric

---

113 *Literally "became his man" — "Ic becom eowr man" was the formula of doing homage.*

of Canterbury, that before remained in his own hand, he transferred to Anselm, who was before Abbot of Bec; to Robert his chancellor the bishopric of Lincoln; and to many minsters he gave land; but that he afterwards took away, when he was better, and annulled all the good laws that he promised us before. Then after this sent the King of Scotland, and demanded the fulfilment of the treaty that was promised him. And the King William cited him to Glocester, and sent him hostages to Scotland; and Edgar Etheling, afterwards, and the men returned, that brought him with great dignity to the king. But when he came to the king, he could not be considered worthy either of our king's speech, or of the conditions that were formerly promised him. For this reason therefore they parted with great dissatisfaction, and the King Malcolm returned to Scotland. And soon after he came home, he gathered his army, and came harrowing into England with more hostility than behoved him; and Robert, the Earl of Northumberland, surrounded him unawares with his men, and slew him. Morel of Barnborough slew him, who was the earl's steward, and a baptismal friend[114] of King Malcolm. With him was also slain Edward his son; who after him should have been king, if he had lived. When the good Queen Margaret heard this—her most beloved lord and son thus betrayed she was in her mind almost distracted to death. She with her priests went to church, and performed her rites, and prayed before God, that she might give up the ghost. And the Scots then chose[115] Dufenal to king, Malcolm's brother, and drove out all the English that formerly were with the King Malcolm. When Duncan, King Malcolm's son, heard all that had thus taken place (he was then in the King William's court,

114 Literally a "gossip"; but such are the changes which words undergo in their meaning as well as in their form, that a title of honour formerly implying a spiritual relationship in God, is now applied only to those whose conversation resembles the contemptible tittle-tattle of a Christening.

115 From this expression it is evident, that though preference was naturally and properly given to hereditary claims, the monarchy of Scotland, as well as of England, was in principle "elective". The doctrine of hereditary, of divine, of indefeasible "right", is of modern growth.

because his father had given him as a hostage to our king's father, and so he lived here afterwards), he came to the king, and did such fealty as the king required at his hands; and so with his permission went to Scotland, with all the support that he could get of English and French, and deprived his uncle Dufenal of the kingdom, and was received as king. But the Scots afterwards gathered some force together, and slew full nigh all his men; and he himself with a few made his escape.[116] Afterwards they were reconciled, on the condition that he never again brought into the land English or French.

A.D. 1094. This year the King William held his court at Christmas in Glocester; and messengers came to him thither from his brother Robert of Normandy; who said that his brother renounced all peace and conditions, unless the king would fulfil all that they had stipulated in the treaty; and upon that he called him forsworn and void of truth, unless he adhered to the treaty, or went thither and explained himself there, where the treaty was formerly made and also sworn. Then went the king to Hastings at Candlemas; and whilst he there abode waiting the weather, he let hallow the minster at Battel, and deprived Herbert Losang, the Bishop of Thetford, of his staff; and thereafter about mid-Lent went over sea into Normandy. After he came, thither, he and his brother Robert, the earl, said that they should come together in peace (and so they did), and might be united. Afterwards they came together with the same men that before made the treaty, and also confirmed it by oaths; and all the blame of breaking the treaty they threw upon the king; but he would not confess this, nor even adhere to the treaty; and for this reason they parted with much dissatisfaction. And the king afterwards won the castle at Bures, and took the earl's men therein; some of whom he sent hither to this land. On the other hand the earl, with the assistance of the King of

---

116 *See the following year towards the end, where Duncan is said to be slain.*

France, won the castle at Argence, and took therein Roger of Poitou,[117] and seven hundred of the king's knights with him; and afterwards that at Hulme; and oft readily did either of them burn the towns of the other, and also took men. Then sent the king hither to this land, and ordered twenty thousand Englishmen to be sent out to Normandy to his assistance; but when they came to sea, they then had orders to return, and to pay to the king's behoof the fee that they had taken; which was half a pound each man; and they did so. And the earl after this, with the King of France, and with all that he could gather together, went through the midst of Normandy, towards Ou, where the King William was, and thought to besiege him within; and so they advanced until they came to Luneville. There was the King of France through cunning turned aside; and so afterwards all the army dispersed. In the midst of these things the King William sent after his brother Henry, who was in the castle at Damfront; but because he could not go through Normandy with security, he sent ships after him, and Hugh, Earl of Chester. When, however, they should have gone towards Ou where the king was, they went to England, and came up at Hamton,[118] on the eve of the feast of All Saints, and here afterwards abode; and at Christmas they were in London. In this same year also the Welshmen gathered themselves together, and with the French that were in Wales, or in the neighbourhood, and had formerly seized their land, stirred up war, and broke into many fastnesses and castles, and slew many men. And when their followers had increased, they divided themselves into larger parties. With some part of them fought Hugh, Earl of Shropshire,[119] and put them to flight. Nevertheless the other part of them all this year omitted no evil that they could do. This year

---

117 *Peitevin, which is the connecting link between "Pictaviensem" and "Poitou".*

118 *Now called Southampton, to distinguish it from Northampton, but the common people in both neighbourhoods generally say "Hamton" to this day (1823).*

119 *The title is now Earl of Shrewsbury.*

also the Scots ensnared their king, Duncan, and slew him; and afterwards, the second time, took his uncle Dufenal to king, through whose instruction and advice he was betrayed to death.

A.D. 1095. In this year was the King William the first four days of Christmas at Whitsand, and after the fourth day came hither, and landed at Dover. And Henry, the king's brother, abode in this land until Lent, and then went over sea to Normandy, with much treasure, on the king's behalf, against their brother, Earl Robert, and frequently fought against the earl, and did him much harm, both in land and in men. And then at Easter held the king his court in Winchester; and the Earl Robert of Northumberland would not come to court. And the king was much stirred to anger with him for this, and sent to him, and bade him harshly, if he would be worthy of protection, that he would come to court at Pentecost. In this year was Easter on the eighth day before the calends of April; and upon Easter, on the night of the feast of St Ambrose, that is, the second before the nones of April,[120] nearly over all this land, and almost all the night, numerous and manifold stars were seen to fall from heaven; not by one or two, but so thick in succession, that no man could tell it. Hereafter at Pentecost was the king at Windsor, and all his council with him, except the Earl of Northumberland; for the king would neither give him hostages, nor own upon truth, that he might come and go with security. And the king therefore ordered his army, and went against the earl to Northumberland; and soon after he came thither, he won many and nearly all the best of the earl's clan in a fortress, and put them into custody; and the castle at Tinemouth he beset until he won it, and the earl's brother therein, and all that were with him; and afterwards went to Bamborough, and beset the earl therein. But when the king saw that he could not win it, then ordered he his

120 *The fourth of April. Vid. "Ord. Vit."*

men to make a castle before Bamborough, and called it in his speech "Malveisin"; that is in English, "Evil Neighbour". And he fortified it strongly with his men, and afterwards went southward. Then, soon after that the king was gone south, went the earl one night out of Bamborough towards Tinemouth; but they that were in the new castle were aware of him, and went after him, and fought him, and wounded him, and afterwards took him. And of those that were with him some they slew, and some they took alive. Among these things it was made known to the king, that the Welshmen in Wales had broken into a castle called Montgomery, and slain the men of Earl Hugo, that should have held it. He therefore gave orders to levy another force immediately, and after Michaelmas went into Wales, and shifted his forces, and went through all that land, so that the army came all together by All Saints to Snowdon. But the Welsh always went before into the mountains and the moors, that no man could come to them. The king then went homeward; for he saw that he could do no more there this winter. When the king came home again, he gave orders to take the Earl Robert of Northumberland, and lead him to Bamborough, and put out both his eyes, unless they that were therein would give up the castle. His wife held it, and Morel who was steward, and also his relative. Through this was the castle then given up; and Morel was then in the king's court; and through him were many both of the clergy and laity surrendered, who with their counsels had conspired against the king. The king had before this time commanded some to be brought into prison, and afterwards had it very strictly proclaimed over all this country, "That all who held land of the king, as they wished to be considered worthy of protection, should come to court at the time appointed." And the king commanded that the Earl Robert should be led to Windsor, and there held in the castle. Also in this same year, against Easter, came the pope's nuncio hither to this land. This was Bishop Walter, a man of very good life, of the town of Albano; and upon the day of Pentecost on the behalf of Pope Urban he gave Archbishop Anselm his pall, and he received him at his archiepiscopal stall in Canterbury. And Bishop Walter remained afterwards in this land a great part of the year; and men then sent by him the Rome-scot,[121] which they had not done for many years before. This same year also the weather was very unseasonable; in consequence of which throughout all this land were all the fruits of the earth reduced to a moderate crop.

A.D. 1096. In this year held the King William his court at Christmas in Windsor; and William Bishop of Durham died there on new-year's day; and on the octave of the Epiphany was the king and all his councillors at Salisbury. There Geoffry Bainard challenged William of Ou, the king's relative, maintaining that he had been in the conspiracy against the king. And he fought with him, and overcame him in single combat; and after he was overcome, the king gave orders to put out his eyes, and afterwards to emasculate him; and his steward, William by name, who was the son of his stepmother, the king commanded to be hanged on a gibbet. Then was also Eoda, Earl of Champagne, the king's son-in-law, and many others, deprived of their lands; whilst some were led to London, and there killed. This year also, at Easter, there was a very great stir through all this nation and many others, on account of Urban, who was declared Pope, though he had nothing of a see at Rome. And an immense multitude went forth with their wives and children, that they might make war upon the heathens. Through this expedition were the king and his brother, Earl Robert, reconciled; so that the king went over sea, and purchased all Normandy of him, on condition that they should be united. And the earl

---

121 *Commonly called "Peter-pence".*

afterwards departed; and with him the Earl of Flanders, and the Earl of Boulogne, and also many other men of rank.[122] And the Earl Robert, and they that went with him, passed the winter in Apulia; but of the people that went by Hungary many thousands miserably perished there and by the way. And many dragged themselves home rueful and hunger-bitten on the approach of winter. This was a very heavy-timed year through all England, both through the manifold tributes, and also through the very heavy-timed hunger that severely oppressed this earth in the course of the year. In this year also the principal men who held this land, frequently sent forces into Wales, and many men thereby grievously afflicted, producing no results but destruction of men and waste of money.

A.D. 1097. In this year was the King William at Christmas in Normandy; and afterwards against Easter he embarked for this land; for that he thought to hold his court at Winchester; but he was weather-bound until Easter-eve, when he first landed at Arundel; and for this reason held his court at Windsor. And thereafter with a great army he went into Wales, and quickly penetrated that land with his forces, through some of the Welsh who were come to him, and were his guides; and he remained in that country from midsummer nearly until August, and suffered much loss there in men and in horses, and also in many other things. The Welshmen, after they had revolted from the king, chose them many elders from themselves; one of whom was called Cadwgan,[123] who was the worthiest of them, being brother's son to King Griffin. And when the king saw that he could do nothing in furtherance of his will, he returned again into this land; and soon after that he let his men build castles on the borders.

---

122 Literally "head-men, or chiefs". The term is still retained with a slight variation in the north of Europe, as the "hetman" Platoff of celebrated memory.

123 This name is now written, improperly, Cadogan; though the ancient pronunciation continues. "Cadung", "Ann. Wav." erroneously, perhaps, for "Cadugn".

Then upon the feast of St. Michael, the fourth day before the nones of October,[124] appeared an uncommon star, shining in the evening, and soon hastening to set. It[125] was seen south-west, and the ray that stood off from it was thought very long, shining south-east. And it appeared on this wise nearly all the week. Many men supposed that it was a comet. Soon after this Archbishop Anselm of Canterbury obtained leave[126] of the king (though it was contrary to the wishes of the king, as men supposed), and went over sea; because he thought that men in this country did little according to right and after his instruction. And the king thereafter upon St. Martin's mass went over sea into Normandy; but whilst he was waiting for fair weather, his court in the county where they lay, did the most harm that ever court or army could do in a friendly and peaceable land. This was in all things a very heavy-timed year, and beyond measure laborious from badness of weather, both when men attempted to till the land, and afterwards to gather the fruits of their tilth; and from unjust contributions they never rested. Many counties also that were confined to London by work, were grievously oppressed on account of the wall that they were building about the tower, and the bridge that was nearly all afloat, and the work of the king's hall that they were building at Westminster; and many men perished thereby. Also in this same year soon after Michaelmas went Edgar Etheling with an army through the king's assistance into Scotland, and with hard fighting won that land, and drove out the King Dufnal; and his nephew Edgar, who was son of King Malcolm and of Margaret the queen, he there appointed king in fealty to the King William; and afterwards again returned to England.

---

124 *It was evidently, therefore, not on Michaelmas day, but during the continuance of the mass or festival which was celebrated till the octave following.*

125 *In the original "he"; so that the Saxons agreed with the Greeks and Romans with respect to the gender of a comet.*

126 *Literally "took leave": hence the modern phrase to signify the departure of one person from another, which in feudal times could not be done without leave or permission formally obtained.*

A.D. 1098. In this year at Christmas was the King William in Normandy; and Walkelin, Bishop of Winchester, and Baldwin, Abbot of St. Edmund's, within this tide[127] both departed. And in this year also died Turold, Abbot of Peterborough. In the summer of this year also, at Finchamstead in Berkshire, a pool welled with blood, as many true men said that should see it. And Earl Hugh was slain in Anglesey by foreign pirates,[128] and his brother Robert was his heir, as he had settled it before with the king. Before Michaelmas the heaven was of such an hue, as if it were burning, nearly all the night. This was a very troublesome year through manifold impositions; and from the abundant rains, that ceased not all the year, nearly all the tilth in the marsh-lands perished.

A.D. 1099. This year was the King William at midwinter in Normandy, and at Easter came hither to land, and at Pentecost held his court the first time in his new building at Westminster; and there he gave the bishopric of Durham to Ranulf his chaplain, who had long directed and governed his councils over all England. And soon after this he went over sea, and drove the Earl Elias out of Maine, which he reduced under his power, and so by Michaelmas returned to this land. This year also, on the festival of St. Martin, the sea-flood sprung up to such a height, and did so much harm, as no man remembered that it ever did before. And this was the first day of the new moon. And Osmond, Bishop of Salisbury, died in Advent.

A.D. 1100. In this year the King William held his court at Christmas in Glocester, and at Easter in Winchester, and at Pentecost in Westminster. And at Pentecost was seen in Berkshire at a certain town blood to well from the earth; as many said that should see it. And thereafter on the morning

---

127 *That is, within the twelve days after Christmas, or the interval between Christmas day, properly called the Nativity, and the Epiphany, the whole of which was called Christmas-tide or Yule-tide, and was dedicated to feasting and mirth.*

128 *The King of Norway and his men. "Vid. Flor."*

after Lammas day was the King William shot in hunting, by an arrow from his own men, and afterwards brought to Winchester, and buried in the cathedral.[129] This was in the thirteenth year after that he assumed the government. He was very harsh and severe over his land and his men, and with all his neighbours; and very formidable; and through the counsels of evil men, that to him were always agreeable, and through his own avarice, he was ever tiring this nation with an army, and with unjust contributions. For in his days all right fell to the ground, and every wrong rose up before God and before the world. God's church he humbled; and all the bishoprics and abbacies, whose elders fell in his days, he either sold in fee, or held in his own hands, and let for a certain sum; because he would be the heir of every man, both of the clergy and laity; so that on the day that he fell he had in his own hand the archbishopric of Canterbury, with the bishopric of Winchester, and that of Salisbury, and eleven abbacies, all let for a sum; and (though I may be tedious) all that was loathsome to God and righteous men, all that was customary in this land in his time. And for this he was loathed by nearly all his people, and odious to God, as his end testified: — for he departed in the midst of his unrighteousness, without any power of repentance or recompense for his deeds. On the Thursday he was slain; and in the morning afterwards buried; and after he was buried, the statesmen that were then nigh at hand, chose his brother Henry to king. And he immediately[130] gave the bishopric of Winchester to William Giffard; and afterwards went to London; and on the Sunday following, before the altar at Westminster, he promised God

---

129 *His monument is still to be seen there, a plain gravestone of black marble, of the common shape called "dos d'ane"; such as are now frequently seen, though of inferior materials, in the churchyards of villages; and are only one remove from the grassy sod.*

130 *i.e. before he left Winchester for London; literally "there-right" — an expression still used in many parts of England. Neither does the word "directly", which in its turn has almost become too vulgar to be used, nor its substitute, "immediately", which has nearly superseded it, appear to answer the purpose so well as the Saxon, which is equally expressive with the French "sur le champ".*

HENRY I.

Henry I (Cassells History of England)

and all the people, to annul all the unrighteous acts that took place in his brother's time, and to maintain the best laws that were valid in any king's day before him. And after this the Bishop of London, Maurice, consecrated him king; and all in this land submitted to him, and swore oaths, and became his men. And the king, soon after this, by the advice of those that were about him, allowed men to take the Bishop Ranulf of Durham, and bring him into the Tower of London, and hold him there. Then, before Michaelmas, came the

275

Archbishop Anselm of Canterbury hither to this land; as the King Henry, by the advice of his ministers had sent after him, because he had gone out of this land for the great wrongs that the King William did unto him. And soon hereafter the king took him to wife Maud, daughter of Malcolm, King of Scotland, and of Margaret the good queen, the relative of King Edward, and of the right royal[131] race of England. And on Martinmas day she was publicly given to him with much pomp at Westminster, and the Archbishop Anselm wedded her to him, and afterwards consecrated her queen. And the Archbishop Thomas of York soon hereafter died. During the harvest of this same year also came the Earl Robert home into Normandy, and the Earl Robert of Flanders, Eustace, Earl of Boulogne, from Jerusalem. And as soon as the Earl Robert came into Normandy, he was joyfully received by all his people; except those of the castles that were garrisoned with the King Henry's men. Against them he had many contests and struggles.

A.D. 1101. In this year at Christmas held the King Henry his court in Westminster, and at Easter in Winchester. And soon thereafter were the chief men in this land in a conspiracy against the king; partly from their own great infidelity, and also through the Earl Robert of Normandy, who with hostility aspired to the invasion of this land. And the king afterwards sent ships out to sea, to thwart and impede his brother; but some of them in the time of need fell back, and turned from the king, and surrendered themselves to the Earl Robert. Then at midsummer went the king out to Pevensey with all his force against his brother, and there awaited him. But in the meantime came the Earl Robert up at Portsmouth twelve nights before Lammas; and the king with all his force came against him. But the chief men interceded between

---

131 *This expression shows the adherence of the writer to the Saxon line of kings, and his consequent satisfaction in recording this alliance of Henry with the daughter of Margaret of Scotland.*

them, and settled the brothers on the condition, "that the king should forego all that he held by main strength in Normandy against the earl; and that all then in England should have their lands again, who had lost it before through the earl, and Earl Eustace also all his patrimony in this land; and that the Earl Robert every year should receive from England three thousand marks of silver; and particularly, that whichever of the brothers should survive the other, he should be heir of all England and also of Normandy, except the deceased left an heir by lawful wedlock." And this twelve men of the highest rank on either side then confirmed with an oath. And the earl afterwards remained in this land till after Michaelmas; and his men did much harm wherever they went, the while that the earl continued in this land. This year also the Bishop Ranulf at Candlemas burst out of the Tower of London by night, where he was in confinement, and went into Normandy; through whose contrivance and instigation mostly the Earl Robert this year sought this land with hostility.

A.D. 1102. In this year at the Nativity was the King Henry at Westminster, and at Easter in Winchester. And soon thereafter arose a dissention between the king and the Earl Robert of Belesme, who held in this land the earldom of Shrewsbury, that his father, Earl Roger, had before, and much territory therewith both on this side and beyond the sea. And the king went and beset the castle at Arundel; but when he could not easily win it, he allowed men to make castles before it, and filled them with his men; and afterwards with all his army he went to Bridgenorth, and there continued until he had the castle, and deprived the Earl Robert of his land, and stripped him of all that he had in England. And the earl accordingly went over sea, and the army afterwards returned home. Then was the king thereafter by Michaelmas at Westminster; and all the principal men in this land, clerk, and laity. And the Archbishop Anselm held a synod of clergy; and there they established many canons that belong to Christianity. And many, both French and English, were there deprived of their staves and dignity, which they either obtained with injustice, or enjoyed with dishonour. And in this same year, in the week of the feast of Pentecost, there came thieves, some from Auvergne,[132] some from France, and some from Flanders, and broke into the minster of Peterborough, and therein seized much property in gold and in silver; namely, roods, and chalices, and candlesticks.

A.D. 1103. In this year, at midwinter, was the King Henry at Westminster. And soon afterwards departed the Bishop William Giffard out of this land; because he would not against right accept his hood at the hands of the Archbishop Gerard of York. And then at Easter held the king his court at Winchester, and afterwards went the Archbishop Anselm from Canterbury to Rome, as was agreed between him and the king. This year also came the Earl Robert of Normandy to speak with the king in this land; and ere he departed hence he forgave the King Henry the three thousand marks that he was bound by treaty to give him each year. In this year also at Hamstead in Berkshire was seen blood [to rise] from the earth. This was a very calamitous year in this land, through manifold impositions, and through murrain of cattle, and deficiency of produce, not only in corn, but in every kind of fruit. Also in the morning, upon the mass day of St. Laurence, the wind did so much harm here on land to all fruits, as no man remembered that ever any did before. In this same year died Matthias, Abbot of Peterborough, who lived no longer than one year after he was abbot. After Michaelmas, on the twelfth day before the calends of November, he was in full procession received as abbot; and on the same day of the

132 *"Auvergne" at that time was an independent province, and formed no part of France. About the middle of the fourteenth century we find Jane, Countess of Auvergne and Boulogne, and Queen of France, assisting in the dedication of the church of the Carmelites at Paris, together with Queen Jeanne d'Evreux, third wife and widow of Charles IV., Blanche of Navarre, widow of Philip VI., and Jeanne de France, Queen of Navarre.—Felib. "Histoire de Paris", vol. I, p. 356.*

next year he was dead at Glocester, and there buried.

A.D. 1104. In this year at Christmas held the King Henry his court at Westminster, and at Easter in Winchester, and at Pentecost again at Westminster. This year was the first day of Pentecost on the nones of June; and on the Tuesday following were seen four circles at mid-day about the sun, of a white hue, each described under the other as if they were measured. All that saw it wondered; for they never remembered such before. Afterwards were reconciled the Earl Robert of Normandy and Robert de Belesme, whom the King Henry had before deprived of his lands, and driven from England; and through their reconciliation the King of England and the Earl of Normandy became adversaries. And the king sent his folk over sea into Normandy; and the head-men in that land received them, and with treachery to their lord, the earl, lodged them in their castles, whence they committed many outrages on the earl in plundering and burning. This year also William, Earl of Moreton[133] went from this land into Normandy; but after he was gone he acted against the king; because the king stripped and deprived him of all that he had here in this land. It is not easy to describe the misery of this land, which it was suffering through various and manifold wrongs and impositions, that never failed nor ceased; and wheresoever the king went, there was full licence given to his company to harrow and oppress his wretched people; and in the midst thereof happened oftentimes burnings and manslaughter. All this was done to the displeasure of God, and to the vexation of this unhappy people.

A.D. 1105. In this year, on the Nativity, held the King Henry his court at Windsor; and afterwards in Lent he went over sea into Normandy against his brother Earl Robert. And whilst he remained there he won of his brother Caen and Baieux;

---

133 *A title taken from a town in Normandy, now generally written Moretaine, or Moretagne; de Moreteon, de Moritonio, Flor.*

and almost all the castles and the chief men in that land were subdued. And afterwards by harvest he returned hither again; and that which he had won in Normandy remained afterwards in peace and subjection to him; except that which was anywhere near the Earl William of Moretaine. This he often demanded as strongly as he could for the loss of his land in this country. And then before Christmas came Robert de Belesme hither to the king. This was a very calamitous year in this land, through loss of fruits, and through the manifold contributions, that never ceased before the king went over [to Normandy], or while he was there, or after he came back again.

A.D. 1106. In this year was the King Henry on the Nativity at Westminster, and there held his court; and at that season Robert de Belesme went unreconciled from the king out of his land into Normandy. Hereafter before Lent was the king at Northampton; and the Earl Robert his brother came thither from Normandy to him; and because the king would not give him back that which he had taken from him in Normandy, they parted in hostility; and the earl soon went over sea back again. In the first week of Lent, on the Friday, which was the fourteenth before the calends of March, in the evening appeared an unusual star; and a long time afterwards was seen every evening shining awhile. The star appeared in the south-west; it was thought little and dark; but the train of light which stood from it was very bright, and appeared like an immense beam shining north-east; and some evening this beam was seen as if it were moving itself forwards against the star. Some said that they saw more of such unusual stars at this time; but we do not write more fully about it, because we saw it not ourselves. On the night preceding the Lord's Supper,[134] that is, the Thursday before Easter, were seen two moons in the heavens before day, the one in the east, and the

---

134 *"Cena Domini"—commonly called Maundy Thursday.*

other in the west, both full; and it was the fourteenth day of the moon. At Easter was the king at Bath, and at Pentecost at Salisbury; because he would not hold his court when he was beyond the sea. After this, and before August, went the king over sea into Normandy; and almost all that were in that land submitted to his will, except Robert de Belesme and the Earl of Moretaine, and a few others of the principal persons who yet held with the Earl of Normandy. For this reason the king afterwards advanced with an army, and beset a castle of the Earl of Moretaine, called Tenerchebrai.[135] Whilst the king beset the castle, came the Earl Robert of Normandy on Michaelmas eve against the king with his army, and with him Robert of Belesme, and William, Earl of Moretaine, and all that would be with them; but the strength and the victory were the king's. There was the Earl of Normandy taken, and the Earl of Moretaine, and Robert of Stutteville, and afterwards sent to England, and put into custody. Robert of Belesme was there put to flight, and William Crispin was taken, and many others forthwith. Edgar Etheling, who a little before had gone over from the king to the earl, was also there taken, whom the king afterwards let go unpunished. Then went the king over all that was in Normandy, and settled it according to his will and discretion. This year also were heavy and sinful conflicts between the Emperor of Saxony and his son, and in the midst of these conflicts the father fell, and the son succeeded to the empire.

A.D. 1107. In this year at Christmas was the King Henry in Normandy; and, having disposed and settled that land to his will, he afterwards came hither in Lent, and at Easter held his court at Windsor, and at Pentecost in Westminster. And afterwards in the beginning of August he was again at Westminster, and there gave away and settled the bishoprics and abbacies that either in England or in Normandy were

---

135 *Now Tinchebrai.*

without elders and pastors. Of these there were so many, that there was no man who remembered that ever so many together were given away before. And on this same occasion, among the others who accepted abbacies, Ernulf, who before was prior at Canterbury, succeeded to the abbacy in Peterborough. This was nearly about seven years after the King Henry undertook the kingdom, and the one and fortieth year since the Franks governed this land. Many said that they saw sundry tokens in the moon this year, and its orb increasing and decreasing contrary to nature. This year died Maurice, Bishop of London, and Robert, Abbot of St. Edmund's bury, and Richard, Abbot of Ely. This year also died the King Edgar in Scotland, on the ides of January, and Alexander his brother succeeded to the kingdom, as the King Henry granted him.

A.D. 1108. In this year was the King Henry on the Nativity at Westminster, and at Easter at Winchester, and by Pentecost at Westminster again. After this, before August, he went into Normandy. And Philip, the King of France, died on the nones of August, and his son Louis succeeded to the kingdom. And there were afterwards many struggles between the King of France and the King of England, while the latter remained in Normandy. In this year also died the Archbishop Girard of York, before Pentecost, and Thomas was afterwards appointed thereto.

A.D. 1109. In this year was the King Henry at Christmas and at Easter in Normandy; and before Pentecost he came to this land, and held his court at Westminster. There were the conditions fully settled, and the oaths sworn, for giving his daughter[136] to the emperor.[137] This year were very frequent storms of thunder, and very tremendous; and the Archbishop Anselm of Canterbury died on the eleventh day before the

136 *Matilda, Mathilde, or Maud.*
137 *Henry V. of Germany, the son of Henry IV.*

calends of April; and the first day of Easter was on "Litania major".

A.D. 1110. In this year held the King Henry his court at Christmas in Westminster, and at Easter he was at Marlborough, and at Pentecost he held his court for the first time in New Windsor. This year before Lent the king sent his daughter with manifold treasures over sea, and gave her to the emperor. On the fifth night in the month of May appeared the moon shining bright in the evening, and afterwards by little and little its light diminished, so that, as soon as night came,[138] it was so completely extinguished withal, that neither light, nor orb, nor anything at all of it was seen. And so it continued nearly until day, and then appeared shining full and bright. It was this same day a fortnight old. All the night was the firmament very clear, and the stars over all the heavens shining very bright. And the fruits of the trees were this night sorely nipt by frost. Afterwards, in the month of June, appeared a star north-east, and its train stood before it towards the south-west. Thus was it seen many nights; and as the night advanced, when it rose higher, it was seen going backward toward the north-west. This year were deprived of their lands Philip of Braiose, and William Mallet, and William Bainard. This year also died Earl Elias, who held Maine in fee-tail[139] of King Henry; and after his death the Earl of Anjou succeeded to it, and held it against the king. This was a very calamitous year in this land, through the contributions which the king received for his daughter's portion, and through the badness of the weather, by which the fruits of the earth were very much marred, and the produce of the trees over all this land almost entirely perished. This year men began first to work at the new minster at Chertsey.

---

138 *Or, "in the early part of the night," etc.*

139 *That is, the territory was not a "fee simple", but subject to "taillage" or taxation; and that particular species is probably here intended which is called in old French "en queuage", an expression not very different from that in the text above.*

A.D. 1111. This year the King Henry bare not his crown at Christmas, nor at Easter, nor at Pentecost. And in August he went over sea into Normandy, on account of the broils that some had with him by the confines of France, and chiefly on account of the Earl of Anjou, who held Maine against him. And after he came over thither, many conspiracies, and burnings, and harrowings, did they between them. In this year died the Earl Robert of Flanders, and his son Baldwin succeeded thereto.[140] This year was the winter very long, and the season heavy and severe; and through that were the fruits of the earth sorely marred, and there was the greatest murrain of cattle that any man could remember.

A.D. 1112. All this year remained the King Henry in Normandy on account of the broils that he had with France, and with the Earl of Anjou, who held Maine against him. And whilst he was there, he deprived of their lands the Earl of Evreux, and William Crispin, and drove them out of Normandy. To Philip of Braiose he restored his land, who had been before deprived of it; and Robert of Belesme he suffered to be seized, and put into prison. This was a very good year, and very fruitful, in wood and in field; but it was a very heavy time and sorrowful, through a severe mortality amongst men.

A.D. 1113. In this year was the King Henry on the Nativity and at Easter and at Pentecost in Normandy. And after that, in the summer, he sent hither Robert of Belesme into the castle at Wareham, and himself soon[141] afterwards came hither to this land.

A.D. 1114. In this year held the King Henry his court on the Nativity at Windsor, and held no other court afterwards during the year. And at midsummer he went with an army into Wales; and the Welsh came and made peace with the king. And he let men build castles therein. And thereafter,

---

140 *i.e. to the earldom of Flanders.*

141 *"Mense Julio".—Flor.*

The Empress Mathilda

in September, he went over sea into Normandy. This year, in the latter end of May, was seen an uncommon star with a long train, shining many nights. In this year also was so great an ebb of the tide everywhere in one day, as no man remembered before; so that men went riding and walking over the Thames eastward of London bridge. This year were very violent winds in the month of October; but it was immoderately rough in the night of the octave of St. Martin; and that was everywhere manifest both in town and country. In this year also the king gave the archbishopric of Canterbury to Ralph, who was before Bishop of Rochester; and Thomas, Archbishop of York, died; and Turstein succeeded thereto, who was before the king's chaplain. About this same time went the king toward the sea, and was desirous of going over, but the weather prevented him; then meanwhile sent he his writ after the Abbot Ernulf of Peterborough, and bade that he should come to him quickly, for that he wished to speak with him on an interesting subject. When he came to him, he appointed him to the bishopric of Rochester; and the archbishops and bishops and all the nobility that were in England coincided with the king. And he long withstood, but it availed nothing. And the king bade the archbishop that he should lead him to Canterbury, and consecrate him bishop whether he would or not.[142] This was done in the town called Bourne[143] on the seventeenth day before the calends of October. When the monks of Peterborough heard of this, they felt greater sorrow than they had ever experienced before; because he was a very good and amiable man, and did much good within and without whilst he abode there. God Almighty abide ever with him. Soon after this gave the king the abbacy to a monk of Sieyes, whose name was John, through the intreaty of the Archbishop of Canterbury. And soon after this the king and the Archbishop of Canterbury sent him to Rome after the archbishop's pall; and a monk also with him, whose name was Warner, and the Archdeacon John, the nephew of the archbishop. And they sped well there. This was done on the seventh day before the calends Of October, in the town that is yclept Rowner. And this same day went the king on board ship at Portsmouth.

---

142 *We have still the form of saying "Nolo episcopari", when a see is offered to a bishop.*
143 *i.e. East Bourne in Sussex; where the king was waiting for a fair wind to carry him over sea.*

A.D. 1115. This year was the King Henry on the Nativity in Normandy. And whilst he was there, he contrived that all the head men in Normandy did homage and fealty to his son William, whom he had by his queen. And after this, in the month of July, he returned to this land. This year was the winter so severe, with snow and with frost, that no man who was then living ever remembered one more severe; in consequence of which there was great destruction of cattle. During this year the Pope Paschalis sent the pall into this land to Ralph, Archbishop of Canterbury; and he received it with great worship at his archiepiscopal stall in Canterbury. It was brought hither from Rome by Abbot Anselm, who was the nephew of Archbishop Anselm, and the Abbot John of Peterborough.

A.D. 1116. In this year was the King Henry on the Nativity at St. Alban's, where he permitted the consecration of that monastery; and at Easter he was at Odiham. And there was also this year a very heavy-timed winter, strong and long, for cattle and for all things. And the king soon after Easter went over sea into Normandy. And there were many conspiracies and robberies, and castles taken betwixt France and Normandy. Most of this disturbance was because the King Henry assisted his nephew, Theobald de Blois, who was engaged in a war against his lord, Louis, the King of France. This was a very vexatious and destructive year with respect to the fruits of the earth, through the immoderate rains that fell soon after the beginning of August, harassing and perplexing men till Candlemas-day. This year also was so deficient in mast, that there was never heard such in all this land or in Wales. This land and nation were also this year oft and sorely swincked by the guilds which the king took both within the boroughs and without. In this same year was consumed by fire the whole monastery of Peterborough, and all the buildings, except the chapter-house and the dormitory, and therewith also all the greater part of the town. All this happened on a Friday, which was the second day before the nones of August.

A.D. 1117. All this year remained the King Henry, in Normandy, on account of the hostility of the King of France and his other neighbours. And in the summer came the King of France and the Earl of Flanders with him with an army into Normandy. And having stayed therein one night, they returned again in the morning without fighting. But Normandy was very much afflicted both by the exactions and by the armies which the King Henry collected against them. This nation also was severely oppressed through the same means, namely, through manifold exactions. This year also, in the night of the calends of December, were immoderate storms with thunder, and lightning, and rain, and hail. And in the night of the third day before the ides of December was the moon, during a long time of the night, as if covered with blood, and afterwards eclipsed. Also in the night of the seventeenth day before the calends of January, was the heaven seen very red, as if it were burning. And on the octave of St. John the Evangelist was the great earthquake in Lombardy; from the shock of which many minsters, and towers, and houses fell, and did much harm to men. This was a very blighted year in corn, through the rains that scarcely ceased for nearly all the year. And the Abbot Gilbert of Westminster died on the eighth day before the ides of December; and Faritz, Abbot of Abingdon, on the seventh day before the calends of March. And in this same year....

A.D. 1118. All this year abode the King Henry in Normandy on account of the war of the King of France and the Earl of Anjou, and the Earl of Flanders. And the Earl of Flanders was wounded in Normandy, and went so wounded into Flanders. By this war was the king much exhausted, and he was a great loser both in land and money. And his own men grieved him most, who often from him turned, and betrayed him; and going over to his foes surrendered to them their castles, to the injury and disappointment of the king. All this England dearly bought through the manifold guilds that all this year abated not. This year, in the week of the Epiphany, there was one evening a great deal of lightning, and thereafter unusual thunder. And the Queen Matilda died at Westminster on the calends of May; and there was buried. And the Earl Robert of Mellent died also this year. In this year also, on the feast of St. Thomas, was so very immoderately violent a wind, that no man who was then living ever remembered any greater; and that was everywhere seen both in houses and also in trees. This year also died Pope Paschalis; and John of Gaeta succeeded to the popedom, whose other name was Gelasius.

A.D. 1119. All this year continued the King Henry in Normandy; and he was greatly perplexed by the hostility of the King of France, and also of his own men, who with treachery deserted from him, and oft readily betrayed him; until the two kings came together in Normandy with their forces. There was the King of France put to flight, and all his best men taken. And afterwards many of King Henry's men returned to him, and accorded with him, who were before, with their castellans, against him. And some of the castles he took by main strength. This year went William, the son of King Henry and Queen Matilda, into Normandy to his father, and there was given to him, and wedded to wife, the daughter of the Earl of Anjou. On the eve of the mass of St. Michael was much earth-heaving in some places in this land; though most of all in Glocestershire and in Worcestershire. In this same year died the Pope Gelasius, on this side of the Alps, and was buried at Clugny. And after him the Archbishop of Vienna was chosen pope, whose name was Calixtus. He afterwards, on the festival of St. Luke the Evangelist, came into France to Rheims, and there held a council. And the Archbishop

The Sinking of the White Ship in the English Channel near the Normandy coast off Barfleur, on November 25, 1120.

Turstin of York went thither; and, because that he against right, and against the archiepiscopal stall in Canterbury, and against the king's will, received his hood at the hands of the pope, the king interdicted him from all return to England. And thus he lost his archbishopric, and with the pope went towards Rome. In this year also died the Earl Baldwin of Flanders of the wounds that he received in Normandy. And after him succeeded to the earldom Charles, the son of his uncle by the father's side, who was son of Cnute, the holy King of Denmark.

A.D. 1120. This year were reconciled the King of England and the King of France; and after their reconciliation all the King Henry's own men accorded with him in Normandy, as well as the Earl of Flanders and the Earl of Ponthieu. From this time forward the King Henry settled his castles and his land in Normandy after his will; and so before Advent came to this land. And in this expedition were drowned the king's two sons, William and Richard, and Richard, Earl of Chester, and Ottuel his brother, and very many of the king's household, stewards, and chamberlains, and butlers, and men of various abodes; and with them a countless multidude of very incomparable folk besides. Sore was their death to their friends in a twofold respect: one, that they so suddenly lost this life; the other, that few of their bodies were found anywhere afterwards. This year came that light to the sepulchre of the Lord in Jerusalem twice; once at Easter, and the other on the assumption of St. Mary, as credible persons said who came thence. And the Archbishop Turstin of York was through the pope reconciled with the king, and came to this land, and recovered his bishopric, though it was very undesirable to the Archbishop of Canterbury.

A.D. 1121. This year was the King Henry at Christmas at Bramton, and afterwards, before Candlemas, at Windsor was given him to wife Athelis; soon afterwards consecrated queen, who was daughter of the Duke of Louvain. And the moon was eclipsed in the night of the nones of April, being a fortnight old. And the king was at Easter at Berkley; and after that at Pentecost he held a full court at Westminster; and afterwards in the summer went with an army into Wales. And the Welsh came against him; and after the king's will they accorded with him. This year came the Earl of Anjou from Jerusalem into his land; and soon after sent hither to fetch his daughter, who had been given to wife to William, the king's son. And in the night of the eve of "Natalis Domini" was a very violent wind over all this land, and that was in many things evidently seen.

A.D. 1122. In this year was the King Henry at Christmas in Norwich, and at Easter in Northampton. And in the Lent-tide before that, the town of Glocester was on fire: the while that the monks were singing their mass, and the deacon had begun the gospel, "Praeteriens Jesus", at that very moment came the fire from the upper part of the steeple, and burned all the minster, and all the treasures that were there within; except a few books, and three mass-hackles. That was on the eighth day before the ides of Marcia. And thereafter, the Tuesday after Palm-Sunday, was a very violent wind on the eleventh day before the calends of April; after which came many tokens far and wide in England, and many spectres were both seen and heard. And the eighth night before the calends of August was a very violent earthquake over all Somersetshire, and in Glocestershire. Soon after, on the sixth day before the ides of September, which was on the festival of St. Mary,[144] there was a very violent wind from the fore part of the day to the depth of the night. This same year died Ralph, the Archbishop of Canterbury; that was on the thirteenth day before the calends of November. After this there were many shipmen on the sea, and on fresh water, who said, that they saw on the north-east, level with the earth, a fire huge and broad, which anon waxed in length up to the welkin; and the welkin undid itself in four parts, and fought against it, as if it would quench it; and the fire waxed nevertheless up to the heaven. The fire they saw in the day-dawn; and it lasted until it was light over all. That was on the seventh day before the ides of December.

A.D. 1123. In this year was the King Henry, at Christmastide at Dunstable, and there came to him the ambassadors of the Earl of Anjou. And thence he went to Woodstock; and his

---

144 *The Nativity of the Virgin Mary.*

bishops and his whole court with him. Then did it betide on a Wednesday, which was on the fourth day before the ides of January, that the king rode in his deer-fold;[145] the Bishop Roger of Salisbury[146] on one side of him, and the Bishop Robert Bloet of Lincoln on the other side of him. And they rode there talking together. Then sank down the Bishop of Lincoln, and said to the king, "Lord king, I die." And the king alighted down from his horse, and lifted him betwixt his arms, and let men bear him home to his inn. There he was soon dead; and they carried him to Lincoln with great worship, and buried him before the altar of St. Mary. And the Bishop of Chester, whose name was Robert Pecceth, buried him. Soon after this sent the king his writ over all England, and bade all his bishops and his abbots and his thanes, that they should come to his wittenmoot on Candlemas day at Glocester to meet him: and they did so. When they were there gathered together, then the king bade them, that they should choose for themselves an Archbishop of Canterbury, whomsoever they would, and he would confirm it. Then spoke the bishops among themselves, and said that they never more would have a man of the monastic order as archbishop over them. And they went all in a body to the king, and earnestly requested that they might choose from the clerical order whomsoever they would for archbishop. And the king granted it to them. This was all concerted before, through the Bishop of Salisbury, and through the Bishop of Lincoln ere he was dead; for that they never loved the rule of monks, but were ever against monks and their rule. And the prior and the monks of Canterbury, and all the other persons of the monastic order that were there, withstood it full two days; but it availed nought: for the Bishop of Salisbury was strong,

---

145 i.e. an inclosure or park for deer. This is now called Blenheim Park, and is one of the few old parks which still remain in this country.

146 This may appear rather an anticipation of the modern see of Salisbury, which was not then in existence; the borough of Old Saturn, or "Saresberie", being then the episcopal seat.

and wielded all England, and opposed them with all his power and might. Then chose they a clerk, named William of Curboil. He was canon of a monastery called Chiche.[147] And they brought him before the king; and the king gave him the archbishopric. And all the bishops received him: but almost all the monks, and the earls, and the thanes that were there, protested against him. About the same time departed the earl's messengers[148] in hostility from the king, reckless of his favour. During the same time came a legate from Rome, whose name was Henry. He was abbot of the monastery of St. John of Angeli; and he came after the Rome-scot. And he said to the king, that it was against right that men should set a clerk over monks; and therefore they had chosen an archbishop before in their chapter after right. But the king would not undo it, for the love of the Bishop of Salisbury. Then went the archbishop, soon after this, to Canterbury; and was there received, though it was against their will; and he was there soon blessed to bishop by the Bishop of London, and the Bishop Ernulf of Rochester, and the Bishop William Girard of Winchester, and the Bishop Bernard of Wales, and the Bishop Roger of Salisbury. Then, early in Lent, went the archbishop to Rome, after his pall; and with him went the Bishop Bernard of Wales; and Sefred, Abbot of Glastonbury; and Anselm, Abbot of St. Edmund's bury; and John, Archdeacon of Canterbury; and Gifard, who was the king's court-chaplain. At the same time went the Archbishop Thurstan of York to Rome, through the behest of the pope, and came thither three days ere the Archbishop of Canterbury came, and was there received with much worship. Then came the Archbishop of Canterbury, and was there full seven nights ere they could come to a conference with the pope. That was, because the pope was made to understand that

---

147 *St. Osythe, in Essex; a priory rebuilt A. 1118, for canons of the Augustine order, of which there are considerable remains.*

148 *i.e. Of the Earl of Anjou.*

he had obtained the archbishopric against the monks of the minster, and against right. But that overcame Rome, which overcometh all the world; that is, gold and silver. And the pope softened, and gave him his pall. And the archbishop (of York) swore him subjection, in all those things, which the pope enjoined him, by the heads of St. Peter and St. Paul; and the pope then sent him home with his blessing. The while that the archbishop was out of the land, the king gave the bishopric of Bath to the Queen's chancellor, whose name was Godfrey. He was born in Louvain. That was on the Annunciation of St. Mary, at Woodstock. Soon after this went the king to Winchester, and was all Easter-tide there. And the while that he was there, gave he the bishopric of Lincoln to a clerk hight Alexander. He was nephew of the Bishop of Salisbury. This he did all for the love of the bishop. Then went the king thence to Portsmouth, and lay there all over Pentecost week. Then, as soon as he had a fair wind, he went over into Normandy; and meanwhile committed all England to the guidance and government of the Bishop Roger of Salisbury. Then was the king all this year[149] in Normandy. And much hostility arose betwixt him and his thanes; so that the Earl Waleram of Mellent, and Hamalric, and Hugh of Montfort, and William of Romare, and many others, went from him, and held their castles against him. And the king strongly opposed them: and this same year he won of Waleram his castle of Pont-Audemer, and of Hugh that of Montfort; and ever after, the longer he stayed, the better he sped. This same year, ere the Bishop of Lincoln came to his bishopric, almost all the borough of Lincoln was burned, and numberless folks, men and women, were consumed: and so much harm was there done as no man could describe to another. That was on the fourteenth day before the calends of June.

149 *The writer means, "the remainder of this year"; for the feast of Pentecost was already past, before the king left England.*

A.D. 1124. All this year was the King Henry in Normandy. That was for the great hostility that he had with the King Louis of France, and with the Earl of Anjou, and most of all with his own men. Then it happened, on the day of the Annunciation of St. Mary, that the Earl Waleram of Mellent went from one of his castles called Belmont to another called Watteville. With him went the steward of the King of France, Amalric, and Hugh the son of Gervase, and Hugh of Montfort, and many other good knights. Then came against them the king's knights from all the castles that were thereabout, and fought with them, and put them to flight, and took the Earl Waleram, and Hugh, the son of Gervase, and Hugh of Montfort, and five and twenty other knights, and brought them to the king. And the king committed the Earl Waleram, and Hugh, the son of Gervase, to close custody in the castle at Rouen; but Hugh of Montfort he sent to England, and ordered him to be secured with strong bonds in the castle at Glocester. And of the others as many as he chose he sent north and south to his castles in captivity. After this went the king, and won all the castles of the Earl Waleram that were in Normandy, and all the others that his enemies held against him. All this hostility was on account of the son of the Earl Robert of Normandy, named William. This same William had taken to wife the younger daughter of Fulke, Earl of Anjou: and for this reason the King of France and all the earls held with him, and all the rich men; and said that the king held his brother Robert wrongfully in captivity, and drove his son William unjustly out of Normandy. This same year were the seasons very unfavourable in England for corn and all fruits; so that between Christmas and Candlemas men sold the acre-seed of wheat, that is two seedlips, for six shillings; and the barley, that is three seedlips, for six shillings also; and the acre-seed of oats, that is four seedlips, for four shillings. That was because that corn was scarce; and the penny was so adulterated,[150] that a man who had a pound at a market could not exchange twelve pence thereof for anything. In this same year died the blessed Bishop Ernulf of Rochester, who before was Abbot of Peterborough. That was on the ides of March. And after this died the King Alexander of Scotland, on the ninth day before the calends of May. And David his brother, who was Earl of Northamptonshire, succeeded to the kingdom; and had both together, the kingdom of Scotland and the earldom in England. And on the nineteenth day before the calends of January died the Pope of Rome, whose name was Calixtus, and Honorius succeeded to the popedom. This same year, after St. Andrew's mass, and before Christmas, held Ralph Basset and the king's thanes a wittenmoot in Leicestershire, at Huncothoe, and there hanged more thieves than ever were known before; that is, in a little while, four and forty men altogether; and despoiled six men of their eyes and of their testicles. Many true men said that there were several who suffered very unjustly; but our Lord God Almighty, who seeth and knoweth every secret, seeth also that the wretched people are oppressed with all unrighteousness. First they are bereaved of their property, and then they are slain. Full heavy year was this. The man that had any property, was bereaved of it by violent guilds and violent moots. The man that had not, was starved with hunger.

A.D. 1125. In this year sent the King Henry, before Christmas, from Normandy to England, and bade that all the mint-men that were in England should be mutilated in their limbs; that was, that they should lose each of them the right hand, and their testicles beneath. This was because the man that had a pound could not lay out a penny at a market. And the Bishop Roger of Salisbury sent over all England, and bade them all that they should come to Winchester at Christmas. When they

---

150 *The pennies, or pence, it must be remembered, were of silver at this time.*

came thither, then were they taken one by one, and deprived each of the right hand and the testicles beneath. All this was done within the twelfth-night. And that was all in perfect justice, because that they had undone all the land with the great quantity of base coin that they all bought. In this same year sent the Pope of Rome to this land a cardinal, named John of Crema. He came first to the king in Normandy, and the king received him with much worship. He betook himself then to the Archbishop William of Canterbury; and he led him to Canterbury; and he was there received with great veneration, and in solemn procession. And he sang the high mass on Easter day at the altar of Christ. Afterwards he went over all England, to all the bishoprics and abbacies that were in this land; and in all he was received with respect. And all gave him many and rich gifts. And afterwards he held his council in London full three days, on the Nativity of St. Mary in September, with archbishops, and diocesan bishops, and abbots, the learned and the lewd;[151] and enjoined there the same laws that Archbishop Anselm had formerly enjoined, and many more, though it availed little. Thence he went over sea soon after Michaelmas, and so to Rome; and (with him) the Archbishop William of Canterbury, and the Archbishop Thurstan of York, and the Bishop Alexander of Lincoln, and the Bishop J. of Lothian, and the Abbot G. of St. Alban's; and were there received by the Pope Honorius with great respect; and continued there all the winter. In this same year was so great a flood on St. Laurence's day, that many towns and men were overwhelmed, and bridges broken down, and corn and meadows spoiled withal; and hunger and qualm[152] in men and in cattle; and in all fruits such unseasonableness as was not known for many years before. And this same year died the Abbot John of Peterborough, on the second day before

---

151 i.e. Clergy and laity.
152 This word is still in use, but in a sense somewhat different; as qualms of conscience, etc.

the ides of October.

A.D. 1126. All this year was the King Henry in Normandy—all till after harvest. Then came he to this land, betwixt the Nativity of St. Mary and Michaelmas. With him came the queen, and his daughter, whom he had formerly given to the Emperor Henry of Lorrain to wife. And he brought with him the Earl Waleram, and Hugh, the son of Gervase. And the earl he sent to Bridgenorth in captivity: and thence he sent him afterwards to Wallingford; and Hugh to Windsor, whom he ordered to be kept in strong bonds. Then after Michaelmas came David, the king of the Scots, from Scotland to this land; and the King Henry received him with great worship; and he continued all that year in this land. In this year the king had his brother Robert taken from the Bishop Roger of Salisbury, and committed him to his son Robert, Earl of Glocester, and had him led to Bristol, and there put into the castle. That was all done through his daughter's counsel, and through David, the king of the Scots, her uncle.

A.D. 1127. This year held the King Henry his court at Christmas in Windsor. There was David the king of the Scots, and all the head men that were in England, learned and lewd. And there he engaged the archbishops, and bishops, and abbots, and earls, and all the thanes that were there, to swear England and Normandy after his day into the hands of his daughter Athelicia, who was formerly the wife of the Emperor of Saxony. Afterwards he sent her to Normandy; and with her went her brother Robert, Earl of Glocester, and Brian, son of the Earl Alan Fergan;[153] and he let her wed the son of the Earl of Anjou, whose name was Geoffry Martel. All the French and English, however, disapproved of this; but the king did it for to have the alliance of the Earl of Anjou, and for to have help against his nephew William. In the Lent-tide of this

---

153 *See an account of him in "Ord. Vit." 544. Conan, another son of this Alan, Earl of Brittany, married a daughter of Henry I.*

same year was the Earl Charles of Flanders slain in a church, as he lay there and prayed to God, before the altar, in the midst of the mass, by his own men. And the King of France brought William, the son of the Earl of Normandy, and gave him the earldom; and the people of that land accepted him. This same William had before taken to wife the daughter of the Earl of Anjou; but they were afterwards divorced on the plea of consanguinity. This was all through the King Henry of England. Afterwards took he to wife the sister of the king's wife of France; and for this reason the king gave him the earldom of Flanders. This same year he[154] gave the abbacy of Peterborough to an abbot named Henry of Poitou, who retained in hand his abbacy of St. John of Angeli; but all the archbishops and bishops said that it was against right, and that he could not have two abbacies on hand. But the same Henry gave the king to understand, that he had relinquished his abbacy on account of the great hostility that was in the land; and that he did through the counsel and leave of the Pope of Rome, and through that of the Abbot of Clugny, and because he was legate of the Rome-scot. But, nevertheless, it was not so; for he would retain both in hand; and did so as long as God's will was. He was in his clerical state Bishop of Soissons; afterwards monk of Clugny; and then prior in the same monastery. Afterwards he became prior of Sevigny; and then, because he was a relation of the King of England, and of the Earl of Poitou, the earl gave him the abbacy of St. John's minster of Angeli. Afterwards, through his great craft, he obtained the archbishopric of Besancon; and had it in hand three days; after which he justly lost it, because he had before unjustly obtained it. Afterwards he procured the bishopric of Saintes; which was five miles from his abbey. That he had full-nigh a week[155] in hand; but the

---

154 *i.e. Henry, King of England.*

155 *"A se'nnight", the space of seven nights; as we still say, "a fortnight", i.e. the space of fourteen nights. The French express the space of one week by "huit jours", the origin of the*

Abbot of Clugny brought him thence, as he before did from Besancon. Then he bethought him, that, if he could be fast-rooted in England, he might have all his will. Wherefore he besought the king, and said unto him, that he was an old man—a man completely broken—that he could not brook the great injustice and the great hostility that were in their land: and then, by his own endeavours, and by those of all his friends, he earnestly and expressly entreated for the abbacy of Peterborough. And the king procured it for him, because he was his relation, and because he was the principal person to make oath and bear witness when the son of the Earl of Normandy and the daughter of the Earl of Anjou were divorced on the plea of consanguinity. Thus wretchedly was the abbacy given away, betwixt Christmas and Candlemas, at London; and so he went with the King to Winchester, and thence he came to Peterborough, and there he dwelt[156] right so as a drone doth in a hive. For as the drone fretteth and draggeth fromward all that the bees drag toward [the hive], so did he.—All that he might take, within and without, of learned and lewd, so sent he over sea; and no good did there— no good left there. Think no man unworthily that we say not the truth; for it was fully known over all the land: that, as soon as he came thither, which was on the Sunday when men sing "Exurge quare o D—— etc." immediately after, several persons saw and heard many huntsmen hunting. The hunters were swarthy, and huge, and ugly; and their hounds were all swarthy, and broad-eyed, and ugly. And they rode on swarthy horses, and swarthy bucks. This was seen in the very deer-fold in the town of Peterborough, and in all the woods from that same town to Stamford. And the monks heard the horn blow that they blew in the night. Credible men, who watched

---

"octave" in English law; of two by "quinte jours". So "septimana" signifies "seven mornings"; whence the French word "semaine".

156 Literally, "woned". Vid Chaucer, "Canterbury Tales", v. 7745. In Scotland, a lazy indolent manner of doing anything is called "droning".

them in the night, said that they thought there might well be about twenty or thirty horn-blowers. This was seen and heard from the time that he[157] came thither, all the Lent-tide onward to Easter. This was his entry; of his exit we can as yet say nought. God provide.

A.D. 1128. All this year was the King Henry in Normandy, on account of the hostility that was between him and his nephew, the Earl of Flanders. But the earl was wounded in a fight by a swain; and so wounded he went to the monastery of St. Bertin; where he soon became a monk, lived five days afterwards, then died, and was there buried. God honour his soul. That was on the sixth day before the calends of August. This same year died the Bishop Randulph Passeflambard of Durham; and was there buried on the nones of September. And this same year went the aforesaid Abbot Henry home to his own minster at Poitou by the king's leave. He gave the king to understand, that he would withal forgo that minster, and that land, and dwell with him in England, and in the monastery of Peterborough. But it was not so nevertheless. He did this because he would be there, through his crafty wiles, were it a twelvemonth or more, and come again afterwards. May God Almighty extend his mercy over that wretched place. This same year came from Jerusalem Hugh of the Temple to the king in Normandy; and the king received him with much honour, and gave him rich presents in gold and in silver. And afterwards he sent him into England; and there he was received by all good men, who all gave him presents, and in Scotland also: and by him they sent to Jerusalem much wealth withal in gold and in silver. And he invited folk out to Jerusalem; and there went with him and after him more people than ever did before, since that the first expedition was in the day of Pope Urban. Though it availed little; for he said, that a mighty war was begun between the Christians and

---

157 *The Abbot Henry of Angeli.*

the heathens; but when they came thither, then was it nought but leasing.[158] Thus pitifully was all that people swinked.[159]

A.D. 1129. In this year sent the King to England after the Earl Waleram, and after Hugh, the son of Gervase. And they gave hostages for them. And Hugh went home to his own land in France; but Waleram was left with the king: and the king gave him all his land except his castle alone. Afterwards came the king to England within the harvest: and the earl came with him: and they became as good friends as they were foes before. Soon after, by the king's counsel, and by his leave, sent the Archbishop William of Canterbury over all England, and bade bishops, and abbots, and archdeacons, and all the priors, monks, and canons, that were in all the cells in England, and all who had the care and superintendence of christianity, that they should all come to London at Michaelmas, and there should speak of all God's rights. When they came thither, then began the moot on Monday, and continued without intermission to the Friday. When it all came forth, then was it all found to be about archdeacons' wives, and about priests' wives; that they should forgo them by St. Andrew's mass; and he who would not do that, should forgo his church, and his house, and his home, and never more have any calling thereto. This bade the Archbishop William of Canterbury, and all the diocesan bishops that were then in England, but the king gave them all leave to go home. And so they went home; and all the ordinances amounted to nothing. All held their wives by the king's leave as they did before. This same year died the Bishop William Giffard of Winchester; and was there buried, on the eighth day before the calends of February. And the King Henry gave the bishopric after Michaelmas to the Abbot Henry of Glastonbury, his nephew, and he was consecrated bishop

---

158 *"Thou shalt destroy them that speak 'leasing,'" etc. "Psalms".*
159 *i.e. Vexed, harassed, fatigued, etc. Milton has used the word in the last sense.*

by the Archbishop William of Canterbury on the fifteenth day before the calends of December. This same year died Pope Honorius. Ere he was well dead, there were chosen two popes. The one was named Peter, who was monk of Clugny, and was born of the richest men of Rome; and with him held those of Rome, and the Duke of Sicily. The other was Gregory: he was a clerk, and was driven out of Rome by the other pope, and by his kinsmen. With him held the Emperor of Saxony, and the King of France, and the King Henry of England, and all those on this side of the Alps. Now was there such division in Christendom as never was before. May Christ consult for his wretched folk. This same year, on the night of the mass of St. Nicholas, a little before day, there was a great earthquake.

A.D. 1130. This year was the monastery of Canterbury consecrated by the Archbishop William, on the fourth day before the nones of May. There were the Bishops John of Rochester, Gilbert Universal of London, Henry of Winchester, Alexander of Lincoln, Roger of Salisbury, Simon of Worcester, Roger of Coventry, Geoffry of Bath, Evrard of Norwich, Sigefrith of Chichester, Bernard of St. David's, Owen of Evreux in Normandy, John of Sieyes. On the fourth day after this was the King Henry in Rochester, when the town was almost consumed by fire; and the Archbishop William consecrated the monastery of St. Andrew, and the aforesaid bishops with him. And the King Henry went over sea into Normandy in harvest. This same year came the Abbot Henry of Angeli after Easter to Peterborough, and said that he had relinquished that monastery[160] withal. After him came the Abbot of Clugny, Peter by name, to England by the king's leave; and was received by all, whithersoever he came, with much respect. To Peterborough he came; and there the Abbot Henry promised him that he would procure him the minster

---

160 *The monastery of Angeli.*

of Peterborough, that it might be subject to Clugny. But it is said in the proverb, "The hedge abideth, that acres divideth." May God Almighty frustrate evil designs. Soon after this, went the Abbot of Clugny home to his country. This year was Angus slain by the army of the Scots, and there was a great multitude slain with him. There was God's fight sought upon him, for that he was all forsworn.

A.D. 1131. This year, after Christmas, on a Monday night, at the first sleep, was the heaven on the northern hemisphere[161] all as if it were burning fire; so that all who saw it were so dismayed as they never were before. That was on the third day before the ides of January. This same year was so great a murrain of cattle as never was before in the memory of man over all England. That was in neat cattle and in swine; so that in a town where there were ten ploughs going, or twelve, there was not left one: and the man that had two hundred or three hundred swine, had not one left. Afterwards perished the hen fowls; then shortened the fleshmeat, and the cheese, and the butter. May God better it when it shall be his will. And the King Henry came home to England before harvest, after the mass of St. Peter "ad vincula". This same year went the Abbot Henry, before Easter, from Peterborough over sea to Normandy, and there spoke with the king, and told him that the Abbot of Clugny had desired him to come to him, and resign to him the abbacy of Angeli, after which he would go home by his leave. And so he went home to his own minster, and there remained even to midsummer day. And the next day after the festival of St. John chose the monks an abbot of themselves, brought him into the church in procession, sang "Te Deum laudamus", rang the bells, set him on the abbot's throne, did him all homage, as they should do their abbot: and the earl, and all the head men, and the monks of the minster, drove the other Abbot Henry out

161 *Aurora Borealis, or the northern lights.*

of the monastery. And they had need; for in five-and-twenty winters had they never hailed one good day. Here failed him all his mighty crafts. Now it behoved him, that he crope in his skin into every corner, if peradventure there were any unresty wrench,[162] whereby he might yet once more betray Christ and all Christian people. Then retired he into Clugny, where he was held so fast, that he could not move east or west. The Abbot of Clugny said that they had lost St. John's minster through him, and through his great sottishness. Then could he not better recompense them; but he promised them, and swore oaths on the holy cross, that if he might go to England he should get them the minster of Peterborough; so that he should set there the prior of Clugny, with a churchwarden, a treasurer, and a sacristan: and all the things that were within the minster and without, he should procure for them. Thus he departed into France; and there remained all that year. Christ provide for the wretched monks of Peterborough, and for that wretched place. Now do they need the help of Christ and of all Christian folk.

A.D. 1132. This year came King Henry to this land. Then came Abbot Henry, and betrayed the monks of Peterborough to the king, because he would subject that minster to Clugny; so that the king was well nigh entrapped, and sent after the monks. But through the grace of God, and through the Bishop of Salisbury, and the Bishop of Lincoln, and the other rich men that were there, the king knew that he proceeded with treachery. When he no more could do, then would he that his nephew should be Abbot of Peterborough. But Christ forbade. Not very long after this was it that the king sent after him, and made him give up the Abbey of Peterborough, and go out of the land. And the king gave the abbacy to a prior of St. Neot's, called Martin, who came on St. Peter's mass-day

---

162 *"Any restless manoeuvre or stratagem." Both words occur in Chaucer. See "Troilus and Criseyde", v. 1355, and "Canterbury Tales", v. 16549. The idea seems to be taken from the habits of destructive and undermining vermin.*

with great pomp into the minster.

A.D. 1135. In this year went the King Henry over sea at the Lammas; and the next day, as he lay asleep on ship, the day darkened over all lands, and the sun was all as it were a three night old moon, and the stars about him at midday. Men were very much astonished and terrified, and said that a great event should come hereafter. So it did; for that same year was the king dead, the next day after St. Andrew's mass-day, in Normandy. Then was there soon tribulation in the land; for every man that might, soon robbed another. Then his sons and his friends took his body, and brought it to England, and buried it at Reading. A good man he was; and there was great dread of him. No man durst do wrong with another in his time. Peace he made for man and beast. Whoso bare his burthen of gold and silver, durst no man say ought to him but good. Meanwhile was his nephew come to England, Stephen de Blois. He came to London, and the people of London received him, and sent after the Archbishop William Curboil, and hallowed him to king on midwinter day. In this king's time was all dissention, and evil, and rapine; for against him rose soon the rich men who were traitors; and first of all Baldwin de Redvers, who held Exeter against him. But the king beset it; and afterwards Baldwin accorded. Then took the others, and held their castles against him; and David, King of Scotland, took to Wessington against him. Nevertheless their messengers passed between them; and they came together, and were settled, but it availed little.

A.D. 1137. This year went the King Stephen over sea to Normandy, and there was received; for that they concluded that he should be all such as the uncle was; and because he had got his treasure: but he dealt it out, and scattered it foolishly. Much had King Henry gathered, gold and silver, but no good did men for his soul thereof. When the King Stephen came to England, he held his council at Oxford; where he

King Stephen

seized the Bishop Roger of Sarum, and Alexander, Bishop of Lincoln, and the chancellor Roger, his nephew; and threw all into prison till they gave up their castles. When the traitors understood that he was a mild man, and soft, and good, and no justice executed, then did they all wonder. They had done him homage, and sworn oaths, but they no truth maintained. They were all forsworn, and forgetful of their troth; for every rich man built his castles, which they held against him: and they filled the land full of castles. They cruelly oppressed the wretched men of the land with castle-works; and when the castles were made, they filled them with devils and evil men. Then took they those whom they supposed to have any goods, both by night and by day, labouring men and women, and threw them into prison for their gold and silver, and inflicted on them unutterable tortures; for never were any martyrs so tortured as they were. Some they hanged up by the feet, and smoked them with foul smoke; and some by the thumbs, or by the head, and hung coats of mail on their feet. They tied knotted strings about their heads, and twisted them till the pain went to the brains. They put them into dungeons, wherein were adders, and snakes, and toads; and so destroyed them. Some they placed in a crucet-house; that is, in a chest that was short and narrow, and not deep; wherein they put sharp stones, and so thrust the man therein, that they broke all the limbs. In many of the castles were things loathsome and grim, called "Sachenteges", of which two or three men had enough to bear one. It was thus made: that is, fastened to a beam; and they placed a sharp iron [collar] about the man's throat and neck, so that he could in no direction either sit, or lie, or sleep, but bear all that iron. Many thousands they wore out with hunger. I neither can, nor may I tell all the wounds and all the pains which they inflicted on wretched men in this land. This lasted the nineteen winters while Stephen was king; and it grew continually worse and worse. They constantly laid guilds on the towns, and called it "tenserie"; and when the wretched men had no more to give, then they plundered and burned all the towns; that well thou mightest go a whole day's journey and never shouldest thou find a man sitting in a town, nor the land tilled. Then was corn dear, and flesh, and cheese, and butter; for none was there in the land. Wretched men starved of hunger. Some had recourse to alms, who were for a while rich men, and some fled out of the land. Never yet was there more wretchedness in the land; nor ever did heathen men worse than they did: for, after a time, they spared neither church nor churchyard, but took all the goods that were therein, and then burned the church and all together. Neither did they spare a bishop's land, or an abbot's, or a priest's, but plundered both monks and clerks; and every man robbed another who could. If two men, or three, came riding to a town, all the township fled for them, concluding them to be robbers. The bishops and learned men cursed them continually, but the effect thereof was nothing to them; for they were all accursed, and forsworn, and abandoned. To till the ground was to plough the sea: the earth bare no corn, for the land was all laid waste by such deeds; and they said openly, that Christ slept, and his saints. Such things, and more than we can say, suffered we nineteen winters for our sins. In all this evil time held Abbot Martin his abbacy twenty years and a half, and eight days, with much tribulation; and found the monks and the guests everything that behoved them; and held much charity in the house; and, notwithstanding all this, wrought on the church, and set thereto lands and rents, and enriched it very much, and bestowed vestments upon it. And he brought them into the new minster on St. Peter's mass-day with much pomp; which was in the year, from the incarnation of our Lord, 1140, and in the twenty-third from the destruction of the place by fire. And he went to Rome, and there was well received by the

A contemporary depiction of King Stephen's family tree, with his mother Adelin at the top, and, left to right, William, Theobald and Stephen

Pope Eugenius; from whom he obtained their privileges:—one for all the lands of the abbey, and another for the lands that adjoin to the churchyard; and, if he might have lived longer, so he meant to do concerning the treasury. And he got in the lands that rich men retained by main strength. Of William Malduit, who held the castle of Rockingham, he won Cotingham and Easton; and of Hugh de Walteville, he won Hirtlingbury and Stanwick, and sixty shillings from Oldwinkle each year. And he made many monks, and planted a vine-yard, and constructed many works, and made the town better than it was before. He was a good monk, and a good man; and for this reason God and good men loved him.

Now we will relate in part what happened in King Stephen's time. In his reign the Jews of Norwich bought a Christian child before Easter, and tortured him after the same manner as our Lord was tortured; and on Long-Friday[163] hanged him on a rood, in mockery of our Lord, and afterwards buried him. They supposed that it would be concealed, but our Lord showed that he was a holy martyr. And the monks took him, and buried him with high honour in the minster. And through our Lord he worketh wonderful and manifold miracles, and is called St. William.

A.D. 1138. In this year came David, King of Scotland, with an immense army to this land. He was ambitious to win this land; but against him came William, Earl of Albemarle, to whom the king had committed York, and other borderers, with few men, and fought against them, and routed the king at the Standard, and slew very many of his gang.

A.D. 1140. In this year wished the King Stephen to take Robert, Earl of Gloucester, the son of King Henry; but he could not, for he was aware of it. After this, in the Lent, the sun and the day darkened about the noon-tide of the day, when men were eating; and they lighted candles to eat by. That was the thirteenth day before the kalends of April. Men were very much struck with wonder. Thereafter died William, Archbishop of Canterbury; and the king made Theobald archbishop, who was Abbot of Bec. After this waxed a very great war betwixt the king and Randolph, Earl of Chester; not because he did not give him all that he could ask him, as he did to all others; but ever the more he gave them, the worse they were to him. The Earl held Lincoln against the king, and took away from him all that he ought to have. And the king went thither, and beset him and his brother William de Romare in the castle. And the earl stole out, and went after Robert, Earl of Glocester, and brought him thither with a large army.

---

163 *Now called "Good-Friday".*

And they fought strenuously on Candlemas day against their lord, and took him; for his men forsook him and fled. And they led him to Bristol, and there put him into prison in close quarters. Then was all England stirred more than ere was, and all evil was in the land. Afterwards came the daughter of King Henry, who had been Empress of Germany, and now was Countess of Anjou. She came to London; but the people of London attempted to take her, and she fled, losing many of her followers. After this the Bishop of Winchester, Henry, the brother of King Stephen, spake with Earl Robert, and with the empress, and swore them oaths, "that he never more would hold with the king, his brother," and cursed all the men that held with him, and told them, that he would give them up Winchester; and he caused them to come thither. When they were therein, then came the king's queen with all her strength, and beset them, so that there was great hunger therein. When they could no longer hold out, then stole they out, and fled; but those without were aware, and followed them, and took Robert, Earl of Glocester, and led him to Rochester, and put him there into prison; but the empress fled into a monastery. Then went the wise men between the king's friends and the earl's friends; and settled so that they should let the king out of prison for the earl, and the earl for the king; and so they did. After this settled the king and Earl Randolph at Stamford, and swore oaths, and plighted their troth, that neither should betray the other. But it availed nothing. For the king afterwards took him at Northampton, through wicked counsel, and put him into prison; and soon after he let him out again, through worse counsel, on the condition that he swore by the crucifix, and found hostages, that he would give up all his castles. Some he gave up, and some gave he not up; and did then worse than he otherwise would. Then was England very much divided. Some held with the king, and some with the empress; for when the king was in prison, the earls and the rich men supposed that he never more would come out: and they settled with the empress, and brought her into Oxford, and gave her the borough. When the king was out, he heard of this, and took his force, and beset her in the tower.[164] And they let her down in the night from the tower by ropes. And she stole out, and fled, and went on foot to Wallingford. Afterwards she went over sea; and those of Normandy turned all from the king to the Earl of Anjou; some willingly, and some against their will; for he beset them till they gave up their castles, and they had no help of the king. Then went Eustace, the king's son, to France, and took to wife the sister of the King of France. He thought to obtain Normandy thereby; but he sped little, and by good right; for he was an evil man. Wherever he was, he did more evil than good; he robbed the lands, and levied heavy guilds upon them. He brought his wife to England, and put her into the castle at...[165] Good woman she was; but she had little bliss with him; and Christ would not that he should long reign. He therefore soon died, and his mother also. And the Earl of Anjou died; and his son Henry took to the earldom. And the Queen of France parted from the king; and she came to the young Earl Henry; and he took her to wife, and all Poitou with her. Then went he with a large force into England, and won some castles; and the king went against him with a much larger force. Nevertheless, fought they not; but the archbishop and the wise men went between them, and made this settlement: That the king should be lord and king while he lived, and after his day Henry should be king: that Henry should take him for a father; and he him for a son: that peace and union should be betwixt them, and in all England. This and the other provisions that they made, swore the king and the earl to observe; and all the bishops,

---

164 *The tower of the castle at Oxford, built by D'Oyley, which still remains.*
165 *The MS. is here deficient.*

and the earls, and the rich men. Then was the earl received at Winchester, and at London, with great worship; and all did him homage, and swore to keep the peace. And there was soon so good a peace as never was there before. Then was the king stronger than he ever was before. And the earl went over sea; and all people loved him; for he did good justice, and made peace.

A.D. 1154. In this year died the King Stephen; and he was buried where his wife and his son were buried, at Faversham; which monastery they founded. When the king died, then was the earl beyond sea; but no man durst do other than good for the great fear of him. When he came to England, then was he received with great worship, and blessed to king in London on the Sunday before midwinter day. And there held he a full court. The same day that Martin, Abbot of Peterborough, should have gone thither, then sickened he, and died on the fourth day before the nones of January; and the monks, within the day, chose another of themselves, whose name was William de Walteville,[166] a good clerk, and good man, and well beloved of the king, and of all good men. And all the monks buried the abbot with high honours. And soon the newly chosen abbot, and the monks with him, went to Oxford to the king. And the king gave him the abbacy; and he proceeded soon afterwards to Peterborough; where he remained with the abbot, ere he came home. And the king was received with great worship at Peterborough, in full procession. And so he was also at Ramsey, and at Thorney, and at.... and at Spalding, and at....

---

166 Or *Vaudeville*.

King Henry II and Eleanor of Aquitaine

The Parker Manuscript (A)

Þy Geare Þe Wæs Agan Fram Cristes Acennesse .Cccc. wintra ⁊ .xciiii. uuintra, þa Cerdic ⁊ Cynric his sunu cuom up æt Cerdicesoran mid .v. scipum; ⁊ se Cerdic wæs Elesing, Elesa Esling, Esla Gewising, Giwis Wiging, Wig Freawining, Freawine Friþugaring, Friþugar Bronding, Brond Bældæging, Bældæg Wodening. Ond þæs ymb .vi. gear þæs þe hie up cuomon geeodon Westseaxna rice, ⁊ þæt uuærun þa ærestan cyningas þe Westseaxna lond on Wealum geeodon; ⁊ he hæfde þæt rice .xvi. gear, ⁊ þa he gefor, þa feng his sunu Cynric to þam rice ⁊ heold .xvii. winter. Þa he gefor, þa feng Ceol to þam rice ⁊ heold .vi. gear. Þa he gefor, þa feng Ceolwulf to his broþur, ⁊ he ricsode .xvii. gear, ⁊ hiera cyn gæþ to Cerdice. Þa feng Cynegils Ceolwulfes broþur sunu to rice ⁊ ricsode .xxxi. wintra, ⁊ he onfeng ærest fulwihte Wesseaxna cyninga, ⁊ þa feng Cenwalh to ⁊ heold .xxxi. wintra, ⁊ se Cenwalh wæs Cynegilses sunu; ⁊ þa heold Seaxburg his cuen an gear þæt rice æfter him. Þa feng Æscwine to rice, þæs cyn gæþ to Cerdice, ⁊ heold .ii. gear. Þa feng Centwine to Wesseaxna rice Cynegilsing ⁊ ricsode .vii. gear. Þa feng Ceadwalla to þam rice, þæs cyn gæþ to Cerdice, ⁊ heold .iii. gear. Ða feng Ine to Seaxna rice, þæs cyn gæþ to Ceardice, ⁊ heold .xxxvii. wintra. Þa feng Æelheard to, þæs cyn gæþ to Ceardice, ⁊ heold .xiiii. winter. Þa feng Cuþred to, þæs cyn gæþ to Cerdice, ⁊ heold .xvii. gear. Þa feng Sigebryht to, þæs cyn gæþ to Cerdice, ⁊ heold an gear. Þa feng Cynewulf to rice, þæs cyn gæþ to Ceardice, ⁊ heold .xxxi. wintra. Þa feng Beorhtric to rice, þæs cyn gæþ to Cerdice, ⁊ heold .xvi. gear. Þa feng Ecgbryht to þam rice ⁊ heold .xxxvii. wintra ⁊ .vii. monaþ, ⁊ feng þa Æþelwulf his sunu to ⁊ heold nigonteoðe healf gear. Se Æþelwulf wæs Ecgbryhting, Ecgbryht Ealhmunding, Ealhmund Eafing, Eafa Eopping, Eoppa Ingilding, Ingild Cenreding, ⁊ Ine Cenreding ⁊ Cuþburg

Cenreding 7 Cuenburg Cenreding, Cenred Ceolwalding, Ceolwald Cuþwulfing, Cuþwulf Cuþwining, Cuþwine Celming, Celm Cynricing, Cynric Cerdicing. Ond þa feng Æþelbald his sunu to rice 7 heold .v. gear. Þa feng Æþelbryht his broþur to 7 heold .v. gear. Þa feng Æþered hiera broþur to rice, 7 heold .v. gear. Þa feng Ælfred hiera broþur to rice, 7 þa was agan his ielde .xxiii. wintra 7 .ccc. 7 .xcvi. wintra þæs þe his cyn ærest Westseaxna lond on Wealum geeodon.

60 BC AER Cristes geflæscnesse .lx. wintra, Gaius Iulius se casere ærest Romana Bretenlond gesohte 7 Brettas mid gefeohte cnysede 7 hie oferswiþde 7 swa þeah ne meahte þær rice gewinnan.

AD 1 Octauianus ricsode .lxvi. wintra, 7 on þam .lxii. geare his rices Crist wæs acenned.

2 Þa tungelwitgan of eastdæle cuomon to þon þæt hie Crist weorþedon 7 þa cild on Bethlem ofslægene wærun for Cristes ehtnesse from Herode.

3 Her swealt Herodus from him selfum ofsticod, 7 Archilaus his sunu feng to rice.

6 From frymþe middangeardes oþ þis gear wæron agan .v. þusendu wintra 7 .cc. wintra.

11 Her onfeng Herodes Antipatres sunu to rice in Iudea.

12 & Philippus 7 Herodes todældun Lyssiam 7 Iudeam feoþericum todældun.

16 Her feng Tiberius to rice.

26 ~~Her onfeng Pilatus gyminge ofer Iudeas.~~

27 Her onfeng Pilatus to gymenne ouer þa Iudeas.

30 Her wæs Crist gefulluhtud 7 Petrus 7 Andreas gehwierfede 7 Iacobus 7 Iohannes 7 Philippus 7 þa .xii. apostolas.

33 Her wæs Crist ahangen, from fruman middangeardes ymb .v. þusendo wintra 7 .cc. 7 .xxvi. wintra.

34 Her wæs Paulus gehwierfed, 7 sanctus Stephanus oftorfod.

35 Her se eadiga Petrus se apostol gesæt biscepsetl in Antiochia
þære ceastre.

39 Her onfeng Gaius rice.

44 Her se eadiga Petrus se apostol gesæt biscepsetl on Rome.

45 Her Herodes aswalt, se þe Iacobum ofslog ane geare ær his
agnum deaþe.

46 Her Claudius oþer Romana cyninga Bretene lond gesohte 7
þone mæstan dæl þæs ealondes on his gewald onfeng, 7 eac
swelce Orcadus þa ealond Romana cynedome underþeodde.
Þis was þes feorðes geares his rices, 7 on þys ylcan geare
gewearð se mycela hunger on Siria þe Lucas recð on þare
boc Actus Apostolorum.

62 Her Iacobus frater Domini þrowode.

63 Her Marcus se godspellere forþferde.

69 Her Petrus 7 Paulus þrowodon.

70 Her Uespassianus onfeng rice.

71 Her Titus Uespassianus sunu in Hierusalem ofslog Iudea .cxi
þusenda.

81 Her Titus feng to rice, se þe sæde þæt he þone dæg forlure þe
he noht to gode on ne gedyde.

83 Her Domittianus Tites broþur feng to rice.

84 Her Iohannes se godspellere in Pathma þam ealonde wrat þa
boc Apocalipsis.

90 ~~Her Simon Petrus wæs ahangen, 7 Iohannes se godspellere
hine gereste in Effesio.~~

92 ~~Her Clemens papa forþferde.~~

99 Her Symon se apostol wæs anhangen 7 Iohannes se
godspellere hine gereste in Epheso.

101 Her Clemens papa forþferde.

110 Her Ignatus biscep þrowude.

155 Her Marcus Antonius 7 Aurelius his broðer fengon to rice.

167 Her Eleutherius on Rome onfeng biscepdom 7 þone wuldorfæstlice .xv. winter geheold. To þam Lucius Bretene kyning sende stafas, bæd þæt he wære cristen gedon, 7 he þurhteah þæt he bæd. 7 hi syððon wunodon on rihton geleauon oððe Diaclitianes rice.

189 Her Seuerus onfeng rice 7 ricsode .xvii. winter, se Bretenlond mid dice begyrdde from sæ oþ sæ. 7 þa geendode on Euerwic, 7 Bassianus his sunu feng to rice.

200 Twa hund gæra.

283 Her þowade sanctus Albanus martyr.

300 Þreo hund gæra.

350 Þreo hund gæ ....

379 Her Gratianus feng to rice.

381 Her Maximianus se casere feng to rice - he wæs on Bretenlonde geboren - 7 þonne for in Gallia 7 he ðar ofsloh ðone casere Gratianum 7 his broðer adraf of æðele, se was gehaten Ualentinianus, 7 se Ualentinianus eft gesanode werod 7 ofsloh Maximum 7 feng to rice. On þam timan aras Pelagies gedwyld geond middaneard.

409 Her Gotan abræcon Romeburg, 7 næfre siþan Romane ne ricsodon on Bretone. Þæt wæs embe .xi. hund wintra 7 .x. wintra þes þe heo getimbred was. Ealles hi ðær rixodon on Brytene feower hund wintra 7 hund seouanti wintra syþþan ærost Gaius Iulius þæt land ærost gesohte.

418 Her Romane gesomnodon al þa goldhord þe on Bretene wæron 7 sume on eorþan ahyddon þæt hie nænig mon siþþan findan ne meahte 7 sume mid him on Gallia læddon.

423 Her Ðeodosius se gingra feng to rice.

430 Her Paladius se biscep wæs onsended to Scottum þæt he hiera geleafan trymede from Cælestino þam papan.

443 Her sendon Brytwalas to Rome 7 heom fultomes bædon

wiþ Piohtas, ac hi þar næfdan nanne, forþan ðe hi fyrdedon wið Ætla Huna cyningæ, 7 þa sendon hi to Anglum 7 Angelcynnes æðelingas ðæs ylcan bædan.

449 Her Mauricius 7 Ualentines onfengon rice 7 ricsodon .vii. winter. 7 On hiera dagum Hengest 7 Horsa from Wyrtgeorne geleaþade Bretta kyninge gesohton Bretene on þam staþe þe is genemned Ypwinesfleot, ærest Brettum to fultume, ac hie eft on hie fuhton. Se cing het hi feohtan agien Pihtas, 7 hi swa dydan 7 sige hæfdan swa hwar swa hi comon. Hi ða sende to Angle 7 heton heom sendan mare fultum 7 heom seggan Brytwalana nahtnesse 7 ðæs landes cysta. Hy ða sendan heom mare fultum. Þa comon þa menn of þrim mægþum Germanie, of Ealdseaxum, of Anglum, of Iotum. Of Iotum comon Cantware 7 Wihtware, þæt ys seo mæið ðe nu eardað on Wiht, 7 ðæt cynn on Westsexum þe man gyt hæt Iutna cyn. Of Ealdseaxon comon Eastsexa 7 Suðsexa 7 WestSexan. Of Angle comon, se a siððan stod westi betwyx Iutum 7 Seaxum, Eastengla, Midelangla, Mearca 7 ealle Norðhymbra.

455 Her Hengest 7 Horsa fuhton wiþ Wyrtgeorne þam cyninge, in þære stowe þe is gecueden Agælesþrep, 7 his broþur Horsan man ofslog; 7 æfter þam Hengest feng to rice 7 Æsc his sunu.

457 Her Hengest 7 Æsc fuhton wiþ Brettas in þære stowe þe is gecueden Crecganford 7 þær ofslogon .iiiim. wera, 7 þa Brettas þa forleton Centlond 7 mid micle ege flugon to Lundenbyrg.

465 Her Hengest 7 Æsc gefuhton uuiþ Walas neah Wippedesfleote 7 þær .xii. wilisce aldormenn ofslogon, 7 hiera þegn an þær wearþ ofslægen, þam wæs noma Wipped.

473 Her Hengest 7 Æsc gefuhton wiþ Walas 7 genamon unarimedlico herereaf, 7 þa Walas flugon þa Englan swa þær fyr.

477 Her cuom Ælle on Bretenlond ⁊ his .iii. suna, Cymen ⁊ Wlencing ⁊ Cissa, mid .iii. scipum on þa stowe þe is nemned Cymenesora, ⁊ þær ofslogon monige Wealas ⁊ sume on fleame bedrifon on þone wudu þe is genemned Andredesleage.

485 Her Ælle gefeaht wiþ Walas neah Mearcrædesburnan stæðe.

488 Her Æsc feng to rice ⁊ was .xxiiii. wintra Cantwara cyning.

491 Her Ælle ⁊ Cissa ymbsæton Andredescester ⁊ ofslogon alle þa þe þærinne eardedon; ne wearþ þær forþon an Bret to lafe.

495 Her cuomon twegen aldormen on Bretene, Cerdic ⁊ Cynric his sunu, mid .v. scipum in þone stede þe is gecueden Cerdicesora ⁊ þy ilcan dæge gefuhtun wiþ Walum.

501 Her cuom Port on Bretene ⁊ his .ii. suna Bieda ⁊ Mægla mid .ii. scipum on þære stowe þe is gecueden Portesmuþa ⁊ ofslogon anne giongne brettiscmonnan, swiþe æþelne monnan.

508 Her Cerdic ⁊ Cynric ofslogon ænne brettisccyning, þam was nama Natanleod, ⁊ .v. þusendu wera mid him. Æfter was þæt lond nemned Natanleaga oþ Cerdicesford.

514 Her cuomon Westseaxe in Bretene mid .iii. scipum in þa stowe þe is gecueden Cerdicesora, ⁊ Stuf ⁊ Wihtgar, ⁊ fuhton wiþ Brettas ⁊ hie gefliemdon.

519 Her Cerdic ⁊ Cynric. Westsexena rice onfengun on þy ilcan geare hie fuhton wiþ Brettas þær mon nu nemneþ Cerdicesford. ⁊ siþþan ricsadan Westsexana cynebearn of þan dæge.

527 Her Cerdic ⁊ Cynric fuhton wiþ Brettas in þære stowe þe is gecueden Cerdicesleaga.

530 Her Cerdic ⁊ Cynric genamon Wihte ealond ⁊ ofslogon feala men on Wihtgarabyrg.

534 Her Cerdic forþferde, ⁊ Cynric his sunu ricsode forþ .xxvi.

wintra; 7 hie saldon hiera tuæm nefum Stufe 7 Wihtgare eall Wiehte ealond.

538 Her sunne aþiestrode .xiiii. dagum ær kalendas Martii from ærmergenne oþ undern.

540 Her sunne aþiestrode on .xii. kalendas Iulius, 7 steorran hie oðiewdon fulneah healfe tid ofer undern.

544 Her Uuihtgar forþferde, 7 hiene mon bebyrgde on Wihtgarabyrg.

547 Her Ida feng to rice, þonon Norþanhymbra cynecyn onwoc 7 rixode twelf gear. 7 he timbrode Bebbanburh. seo wæs ærost mid hegge betyned. 7 þaræfter mid wealle. ~~Ida wæs Eopping, Eoppa wæs Esing, Esa Inguing. Ingui Angenwiting. Angenwit Aloching. Aloc Beonocing. Beonoc Branding. Brand Bældæging. Bældæg Wodening. Woden Friþowulfing. Friþowulf Finning. Finn Godwulfing. Godwulf Geating.~~

552 Her Cynric gefeaht wiþ Brettas in þære stowe þe is genemned æt Searobyrg. 7 þa Bretwalas gefliemde. Cerdic wæs Cynrices ~~fæder. Cerdic Elesing. Elesa Esling. Esla Gewising. Gewis Wiging. Wig Freawining. Freawine Friþogaring. Friþogar Branding. Brand Bældæging. Bældæg Wodening.~~

556 Her Cynric 7 Ceawlin fuhton wiþ Brettas æt Beranbyrg.

560 Her Ceawlin feng to rice on Wesseaxum, 7 ælle feng to Norþanhymbra ~~rice 7 heold .xxx.wintra. Ælle wæs Yffing. Yffe Uscfreaing. Uscfrea Wilgisling. Wilgisl Westerfalcning. Westerfalcna Sæfugling. Sæfugl Sæbalding. Sæbald Sigegeating. Sigegeat Swæfdæging. Swæfdæg Sigegearing. Sigegear Wægdæging. Wægdæg Wodening. Woden Friþowulfing.~~ rice, Idan forðgefarenum. 7 heora ægðer rixade .xxx. wintra.

565 Her ~~Columba mæssepreost of Scottum com in Brettas to lærenne Peohtas 7 in Hi þam ealonde mynster worhte.~~ Her

feng Æðelbriht to Cantwara rice. 7 heold .liii. wintra. On his dagum sende Gregorius us fulluht 7 Columba mæssepreost com to Pihtum. 7 hi gecyrde to Cristes geleauan. Þæt synd þonne wærteras be norðum morum. 7 heora cyng him gesealde þæt igland þe man Ii nemnað. þar syndon fif hida. þæs ðe man seggað. Þar se Columban getimbrade mynster, 7 he þarr wæs abbod .xxxii. wintra 7 þar forðferde. þa he was .lxxvii. wintra. Ða stowe habbað gyt his yrfnuman. Suþ Pihtas wæron ær gefullode of Ninna biscope. se was on Rome gelæred. His mynster ys Hwiterne on Sanctus Martines naman gehalgod. þar he resteð mid manegum halgum. Nu sceal beon æfre on Ii abbod, 7 na biscop. 7 þan sculon beon underðeodde ealle Scotta biscopas. for þan þe Columban was abbod, na biscop.

568 Her Ceaulin 7 Cuþa gefuhton wiþ Æþelbryht. 7 hine in Cent gefliemdon, 7 tuegen aldormen on Wibban dune ofslogon, Oslaf 7 Cnebban.

571 Her Cuþwulf feaht wiþ Bretwalas æt Bedcan forda. 7 .iiii. tunas genom, Lygeanburg. 7 ægelesburg. Benningtun. 7 Egonesham. 7 þy ilcan geare he gefor.

577 Her Cuþwine 7 Ceawlin fuhton wiþ Brettas, 7 hie .iii. kyningas ofslogon, Coinmail, 7 Condidan, 7 Farinmail, in þære stowe þe is gecueden Deorham. 7 genamon .iii. ceastro Gleawanceaster, 7 Cirenceaster, 7 Baþanceaster.

583 Her Mauricius feng to Romana rice.

584 Her Ceawlin 7 Cuþa fuhton wiþ Brettas, in þam stede þe mon nemneþ Feþanleag. 7 Cuþan mon ofslog. 7 Ceaulin monige tunas genom, 7 unarimedlice herereaf, 7 ierre he hwearf þonan to his agnum.

588 Her ælle cyning forþferde, 7 æþelric ricsode æfter him .v. gear.

591 Her Ceolric ricsode .v. gear.

592 Her micel wælfill wæs æt Woddes beorge, ⁊ Ceawlin wæs
ut adrifen. ⁊ Gregorius feng to papdome on Rome.

593 Her Ceawlin ⁊ Cuichelm ⁊ Crida forwurdon, ⁊ æþelfriþ
feng to rice on Norðhymbrum.

595 Her Gregorius papa sende to Brytene Augustinum. mid
wel manegum munecum. þe Godes word Engla ðeoda
godspelledon.

596 ~~Her Gregorius papa sende to Bretene Augustinum. mid
wel monegum munecum. þa Godes word Engla þeode
godspellian.~~

597 Her ongon Ceolwulf ricsian on Wesseaxum, ⁊ simle he
feaht. ⁊ won, oþþe wiþ Angelcyn, oþþe uuiþ Walas, oþþe
wiþ Peohtas, oþþe wiþ Scottas; Se wæs Cuþaing. Cuþa
Cynricing, Cynric Cerdicing, Cerdic Elesing, Elesa Esling,
Esla Gewising, Giwis Wiging, Wig Freawining, Freawine
Friðugaring, Friðugar Bronding, Brond Bældæging, Bældæg
Wodening.

601 Her sende Gregorius papa Agustino ærcebiscepe pallium in
Bretene, ⁊ wel monige godcunde lareowas him to fultome;
⁊ Paulinus biscep gehwerfde Edwine Norþhymbra cyning
to fulwihte.

603 Her ~~wæs gefeoht æt Egesan stane.~~ Ægþan Scotta cyng
feaht wið Dælreoda, ⁊ wið æðelferþe Norþhymra cynge æt
Dægstane, ⁊ man ofsloh mæst ealne his here.

604 Her ~~East Seaxe onfengon geleafan~~ ⁊ ~~fulwihtes bæð.
under Sæbryhte cyninge~~ Augustinus gehalgode .ii. biscopas.
Mellitum ⁊ Iustum. Mellitum he sende to bodiende East
Seaxum fulluht. ðar was se cing gehaten Sæbyrht. Ricolan
sunu. æðelberhtes swyster. ðone æðelbyrht gesette to cynge.
⁊ æðelberht gesealde Mellite biscopsetl on Lundewic. ⁊
Iusto on Hrouecystre. seo ys .xxiiii. mila fram Dorwitceastre.

606 Her forþferde Gregorius ymb .x. gear þæs þe he us fulwiht

sende ⁊ ~~his fæder wæs haten Gordianus~~ And her Æðelfrið lædde his færde to Legercyestre, ⁊ ðar ofsloh unrim Walena. ⁊ swa wearþ gefyld Augustinus witegunge. þe he cwæþ. Gif Wealas nellað sibbe wið us. hi sculan æt Seaxana handa farwurþan. Þar man sloh eac .cc. preosta ða comon ðyder þæt hi scoldon gebiddan for Walena here. Scrocmail was gehaten heora ealdormann. se atbærst ðanon fiftiga sum.

607 Her Ceolwulf gefeaht wiþ Suþ Seaxe.

611 Her Cynegils feng to rice on Wesseaxum, ⁊ heold .xxxi. wintra. ~~Cynegils wæs Ceoling. Ceol Cuþaing. Cuþa Cynricing.~~

614 Her Cynegils ⁊ Cuichelm gefuhton on Beandune, ⁊ ofslogon .ii. þusendo Wala ⁊ .lxvi.

616 Her Æþelbryht Contwara cyning forþferde, ⁊ Eadbald his sunu feng to rice. ⁊ ~~þy ilcan geare wæs agan fram frymþe middangeardes fif þusendu wintra ⁊ .dccc.~~ Se forlet his fulluht, ⁊ leouode on hæðenum þeawe swa þæt he hæfde his fæder laue to wiue. Þa mynte Laurentius ðe þa was ercebiscop on Cent þæt he wolde suð ofer sæ ⁊ eall forlæton. Ac him com to on niht se apostol Petrus ⁊ hine hetelice swang, forðan ðe he wolde Godes hyrde forlæton ⁊ het hine gan to þam cynge ⁊ bodian him rihtne geleafan. ⁊ he swa dyde ⁊ se cing gecyrde to rihtan geleauan. On þyses cinges dagum Laurentius ercebiscop se was on Cent æfter Agustine forþferde .iiii. nonas Februarii ⁊ he was bebyred be Agustine. Æfter him feng Mellitus to arcebiscopdome se was biscop of Lundene ⁊ þas binnan fif wintre Mellitus forðferde. Þa æfter him feng to arcebiscopdome Iustus, se was biscop of Hrouecistre, ⁊ þar to gehalgode Romanum to biscope.

625 Her Paulinus fram Iusto þam ercebiscop wæs gehadod Norþhymbrum to biscepe.

626 Her Eanflæd Edwines dohtor cyninges wæs gefulwad in

þone halgan æfen Pentecosten; 7 Penda hæfde .xxx. wintra rice. 7 he hæfde .L. wintra þa þa he to rice feng. ~~Penda wæs Pybbing. Pybba Cryding. Cryda Cynewolding. Cynewold Cnebbing. Cnebba Iceling. Icel Eomæring. Eomær Angelþeowing. Angelþeow Offing. Offa Wærmunding. Wærmund Wihtlæging. Wihtlæg Wodening.~~

627 Her Edwine kyning wæs gefulwad mid his þeode on Eastron.

628 Her Cynegils 7 Cuichelm gefuhtun wiþ Pendan æt Cirenceastre, 7 geþingodan þa.

632 Her was Eorpwald gefulwad.

633 Her Edwine wæs ofslægen, 7 Paulinus huerf eft to Cantwarum, 7 gesæt þæt biscepsetl on Hrofesceastre.

634 Her Birinus biscep bodude West Seaxum fulwuht.

635 Her Cynegils wæs gefulwad from Birino þæm biscep in Dorkeceastre, 7 Oswold his onfeng.

636 Her Cuichelm wæs gefulwad in Dorcesceastre, 7 þy ilcan geare forþferde; 7 Felix biscep bodade East Englum Cristes geleafan.

639 Her Birinus fulwade Cuþræd on Dorcesceastre, 7 onfeng hine him to suna.

640 Her Redbald Cantwara cyning forþferde, 7 he ricsode .xxv. wintra. He hæfde twegene sunu Ermenred 7 Ercenberht. 7 þes Ercenberht rixode æfter his fæder. 7 Ermenred gestrynde twegen sunu. þa syððan wurðan gemartirode of Đunore.

642 Her Oswald Norþanhymbra cyning ofslægen wæs.

643 Her Cenwalh feng to Wesseaxna rice, 7 heold .xxxi. wintra. 7 se Cenwalh het atimbran þa ciricean on Wintunceastre.

644 Her Paulinus forþferde se was ærcebiscep on Eoforwicceastre, 7 eft on Hrofesceastre.

645 Her Cenwalh adrifen wæs from Pendan cyninge.

646 Her Cenwalh wæs gefulwad.

648 Her Cenwalh gesalde Cuþrede his mæge .iii. þusendo londes be æscesdune; se Cuþred wæs Cuichelming. Cuichelm Cynegilsing.

650 Her ægelbryht of Galwalum. æfter Birine þam Romaniscan biscep onfeng Wesseaxna biscepdome.

651 Her Oswine kyning wæs ofslægen, ⁊ Aidan biscep forþferde.

652 Her Cenwalh gefeaht æt Bradanforda be Afne.

653 Her Middel Seaxe onfengon under Peadan aldormen ryhtne geleafan.

654 Her Onna cyning wearþ ofslægen. ⁊ Botulf ongon mynster timbran æt Icanho.

655 Her Penda forwearþ, ⁊ Mierce wurdon Cristne. Þa was agan from fruman middangeardes .v. þusendo wintra. ⁊ .dccc. ⁊ .l. wintra. ⁊ Peada feng to Mercna rice. Pending.

657 Her forþferde Peada, ⁊ Wulfhere Pending feng to Miercna rice.

658 Her Cenwalh gefeaht æt Peonnum wiþ Walas, ⁊ hie gefliemde oþ Pedridan; þis wæs gefohten siþþan he of East Englum com. He wæs þær .iii. gear on wrece, hæfde hine Penda adrifenne, ⁊ rices benumenne. forþon he his swostor anforlet.

660 Her ægelbryht biscep geewat from Cenwale, ⁊ Wine heold þone biscepdom .iii. gear; ⁊ se ægelbryht onfeng Persa biscepdomes on Galwalum bi Signe.

661 Her Cenwalh gefeaht in Eastron on Posentesbyrg, ⁊ gehergeade Wulfhere Pending oþ æscesdune; ⁊ Cuþred Cuichelming, ⁊ Coenbryht cyning on anum geare forþferdun; ⁊ on Wiht gehergade Wulfhere Pending, ⁊ gesalde Wihtwaran æþelwalde Suþ Seaxna cyninge. forþon Wulfhere hine onfeng æt fulwihte. ⁊ Eoppa mæssepreost.

be Wilferþes worde ⁊ Wulfhere cyning brohte Wihtwarum fulwiht ærest.

664 Her sunne aþiestrode, ⁊ Arcenbryht Cantwara cyng forþferde; ⁊ Colman mid his geferum for to his cyððe. Þy ilcan geare wæs micel mancuealm; ⁊ Ceadda ⁊ Wilferþ wæron gehadode, ⁊ þy ilcan geare Deusdedit forþferde.

668 Her þeodorus mon hadode to ercebiscep:

669 Her Ecgbryht cyning salde Basse mæsseprioste Reculf mynster on to timbranne.

670 Her forþferde Osweo Norþanhymbra cyning, ⁊ Ecgferþ ricsode æfter him; ⁊ Hloþhere feng to biscepdome ofer Wesseaxan ægelbryhtes biscepes nefa. ⁊ heold .vii. gear, þeodor biscep hine gehalgode; ⁊ se Oswio wæs æþelferþing, æþelferþ æþelricing, æþelric Iding, Ida Eopping.

671 Her wæs þæt micle fugla wæl.

672 Her forþferde Cenwalh ⁊ Seaxburg an gear ricsode his cuen æfter him.

673 Her Ecgbryht Cantwara cyning forþferde; ⁊ þy geare wæs senoð æt Heorotforda, ⁊ Sancte æþeldryht ongon þæt mynstær æt Elige:

674 Her feng æscwine to rice on Wesseaxum, se wes Cenfusing, Cenfus Cenferþing, Cenferþ Cuþgilsing, Cuþgils Ceolwulfing, Ceolwulf Cynricing, Cynric Cerdicing.

675 Her Wulfhere Pending ⁊ æscwine gefuhton æt Biedanheafde; ⁊ þy ilcan geare Wulfhere forþferde, ⁊ æþelred feng to rice.

676 Her æscwine forþferde, ⁊ Hedde feng to biscepdome, ⁊ Centwine feng to rice; ⁊ Centwine was Cynegilsing, Cynegils Ceolwulfing; ⁊ æþered Miercna cyning oferhergeada Centlond.

678 Her oþiewde cometa se steorra. ⁊ Wilfriþ biscop wæs adrifen of his biscopdome from Ecgferþe cyninge.

679 Her ælfwine wæs ofslægen, ⁊ Sancte æþelþryþ forþferde.

680 Her gesæt þeodorius ærcebiscop senoþ on Hæþfelda, forþon he wolde þone Cristes geleafan geryhtan; 7 þy ylcan geare forþferde Hild abbodesse on Streonesheale.

682 On þissum geare Centwine gefliemde Bretwealas oþ sæ.

685 Her Ceadwalla ongan æfter rice winnan; Se Ceadwalla was Coenbryhting. Coenbryht Cading, Cadda Cuþaing, Cuþa Ceawlining, Ceawlin Cynricing, Cynric Cerdicing; 7 Mul was Ceadwallan broþur, 7 þone mon eft on Cent forbærnde; 7 þy ilcan geare Ecgferþ cyning mon ofslog; Se Ecgferþ was Osweoing, Osweo æþelferþing, æþelferþ æþelricing, æþelric Iding, Ida Eopping; 7 Hloþhere þy ilcan geare forþferde.

686 Her Ceadwalla 7 Mul Cent 7 Wieht forhergedon.

687 Her Mul wearþ on Cent forbærned, 7 oþre .xii. men mid him, 7 þy geare Ceadwalla eft Cent forhergeada.

688 Her Ine feng to Wesseaxna rice, 7 heold .xxxvii. wintra. 7 he getimbrade þæt menster æt Glæstingabyrig. 7 þy ilcan geare Ceadwalla for to Rome, 7 fulwihte onfeng from þam papan, 7 se papa hine heht Petrus. 7 ymb .vii. niht he forþferde. Þonne was se Ine Cenreding, Cenred Ceolwalding, Ceolwald was Cynegilses broþur, 7 þa wæron Cuþwines suna Ceaulininges, Ceaulin Cynricing, Cynric Cerdicing.

690 Her þeodorius ærcebiscop forþferde, 7 feng Beorhtwald to þam biscepdome. Ær wærun Romanisce biscepas, siþþan wærun Englisce.

694 Her Cantware geþingodan wiþ Ine, 7 him gesaldon .xxx m.. forþon þe hie ær Mul forbærndon; 7 Wihtred feng to Cantwara rice, 7 heold .xxxiii. wintra; Se Wihtred was Ecgbryhting, Ecgbryht Arcenbryhting, Erconbryht Eadbalding, Eadbald æþelbryhting.

703 Her Hedde biscep forþferde, 7 he heold þone biscepdom .xxvii. wintra on Wintaceastre.

704 Her æþelred Pending Miercna cyning onfeng munuchade,

7 þæt rice heold .xxviiii. wintra. þa feng Coenred to.

705 Her Aldferþ Norþanhymbra cyning forþferde ⁊ Seaxuulf biscep.

709 Her Aldhelm biscep forþferde, se wæs be westan wuda biscep, ⁊ wæs todæled in foreweardum Danieles dagum in tua biscepscira West Seaxna lond, ⁊ ær hit wæs an. oþer heold Daniel, oþer Aldhelm; Æfter Aldhelme feng Forþhere to; ⁊ Ceolred feng to Miercna rice, ⁊ Coenred for to Rome ⁊ Offa mid him.

710 : Her Beorhtfriþ ealdormon feaht wiþ Peohtas, ⁊ Ine ⁊ Nun his mæg gefuhton wiþ Gerente Wala cyninge.

714 Her forþferde Guþlac se halga.

715 Her Ine ⁊ Ceolred fuhton æt Woddes beorge.

716 Her Osred Norþanhymbra cyning wearþ ofslægen, se hæfde .vii. winter rice æfter Aldferþe; þa feng Coenred to rice, ⁊ heold .ii. gear; þa Osric ⁊ heold .xi. gear; ⁊ on þam ilcan geare Ceolred Miercna cyning forþferde, ⁊ his lic resteþ on Licetfelda, ⁊ æþelrædes Pendinges on Bearddanigge; ⁊ þa feng Æþelbald to rice on Mercium, ⁊ heold .xli. wintra Æþelbald wæs Alweoing, Alweo Eawing, Eawa Pybing, þæs cyn is beforan awriten; ⁊ Ecgbryht se arwierþa wer on Hii þam ealonde þa munecas on ryht gecierde. þæt hie Eastron onryht heoldon, ⁊ þa ciriclecan scare.

718 Her Ingild forþferde Ines broþur, ⁊ hiera swostur wærun Cuenburg ⁊ Cuþburg, ⁊ sio Cuþburg þæt liif æt Winburnan arærde, ⁊ hio wæs forgifen Norþanhymbra cyninge Aldferþe, ⁊ hie be him lifgendum hie gedældun.

721 Her Daniel ferde to Rome; ⁊ þy ilcan geare Ine ofslog Cynewulf.

722 Her Æþelburg cuen towearp Tantun ⁊ Ine ær timbrede; ⁊ Aldbryht wræccea gewat on Suþrige ⁊ on Suþ Seaxe; ⁊ Ine gefeaht wiþ Suþ Seaxum.

725 Her Wihtræd Cantwara cyning forþferde. þæs cyn is beforan. ⁊ Eadberht feng to Centrice. ⁊ Ine feaht wiþ Suþ Seaxan, ⁊ þær ofslog Aldbryht.

728 Her Ine ferde to Rome. ⁊ þær his feorh gesealde ⁊ feng æþelheard to Wesseaxna rice ⁊ heold .xiiii. gear. ⁊ þy geare gefuhton æþelheard ⁊ Oswald se æþeling; ⁊ se Oswald was æþelbalding, æþelbald Cynebalding, Cynebald Cuþwining, Cuþwine Ceaulining.

729 Her cometa se steorra hiene oþiewde, ⁊ Sanctus Ecgbryht forþferde;

730 Her Oswald se æþeling forþferde.

731 Her was ofslægen Osric Norþanhymbra cyning, ⁊ feng Ceoluulf to þam rice, ⁊ heold .viii. gear. ⁊ se Ceolwulf wæs Cuþaing, Cuþa Cuþwining, Cuþwine Leodwalding. Leodwald Ecgwalding, Ecgwald Aldhelming, Aldhelm Ocging, Ocga Iding, Ida Eopping; ⁊ Beorhtwald ærcebiscep gefor; ⁊ þy ilcan geare Tatwine wæs gehalgod to ærcebiscepe.

733 Her æþelbald geeode Sumurtun; ⁊ sunne aþiestrode.

734 Her wæs se mona swelce he wære mid blode begoten; ⁊ ferdon forþ Tatwine ⁊ Bieda.

736 Her Noþhelm ærcebiscep onfeng pallium from Romana biscep.

737 Her Forþhere biscep ⁊ Friþogiþ cuen ferdun to Rome.

738 Her Eadbryht Eating, Eata Leodwalding, feng to Norþanhymbra rice. ⁊ heold .xxi. wintra. ⁊ his broþor wæs Ecgbryht Eating ærcebiscep, ⁊ hie restaþ begen on Eoforwicceastre on anum portice.

741 Her æþelheard cyning forþferde, ⁊ feng Cuþræd to Wesseaxna rice, ⁊ heold .xvi. wintra, ⁊ heardlice gewon wiþ æþelbald cyning; ⁊ cuþbryht wæs to ærcebiscepe gehalgod, ⁊ Dun biscep to Hrofesceastre.

743 Her æþelbald ⁊ Cuþræd fuhton wiþ Walas.

744 Her Danihel gesæt on Wintanceastre, 7 Hunferþ feng to biscepdome.

745 Her Danihel forþferde, þa was .xliii. wintra agan siþþan he onfeng biscepdome.

746 Her mon slog Selred cyning.

748 Her wæs ofslægen Cynric Wesseaxna æþeling, 7 Eadbryht Cantwara cyning forþferde. 7 æthelbyrht Wihtredes sunu cinges feng to þam rice.

750 Her Cuþred cyning gefeaht uuiþ Æþelhun þone ofermedan aldormonn.

752 Her Cuþred gefeaht þy .xii. geare his rices æt Beorgfeorda wiþ Æþelbald.

753 Her Cuþred feaht wiþ Walas.

754 actually 756 Her Cuþred forþferde, 7 Cyneheard onfeng biscepdome æfter Hunferþe on Wintanceastre; 7 Cantwaraburg forbærn þy geare 7 Sigebryht feng to Wesseaxna rice 7 heold an gear.

755 actually 757 Her Cynewulf benam Sigebryht his rices 7 West Seaxna wiotan for unryhtum dædum buton Hamtunscire 7 he hæfde þa oþ he ofslog þone aldormon þe him lengest wunode 7 hiene þa Cynewulf on Andred adræfde 7 he þær wunade oþ þæt hiene an swan ofstang æt Pryfetesflodan 7 he wræc þone aldormon Cumbran 7 se Cynewulf oft miclum gefeohtum feaht uuiþ Bretwalum 7 ymb .xxxi. wintra þæs þe he rice hæfde he wolde adræfan anne æþeling se was Cyneheard haten 7 se Cyneheard wæs þæs Sigebryhtes broþur 7 þa geascode he þone cyning lytle werode on wifcyþþe on Merantune 7 hine þær berad 7 þone bur utan beeode ær hine þa men onfunden þe mid þam kyninge wærun 7 þa ongeat se cyning þæt 7 he on þa duru eode 7 þa unheanlice hine werede oþ he on þone æþeling locude 7 þa utræsde on hine 7 hine miclum gewundode. 7

hie alle on þone Cyning wærun feohtende oþ þæt hie hine
ofslægenne hæfdon 7 þa on þæs wifes gebærum onfundon
þæs cyninges þegnas þa unstilnesse 7 þa þider urnon swa
hwelc swa þonne gearo wearþ 7 radost 7 hiera se æþeling
gehwelcum feoh 7 feorh gebead 7 hiera nænig hit geþicgean
nolde'. Ac hie simle feohtende wæran oþ hie alle lægon
butan anum Bryttiscum gisle 7 se swiþe gewundad wæs.
Þa on morgenne gehierdun þæt þæs cyninges þegnas þe him
beæftan wærun þæt se cyning ofslægen wæs þa ridon hie
þider 7 his aldormon Osric 7 Wiferþ his þegn 7 þa men
þe he beæftan him læfde ær 7 þone æþeling on þære byrig
metton þær se cyning ofslægen læg 7 þa gatu him to belocen
hæfdon 7 þa þærto eodon 7 þa gebead he him hiera agenne
dom feos 7 londes gif hie him þæs rices uþon 7 him cyþdon
þæt hiera mægas him mid wæron þa þe him from noldon 7
þa cuædon hie þæt him nænig mæg leofra nære þonne hiera
hlaford 7 hie næfre his banan folgian noldon 7 þa budon hie
hiera mægum þæt hie gesunde from eodon 7 hie cuædon þæt
tæt ilce hiera geferum geboden wære þe ær mid þam cyninge
wærun þa cuædon hie þæt hie hie þæs ne onmunden þon ma
þe eowre geferan þe mid þam cyninge ofslægene wærun. 7
hie þa ymb þa gatu feohtende wæron oþ þæt hie þærinne
fulgon 7 þone æþeling ofslogon 7 þa men þe him mid
wærun alle butan anum se wæs þæs aldormonnes godsunu
7 he his feorh generede 7 þeah he wæs oft gewundad. 7 se
Cynewulf ricsode .xxxi. wintra 7 his lic liþ æt Wintanceastre
7 þæs æþlinges æt Ascanmynster 7 hiera ryhtfæder cyn gæþ
to Cerdice 7 þy ilcan geare mon ofslog Æþelbald Miercna
cyning on Seccandune 7 his lic liþ on Hreopadune 7
Beornræd feng to rice 7 lytle hwile heold 7 ungefealice
7 þy ilcan geare Offa feng to rice 7 heold .xxxviiii. wintra
7 his sunu Egferþ heold .xli. daga 7 .c. daga. Se Offa wæs
Þincgferþing Þincgferþ Eanwulfing, Eanwulf Osmoding,
Osmod Eawing, Eawa Pybing, Pybba Creoding, Creoda

334

Cynewalding, Cynewald Cnebing, Cnebba Iceling, Icel
Eomæring, Eomær Angelþowing, Angelþeow Offing, Offa
Wærmunding, Wærmund Wyhtlæging, Wihtlæg Wodening.

758 actually 760 Her Cuþbryht arcebiscep forþferde.

759 actually 761 Her Bregowine wæs to ercebiscepe gehadod to
Sancte Michaeles tide.

760 actually 762 Her Æþelbryht Cantwara cyning forþferde se
was Wihtredes cinges sunu.

761 actually 763-4 Her wæs se micla winter.

763 actually 765 Her Ianbryht wæs gehadod to ærcebiscepe on
þone feowertegan dæg ofer midne winter.

764 actually 766 Her Iaenbryht ærcebiscep onfeng pallium.

768 actually 770 Her forþferde Eadberht ~~Cantwara~~ Eating cinc.

772 actually 774 Her Milred biscep forþferde.

773 actually 775 Her oþiewde read Cristesmæl on hefenum æfter
sunnan setlgonge; 7 þy geare gefuhton Mierce 7 Cantware
æt Ottanforda; 7 wunderleca nædran wæron gesewene on
Suþ Seaxna londe.

777 actually 779 Her Cynewulf 7 Offa gefuhton ymb
Benesingtun 7 Offa nam þone tuun.

780 actually 782 Her Ald Seaxe 7 Francan gefuhtun.

784 actually 786 Her Cyneheard ofslog Cynewulf cyning, 7
he þær wearþ ofslægen, 7 .lxxxiiii. monna mid him; 7 þa
onfeng Beorhtric Wesseaxna rices, 7 he ricsode .xvi. gear, 7
his lic liþ æt Werham, 7 his ryhtfædren cyn gæþ to Cerdice.
To þysan timan rixode Ealhmund cing innon Cent.

785 actually 787 Her wæs geflitfullic senoþ æt Cealchyþe, 7
Iaenbryht ærcebiscep forlet sumne dæl his biscepdomes, 7
from Offan kyninge Hygebryht wæs gecoren, 7 Ecgferþ to
cyninge gehalgod.

787 actually 789 Her nom Beorhtric cyning Offan dohtor
Eadburge; 7 on his dagum cuomon ærest .iii. scipu, 7 þa

se gerefa þærto rad, 7 hie wolde drifan to þæs cyninges tune þy he nyste hwæt hie wæron; 7 hiene mon ofslog; Þæt wæron þa ærestan scipu Deniscra monna þe Angelcynnes lond gesohton.

790 actually 792 Her Iaenbryht ærcebiscep forþferde, 7 þy ilcan geare wæs gecoren æþelheard abbud to biscepe.

792 actually 794 Her Offa Miercna cyning het æþelbryhte rex þæt heafod ofaslean.

794 actually 796 Her Adrianus papa 7 Offa cyning forþferdon; 7 æþelred Norþanhymbra cyning wæs ofslægen from his agenre þeode, 7 Ceolwulf biscep 7 Eadbald biscep of þæm londe aforon; 7 Ecgferþ feng to Miercna rice. 7 þy ilcan geare forþferde; 7 Eadbryht onfeng rice on Cent. þam was oþer noma nemned Præn.

796 actually 798 Her Ceolwulf Miercna cyning oferhergeade Cantware oþ Mersc, 7 gefengun Praen hiera cyning, 7 gebundenne hine on Mierce læddon;

797 actually 799 Her Romane Leone þæm papan his tungon forcurfon, 7 his eagan astungon, 7 hine of his setle afliemdon; 7 þa sona eft Gode fultomiendum he meahte geseon 7 sprecan, 7 eft was papa swa he ær wæs.

799 actually 801 Her æþelheard ærcebiscep 7 Cynebryht Wesseaxna biscep foron to Rome.

800 actually 802 Her Beorhtric cyning forþferde 7 Worr aldormon; 7 Ecgbryht feng to Wesseaxna rice; 7 þy ilcan dæge rad æþelmund aldorman of Hwiccium ofer æt Cynemæresforda, þa mette hine Weoxstan aldorman mid Wilsætum; þær wearþ micel gefeoht, 7 þær begen ofslægene þa aldormen, 7 Wilsætan namon sige.

802 actually 804 Her wæs gehadod Beornmod biscep to Hrofesceastre.

803 actually 805 Her æþelheard ærcebiscep forþferde, 7

Wulfred wæs to ærcebiscepe gehadod, 7 Forþred abbud forþferde.

804 actually 806 Her Wulfred ærcebiscep pallium onfeng.

805 actually 807 Her Cuþred cyning forþferde on Cantwarum, 7 Ceolburg abbudesse, 7 Heabryht aldorman.

812 actually 814 Her Carl cyning forþferde, 7 he ricsode .xlv. wintra. 7 Wulfred arcebiscep 7 Wigbryht Wesseaxna biscep foron begen to Rome;

813 actually 815 Her Wulfred ærcebiscep mid bledsunge þæs papan Leon hwearf eft to his agnum biscepdome; 7 þy geare gehergade Ecgbryht cyning on West Walas from easteweardum oþ westewearde.

814 actually 816 Her Leo se æþela papa 7 se halga forþferde, 7 æfter him Stephanus feng to rice.

816 actually 818 Her Stephanus papa forþferde, 7 æfter him was Paschalis to papan gehadod; 7 þy ilcan geare forborn Ongolcynnes scolu.

819 actually 821 Her Cenwulf Miercna cyning forþferde, 7 Ceolwulf feng to rice, 7 Eadbryht aldormon forþferde.

821 actually 823 Her wearþ Ceolwulf his rices besciered.

822 actually 824 Her tuegen aldormen wurdon ofslægene, Burghelm 7 Muca; 7 senoþ wæs æt Clofeshoo.

823 actually 825 Her wæs Wala gefeoht 7 Defna æt Gafulforda 7 þy ilcan geare gefeaht Ecbryht cyning 7 Beornwulf cyning on Ellendune 7 Ecgbryht sige nam 7 þær wæs micel wæl geslægen. Þa sende he Æþlwulf his sunu of þære fierde 7 Ealhstan his biscep 7 Wulfheard his aldormon to Cent micle werede 7 hie Baldred þone cyning norþ ofer Temese adrifon 7 Cantware him to cirdon 7 Suþrige 7 SuþSeaxe 7 EastSeaxe þy hie from his mægum ær mid unryhte anidde wærun 7 þy ilcan geare EastEngla cyning 7 seo þeod gesohte Ecgbryht cyning him to friþe 7 to mundboran

for Miercna ege ⁊ þy geare slogon EastEngle Beornwulf Miercna cyning.

825 actually 827 Her Ludecan Miercna cyning ⁊ his .v. aldormen mon ofslog mid him ⁊ Wiiglaf feng to rice.

827 actually 829 Her mona aþistrode on middes wintres mæsseniht ⁊ þy ilcan geare geeode Ecgbryht cyning Miercna rice ⁊ al þæt be suþan Humbre wæs ⁊ he wæs se eahteþa cyning se þe Bretwalda wæs Ærest Ælle SuþSeaxna cyning se þus micel rice hæfde se æftera wæs Ceawlin Wesseaxna cyning se þridda wæs Æþelbryht Cantwara cyning se feorþa wæs Rædwald EastEngla cyning fifta was Eadwine Norþanhymbra cyning siexta wæs Oswald se æfter him ricsode seofoþa wæs Oswio Oswaldes broþur eahtoþa wæs Ecgbryht Wesseaxna cyning ⁊ se Ecgbryht lædde fierd to Dore wiþ Norþanhymbre ⁊ hie him þær eaþmedo budon ⁊ geþuærnesse ⁊ hie on þam tohwurfon.

828 actually 830 Her eft Wilaf onfeng Miercna rices ⁊ Æþelwald biscep forþferde ⁊ þy ilcan geare lædde Ecgbryht cyning fierd on NorþWalas ⁊ he hie to eaþmodre hersumnesse gedyde.

829 actually 831 Her Wulfred ærcebiscep forþferde.

830 actually 832 Her Ceolnoþ wæs gecoren to biscepe ⁊ gehadod ⁊ Feologid abbud forþferde.

831 actually 833 Her Ceolnoþ ærcebiscep onfeng pallium.

832 actually 835 Her hæþen men oferhergeadon Sceapige.

833 actually 836 Her gefeaht Ecgbryht cyning wiþ .xxxv. sciphlæsta æt Carrum ⁊ þær wearþ micel wæl geslægen, ⁊ þa Denescan ahton wælstowe gewald; ⁊ Hereferþ ⁊ Wigþen tuegen biscepas forþferdon, ⁊ Dudda ⁊ Osmod tuegen aldormen forþferdon.

835 actually 838 Her cuom micel sciphere on Westwalas ⁊ hie to anum gecierdon, ⁊ wiþ Ecgbryht West Seaxna cyning

winnende wæron. Þa he þæt hierde 7 mid fierde ferde 7
him wiþ feaht æt Hengestdune 7 þær gefliemde ge þa Walas
ge þa Deniscan.

836 actually 839 Her Ecgbryht cyning forþferde, 7 hine hæfde
ær Offa Miercna cyning 7 Beorhtric Wesseaxna cyning
afliemed .iii. gear of Angelcynnes lande on Fronclond,
ær he cyning wære, 7 þy fultomode Beorhtric Offan þy
he hæfde his dohtor him to cuene; 7 se Ecgbyht ricsode
.xxxvii. wintra, .vii. monaþ, 7 feng Æþelwulf Ecgbrehting
to Wesseaxna rice, 7 he salde his suna Æþelstane Cantwara
rice 7 Eastseaxna 7 Suþrigea 7 Suþseaxna.

837 probably 840 Her Wulfheard aldormon gefeaht æt Hamtune
wiþ .xxxiii. sciphlæsta 7 þær micel wæl geslog 7 sige nom.
7 þy geare forþferde Wulfheard. 7 þy ilcan geare gefeaht
Æþelhelm dux wiþ Deniscne here on Port mid Dornsætum
7 gode hwile þone here gefliemde, 7 þa Deniscan ahton
wælstowe gewald 7 þone aldormon ofslogon.

838 actually 841 Her Herebryht aldormon wæs ofslægen from
hæþnum monnum 7 monige mid him on Merscwarum, 7 þy
ilcan geare eft on Lindesse 7 on Eastenglum 7 on Cantwarum
wurdon monige men ofslægene from þam herige.

839 actually 842 Her wæs micel wæsliht on Lundenne 7 on
Cwantawic 7 on Hrofesceastre.

840 probably 843 Her Æþelwulf cyning gefeaht æt Carrum wiþ
.xxxv. schiplæsta, 7 þa Deniscan ahton wæstowe gewald.

845 probably 848 Her Eanulf aldorman gefeaht mid Sumursætum
7 Ealchstan biscep 7 Osric aldorman mid Dornsætnum
gefuhton æt Pedridan muþan wiþ Deniscne here 7 þær micel
wæl geslogon 7 sige namon. þy ilcan geare Æþelstan rex 7
Ealchere dux micelne here ofslogon æt Sondwic on Kent 7
.viiii. scipu gefengon 7 þa oþru geflimdon

851 Her Ceorl aldormon gefeaht wiþ hæþene men min
Defenascire æt Wicganbeorge, 7 þær micel wæl geslogon

7 sige namon. 7 þy ilcan geare Æþelstan cyning 7
Ealchere dux micelne here ofslogon æt Sondwic on Cent 7
.ix .scipu gefengun 7 þa oþre gefliemdon. 7 hæþne men
ærest ofer winter sæton. 7 þy ilcan geare cuom feorðe healf
hund scipa on Temese muþan 7 bræcon Contwaraburg 7
Lundenburg, 7 gefliemdon Beorhtwulf Miercna cyning mid
his fierde, 7 foron þa suþ ofer Temese on Suþrige 7 him
gefeaht wiþ Æþelwulf cyning 7 Æþelbald his sunu æt Aclea
mid Westseaxna fierde, 7 þær þæt mæste wæl geslogon on
hæþnum herige þe we secgan hierdon oþ þisne ondweardan
dæg, 7 þær sige namon.

853 Her bæd Burgred Miercna cyning 7 his wiotan (bædon)
Æþelwulf cyning þæt he (he) him gefultumade þæt him
Norþwalas gehiersumade. He þa swa dyde, 7 mid fierde
fór ofer Mierce on Norþwalas, 7 hie him alle gehiersume
dydon. 7 þy ilcan geare sende Æþelwulf cyning Ælfred his
sunu to Rome. Þa was domne Leo papa on Rome, 7 he hine
to cyninge gehalgode 7 hiene him to biscepsuna nam. Þa þy
ilcan geare Ealhere mid Cantwarum 7 Huda mid Suþrigium
gefuhton on Tenet wiþ hæþnum herige 7 ærest sige namon,
7 þær wearþ monig mon ofslægen 7 adruncen on gehwæþere
hond. On þæs ofer Eastron geaf Æþelwulf cyning his dohtor
Burgrede cyninge of Wesseaxum on Merce.

855 Her hæþne men ærest on Sceapige ofer winter sætun. 7 þy
ilcan geare gebocude Æþelwulf cyning teoþan dæl his londes
ofer al his rice Gode to lofe 7 him selfum to ecere hælo,
7 þy ilcan geare ferde to Rome mid micelre weorþnesse 7
þær was .xii. monaþ wuniende 7 þa him hamweard fór, 7
him þa Carl Francna cyning his dohtor geaf him to cuene, 7
æfter þam to his leodum cuom 7 hie þæs gefægene wærun.
7 ymb .ii. gear þæs ðe he on Francum com he gefór, 7 his
lic liþ æt Wintanceastre, 7 he ricsode nigonteoþe healf gear.
On se Æþelwulf wæs Ecgbrehting, Ecgbryht Ealhmunding,
Ealhmund Eafing, Eafa Eopping, Eoppa Ingilding; Ingild

wæs Ines broþur Westseaxna cyninges, þæs þe eft ferde to
Sancte Petre ⁊ þær eft his feorh gesealde; ⁊ hie wæron
Cendredes suna, Cenred wæs Ceolwalding, Ceolwald
Cuþaing, Cuþa Cuþwining, Cuþwine Ceaulining, Ceawlin
Cynricing, Cynric Cerdicing, Cerdic Elesing, Elesa Esling,
Esla Giwising, Giwis Wiging, Wig Freawining, Freawine
Friþogaring, Friþogar Bronding, Brond Bældæging, Bældæg
Wodening, Woden Friþowalding, Friþuwald Freawining,
Frealaf Friþuwulfing, Friþuwulf Finning, Fin Godwulfing,
Godwulf Geating, Geat Tætwaing, Tætwa Beawing, Beaw
Sceldwaing, Sceldwea Heremoding, Heremod Itermoning,
Itermon Hraþraing, se wæs geboren in þære earce: Noe,
Lamach, Matusalem, Enoh, Iaered, Maleel, Camon, Enos,
Sed, Adam primus homo et pater noster est Christus, Amen.
On þa fengon Æþelwulfes suna twegen to rice, Æþelbald
to Wesseaxna rice ⁊ Æþelbryht to Cantwara rice ⁊ to
Eastseaxna rice ⁊ to Suþrigea ⁊ to Suþseaxna rice; ⁊ þa
ricsode Æþelbald .v. gear.

860 Her æþelbald cyng forþferde, ⁊ his lic liþ æt Sciraburnan,
⁊ feng æþelbryht to allum þam rice his broþur, ⁊ he hit heold
on godre geþuærnesse ⁊ on micelre sibsumnesse; ⁊ on his
dæge cuom micel sciphere up ⁊ abræcon Wintanceastre. ⁊
wiþ þone here gefuhton Osric aldorman mid Hamtunscire,
⁊ æþelwulf aldormon mid Bearrucscire, ⁊ þone here
gefliemdon, ⁊ wælstowe gewald ahton; ⁊ se æþelbryht
ricsode .v. gear, ⁊ his lic liþ æt Scireburnan.

865 Her sæt hæþen here on Tenet, ⁊ genamon friþ wiþ
Cantwarum, ⁊ Cantware him feoh geheton wiþ þam friþe,
⁊ under þam friþe ⁊ þam feohgehate se here hiene on niht
up bestæl, ⁊ oferhergeade alle Cent eastewearde;

866 Her feng æþered æþelbryhtes broþur to Wesseaxna rice;
⁊ þy ilcan geare cuom micel here on Angelcynnes lond, ⁊
wintersetl namon on Eastenglum, ⁊ þær gehorsude wurdon,
⁊ hie him friþ wiþ namon.

867 Her for se here of East Englum ofer Humbre muþan
to Eoforwicceastre on Norþhymbre, 7 þær wæs micel
ungeþuærnes þære þeode betweox him selfum, 7 hie hæfdun
hiera cyning aworpenne Osbryht, 7 ungecyndne cyning
underfengon ællan; 7 hie late on geare to þam gecirdon
þæt hie wiþ þone here winnende wærun, 7 hie þeah micle
fierd gegadrodon, 7 þone here sohton æt Eoforwicceastre,
7 on þa ceastre bræcon, 7 hie sume inne wurdon, 7 þær
was ungemetlic wæl geslægen Norþanhymbra, sume binnan,
sume butan; 7 þa cyningas begen ofslægene, 7 sio laf wiþ
þone here friþ nam; 7 þy ilcan geare gefor Ealchstan biscep,
7 he hæfde þæt bisceprice .l. wintra æt Scireburnan, 7 his
lic liþ þær on tune.

868 Her for se ilca here innan Mierce to Snotengaham, 7 þær
wintersetl namon; 7 Burgræd Miercna cyning 7 his wiotan
bædon æþered Westseaxna cyning 7 ælfred his broþur þæt
hie him gefultumadon, þæt hie wiþ þone here gefuhton;
7 þa ferdon hie mid Wesseaxna fierde innan Mierce oþ
Snotengaham, 7 þone here þær metton on þam geweorce,
7 þær nan hefelic gefeoht ne wearþ, 7 Mierce friþ namon
wiþ þone here;

869 Her for se here eft to Eoforwicceastre, 7 þær sæt .i. gear.

870 Her rad se here ofer Mierce innan Eastengle 7 wintersetl
namon. æt þeodforda, 7 þy wintra Eadmund cyning him wiþ
feaht, 7 þa Deniscan sige namon, 7 þone cyning ofslogon, 7
þæt lond all geeodon; 7 þy geare gefor Ceolnoþ ærcebiscep.
7 Æþered Wiltunscire biscop wearþ gecoren to ærcebiscpe
to Cantuareberi.

871 Her cuom se here to Readingum on Westseaxe, 7 þæs
ymb .iii. niht ridon .ii. eorlas up; Þa gemette hie æþelwulf
aldorman on Englafelda, 7 him þær wiþ gefeaht 7 sige
nam; Þæs ymb .iiii. niht æþered cyning 7 ælfred his broþur
þær micle fierd to Readingum gelæddon, 7 wiþ þone here

gefuhton, 7 þær wæs micel wæl geslægen on gehwæþre hond, 7 æþelwulf aldormon wearþ ofslægen, 7 þa Deniscan ahton wælstowe gewald; 7 þæs ymb .iiii. niht gefeaht æþered cyning 7 ælfred his broþur wiþ alne þone here on æscesdune, 7 hie wærun on twæm gefylcum, on oþrum wæs Bachsecg 7 Halfdene þa hæþnan cyningas, 7 on oþrum wæron þa eorlas; 7 þa gefeaht se cyning æþered wiþ þara cyninga getruman, 7 þær wearþ se cyning Bagsecg ofslægen; 7 ælfred his broþur wiþ þara eorla getruman, 7 þær wearþ Sidroc eorl ofslægen se alda, 7 Sidroc eorl se gioncga, 7 Osbearn eorl, 7 Fræna eorl, 7 Hareld eorl, 7 þa hergas begen gefliemde, 7 fela þusenda ofslægenra, 7 onfeohtende wæron oþ niht. 7 þæs ymb .xiiii. niht gefeaht æþered cyning 7 ælfred his broður wiþ þone here æt Basengum, 7 þær þa Deniscan sige namon; 7 þæs ymb .ii. monaþ gefeaht æþered cyning 7 ælfred his broþur wiþ þone here æt Meretune, 7 hie wærun on tuæm gefylcium, 7 hie butu gefliemdon, 7 longe on dæg sige ahton, 7 þær wearþ micel wælsliht on gehwæþere hond, 7 þa Deniscan ahton wælstowe gewald; 7 þær wearþ Heahmund biscep ofslægen, 7 fela godra monna; 7 æfter þissum gefeohte cuom micel sumorlida; 7 þæs ofer Eastron gefor æþered cyning, 7 he ricsode .v. gear, 7 his lic liþ æt Winburnan. Þa feng ælfred æþelwulfing his broþur to Wesseaxna rice; 7 þæs ymb anne monaþ gefeaht ælfred cyning wiþ alne þone here lytle werede æt Wiltune, 7 hine longe on dæg gefliemde, 7 þa Deniscan ahton wælstowe gewald; 7 þæs geares wurdon .viiii. folc gefeoht gefohten wiþ þone here on þy cynerice be suþan Temese, 7 butan þam þe him ælfred þæs cyninges broþur, 7 anlipig aldormon, 7 cyninges þegnas oft rade onridon þe mon na ne rimde, 7 þæs geares wærun ofslægene .viiii. eorlas 7 an cyning; 7 þy geare namon Westseaxe friþ wiþ þone here.

872 Her for se here to Lundenbyrig from Readingum, 7 þær wintersetl nam, 7 þa namon Mierce friþ wiþ þone here.

873 Her for se here on Norþhymbre, 7 he nam wintersetl on Lindesse æt Tureces iege, 7 þa namon Mierce friþ wiþ þone here.

874 Her for se here from Lindesse to Hreopedune, 7 þær wintersetl nam, 7 þone cyning Burgræd ofer sæ adræfdon ymb .xxii. wintra þæs þe he rice hæfde, 7 þæt lond all geeodon; 7 he for to Rome 7 þær gesæt 7 his lic liþ on Sancta Marian ciricean on Angelcynnes scole; 7 þy ilcan geare hie sealdon anum unwisum cyninges þegne Miercna rice to haldanne, 7 he him aþas swor 7 gislas salde, þæt he him gearo wære swa hwelce dæge swa hie hit habban wolden, 7 he gearo wære mid him selfum, 7 on allum þam þe him læstan woldon. to þæs heres þearfe.

875 Her for se here from Hreopedune, 7 Healfdene for mid sumum þam here on Norþhymbre. 7 nam wintersetl be Tinan þære ea, 7 se here þæt lond geeode. 7 oft hergade on Peohtas, 7 on Stræcledwalas; 7 for Godrum 7 Oscytel 7 Anwynd. þa .iii. cyningas, of Hreopedune to Grantebrycge mid micle here, 7 sæton þær an gear; 7 þy sumera for ælfred cyning ut on sæ mid sciphere, 7 gefeaht wiþ .vii. sciphlæstas, 7 hiera an gefeng. 7 þa oþru gefliemde.

876 Her hiene bestæl se here into Werham Wesseaxna fierde, 7 wiþ þone here se cyning friþ nam, 7 him þa aþas sworon on þam halgan beage, þe hie ær nanre þeode noldon, þæt hie hrædlice of his rice foren; 7 hie þa under þam hie nihtes bestælon þære fierde se gehorsoda here into Escanceaster; 7 þy geare Healfdene Norþanhymbra lond gedælde. 7 ergende wæron 7 hiera tilgende.

877 Her cuom se here into Escanceastre from Werham, 7 se sciphere sigelede west ymbutan, 7 þa mette hie micel yst on sæ, 7 þær forwearþ .cxx. scipa æt Swanawic; 7 se cyning ælfred æfter þam gehorsudan here mid fierde rad oþ Exanceaster 7 hie hindan ofridan ne meahte ær hie on þam

fæstene wæron, þær him mon to ne meahte; ⁊ hie him þær
foregislas saldon. swa fela swa he habban wolde, ⁊ micle
aþas sworon, ⁊ þa godne friþ heoldon; ⁊ þa on hærfæste
gefor se here on Miercna lond, ⁊ hit gedældon sum, ⁊ sum
Ceolwulfe saldon.

878 Her hiene bestæl se here on midne winter ofer tuelftan niht
to Cippanhamme, ⁊ geridon Wesseaxna lond ⁊ gesæton ⁊
micel þæs folces (7) ofer sæ adræfdon, ⁊ þæs oþres þone
mæstan dæl hie geridon, ⁊ him to gecirdon buton þam
cyninge Ælfrede. ⁊ he lytle werede unieþelice æfter wudum
for, ⁊ on morfæstenum; ⁊ þæs ilcan wintra wæs Inwæres
broþur ⁊ Healfdenes on Westseaxum on Defenascire mid
.xxiii. scipum, ⁊ hiene mon þær ofslog, ⁊ .dccc. monna
mid him. ⁊ .xl. monna his heres; ⁊ þæs on Eastron worhte
ælfred cyning lytle werede geweorc æt Æþelingaeigge, ⁊ of
þam geweorce was winnende wiþ þone here, ⁊ Sumursætna
se dæl, se þær niehst wæs; Þa on þære seofoðan wiecan ofer
Eastron he gerad to Ecgbryhtes stane be eastan Sealwyda, ⁊
him to comon þær ongen Sumorsæte alle, ⁊ Wilsætan, ⁊
Hamtunscir se dæl, se hiere behinon sæ was, ⁊ his gefægene
wærun; ⁊ he for ymb ane niht of þam wicum to Iglea, ⁊
þæs ymb ane to Eþandune, ⁊ þær gefeaht wiþ alne þone
here, ⁊ hiene gefliemde, ⁊ him æfter rad oþ þæt geweorc,
⁊ þær sæt .xiiii. niht; ⁊ þa salde se here him foregislas ⁊
micle aþas þæt hie of his rice uuoldon ⁊ him eac geheton
þæt kyning fulwihte onfon wolde ⁊ hie þæt gelæston swa,
⁊ þæs ymb .iii. wiecan com se cyning to him Godrum þritiga
sum þara monna þe in þam here weorþuste wæron æt Alre,
⁊ þæt is wiþ Æþelinggaeige; ⁊ his se cyning þær onfeng æt
fulwihte, ⁊ his crismlising was æt Weþmor, ⁊ he was .xii.
niht mid þam cyninge, ⁊ he hine miclum ⁊ his geferan mid
feo weorðude.

879 Her for se here to Cirenceastre of Cippanhamme. ⁊ sæt þær
an gear; ⁊ þy geare gegadrode on hloþ wicenga, ⁊ gesæt æt

Fullanhamme be Temese; 7 þy ilcan geare aþiestrode sio sunne ane tid dæges.

880 Her for se here of Cirenceastre on Eastengle, 7 gesæt þæt lond, 7 gedælde. 7 þy ilcan geare for se here ofer sæ þe ær on Fullanhomme sæt on Fronclond to Gend, 7 sæt þær an gear.

881 Her for se here ufor on Fronclond, 7 þa Francan him wiþ gefuhton, 7 þær þa wearþ se here gehorsod æfter þam gefeohte.

882 Her for se here up onlong Mæse feor on Fronclond, 7 þær sæt an gear. 7 þy ilcan geare for ælfred cyning mid scipum ut on sæ. 7 gefeaht wiþ feower sciphlæstas Deniscra monna, 7 þara scipa tu genam, 7 þa men ofslægene wæron þe ðæron wæron, 7 tuegen sciphlæstas him on hond eodon, 7 þa wæron miclum forslægene 7 forwundode ær hie on hond eodon.

883 Her for se here up on Scald to Cundoþ, 7 þær sæt an gear.

884 Her for se here up on Sunnan to Embenum, 7 þær sæt an gear.

885 Her todælde se foresprecena here on tu, oþer dæl east. oþer dæl to Hrofesceastre; 7 ymbsæton ða ceastre, 7 worhton oþer fæsten ymb hie selfe. 7 hie þeah þa ceastre aweredon oþþæt ælfred com utan mid fierde; Þa eode se here to hiera scipum, 7 forlet þæt geweorc. 7 hie wurdon þær behorsude, 7 sona þy ilcan sumere ofer sæ gewiton; 7 þy ilcan geare sende ælfred cyning sciphere on Eastengle; sona swa hie comon on Stufe muþan, þa metton hie .xvi. scipu wicenga, 7 wiþ ða gefuhton, 7 þa scipo alle geræhton, 7 þa men ofslogon; Þa hie þa hamweard wendon mid þære herehyþe, þa metton hie micelne sciphere wicenga, 7 þa wiþ þa gefuhton þy ilcan dæge, 7 þa Deniscan ahton sige; Þy ilcan geare ær middum wintra. forþferde Carl Francna cyning, 7 hiene ofslog an efor, 7 ane geare ær his broður forþferde, se hæfde eac þæt

346

westrice, 7 hie wæron begen Hloþwiges suna. Se hæfde eac þæt westrice, 7 forþferde þy geare þe sio sunne aþiestrode. Se wæs Karles sunu þe æþelwulf Westseaxna cyning his dohtor hæfde him to cuene. 7 þy ilcan geare gegadrode micel sciphere on Aldseaxum, 7 þær wearþ micel gefeoht tua on geare, 7 þa Seaxan hæfdun sige, 7 þær wæron Frisan mid. Þy ilcan geare feng Carl to þam westrice, 7 to allum þam westrice behienan Wendelsæ, 7 begeondan þisse sæ, swa hit his þridda fæder hæfde, butan Lidwiccium. Se Carl was Hloþwiges sunu, se Hloþwig was Carles broþur, se wæs Iuþyttan fæder þe æþelwulf cyning hæfde, 7 hie wæron Hloþwiges suna, se Hloþwig was þæs aldan Carles sunu, se Carl was Pippenes sunu. 7 þy ilcan geare forþferde se goda papa Marinus, se gefreode Ongelcynnes scole be ælfredes bene Westseaxna cyninges, 7 he sende him micla gifa, 7 þære rode dæl þe Crist on þrowude. 7 þy ilcan geare se here on Eastenglum bræc friþ wiþ ælfred cyning.

886 Her for se here eft west þe ær east gelende, 7 þa up on Sigene, 7 þær wintersetl namon. Þy ilcan geare gesette ælfred cyning Lundenburg, 7 him all Angelcyn to cirde, þæt buton Deniscra monna hæftniede was, 7 hie þa befæste þa burg æþerede aldormen to haldonne.

887 Her for se here up þurh þa brycge æt Paris, 7 þa up andlang Sigene oþ Mæterne, oþ Cariei; 7 þa sæton þara 7 innan Ionan tu winter on þam twam stedum; 7 þy ilcan geare forþferde Karl Francna cyning, 7 Earnulf his broþur sunu hine .vi. wicum ær he forþferde berædde æt þam rice, 7 þa wearþ þæt rice todæled on .v. 7 .v. kyningas to gehalgode. Þæt wæs þeah mid Earnulfes geþafunge, 7 hi cuædon þæt hie þæt to his honda healdan sceoldon. forþæm hira nan næs on fædren healfe to geboren. buton him anum. Earnulf þa wunode on þæm londe be eastan Rin, 7 Roþulf þa feng to þæm middelrice, 7 Oda to þæm westdæle, 7 Beorngar 7 Wiþa to Longbeardna londe, 7 to þæm londum on þa

healfe muntes, ⁊ þæt heoldun mid micelre unsibbe, ⁊ tu folcgefeoht gefuhton, ⁊ þæt lond oft ⁊ gelome forhergodon, ⁊ æghwæþer oþerne oftrædlice ut dræfde; ⁊ þy ilcan geare þe se here for forþ up ofer þa brycge æt Paris. (7) Æþelhelm aldormon lædde Wesseaxna ælmessan ⁊ ælfredes cyninges to Rome.

888 Her lædde Beocca aldormon Wesseaxna ælmessan ⁊ ælfredes cyninges to Rome. ⁊ æþelswiþ cuen, sio wæs ælfredes sweostor cyninges, forþferde, ⁊ hire lic liþ æt Pafian; ⁊ þy ilcan geare æþelred ercebiscep ⁊ æþelwold aldormon. forþferdon on anum monþe.

889 On þissum geare næs nan færeld to Rome, buton tuegen hleaperas ælfred cyning sende mid gewritum.

890 Her lædde Beornhelm abbud Westseaxna ælmessan to Rome ⁊ ælfredes cyninges; ⁊ Godrum se norþerna cyning forþferde, þæs fulluhtnama wæs æþelstan, se wæs ælfredes cyninges godsunu, ⁊ he bude on Eastenglum, ⁊ þæt lond ærest gesæt; ⁊ þy ilcan geare for se here of Sigene to Sant Laudan, þæt is butueoh Brettum ⁊ Francum, ⁊ Brettas him wiþ gefuhton, ⁊ hæfdon sige, ⁊ hie bedrifon ut on ane ea, ⁊ monige adrencton. Her wæs Plegemund gecoron of Gode ⁊ of eallen his halechen.

891 Her for se here east. ⁊ Earnulf cyning gefeaht wið ðæm ræde here ær þa scipu cuomon, mid Eastfrancum, ⁊ Seaxum, ⁊ Bægerum. ⁊ hine gefliemde; ⁊ þrie Scottas comon to ælfrede cyninge, on anum bate butan ælcum gereþrum of Hibernia, þonon hi hi bestælon forþon þe hi woldon for Godes lufan on elþiodignesse beon, hi ne rohton hwær. Se bat wæs geworht of þriddan healfre hyde þe hi on foron, ⁊ hi namon mid him þæt hi hæfdun to seofon nihtum mete; ⁊ þa comon hie ymb .vii. niht to londe on Cornwalum. ⁊ foron þa sona to ælfrede cyninge; Þus hie wæron genemnde, Dubslane ⁊ Maccbethu. ⁊ Maelinmun. ⁊ Swifneh se betsta

lareow þe on Scottum wæs gefor.

(892)

(891 cont'd) ⁊ þy ilcan geare ofer Eastron. ymbe gang dagas oþþe ær, æteowde se steorra þe mon on boclæden hæt cometa, Sume men cweþaþ on Englisc þæt hit sie feaxede steorra. forþæm þær stent lang leoma of, hwilum on ane healfe hwilum on ælce healfe:

892 Her on þysum geare for se micla here. þe we gefyrn ymbe spræcon, eft of þæm eastric westweard to Bunann. ⁊ þær wurdon gescipode, swa þæt hie asettan him on anne siþ ofer mid horsum mid ealle, ⁊ þa comon up on Limene muþan. mid .ccl. (hunde) scipa. Se muþa is on easte weardre Cent. æt þæs miclan wuda eastende þe we Andred hatað; se wudu is eastlang ⁊ westlang hund twelftiges mila lang oþþe lengra, ⁊ þritiges mila brad; seo ea þe we ær ymbe spræcon lið ut of þæm wealda; On þa ea hi tugon up hiora scipu oþ þone weald .iiii. mila fram þæm muþan uteweardum. ⁊ þær abræcon an geweorc. inne on þæm fenne sæton feawa cirlisce men on, ⁊ wæs samworht. Þa sona æfter þæm com Hæsten mid .lxxx. scipa up on Temese muðan, ⁊ worhte him geweorc æt Middeltune, ⁊ se oþer here æt Apuldre.

893 On þys geare, þæt wæs ymb twelf monað þæs þe hie on þæm eastrice geweorc geworht hæfdon, Norþhymbre ⁊ Eastengle hæfdon ælffrede cyninge aþas geseald, ⁊ Eastengle foregisla .vi. ⁊ þeh ofer þa treowa, swa oft swa þa oþre hergas mid ealle herige ut foron, þonne foron hie, oþþe mid, oþþe on heora healfe an. Þa gegaderade ælfred cyning his fierd, ⁊ for þæt he gewicode betwuh þæm twam hergum. þær þær he niehst rymet hæfde for wudufæstenne ond for wæterfæstenne swa þæt he mehte ægþerne geræcan gif hie ænigne feld secan wolden; Þa foron hie siþþan æfter þæm wealda hloþum ⁊ flocradum. bi swa hwaþerre efes swa hit þonne fierdleas wæs. ⁊ him mon eac mid oþrum

floccum sohte mæstra daga ælce, oþþe on niht. ge of þære fierde, ge eac of þæm burgum; Hæfde se cyning his fierd on tu tonumen, swa þæt hie wæron simle healfe æt ham, healfe ute, butan þæm monnum þe þa burga healdan scolden. Ne com se here oftor eall ute of þæm setum þonne tuwwa. oþre siþe þa hie ærest to londe comon, ær sio fierd gesamnod wære, oþre siþe þa hie of þæm setum faran woldon; Þa hie gefengon micle herehyð, 7 þa woldon ferian norþweardes ofer Temese in on Eastseaxe ongean þa scipu. Þa forrad sio fierd hie foran, 7 him wið gefeaht æt Fearnhamme, 7 þone here gefliemde, 7 þa herehyþa ahreddon, 7 hie flugon ofer Temese buton ælcum forda þa up be Colne on anne iggað. Þa besæt sio fierd hie þær utan þa hwile þe hie þær lengest mete hæfdon. Ac hie hæfdon þa heora stemn gesetenne, 7 hiora mete genotudne, 7 wæs se cyng þa þiderweardes on fære. mid þære scire þe mid him fierdedon; Þa he þa wæs þiderweardes, 7 sio oþeru fierd wæs hamweardes, 7 ða Deniscan sæton þær behindan, forþæm hiora cyning wæs gewundod on þæm gefeohte, þæt hi hine ne mehton ferian; Þa gegaderedon þa þe in Norþhymbrum bugeað, 7 on Eastenglum, sum hund scipa, 7 foron suð ymbutan, 7 sum feowertig scipa norþ ymbutan, 7 ymbsæton an geweorc on Defnascire be þære norþsæ; 7 þa þe suð ymbutan foron. ymbsæton Exancester. Þa se cyng þæt hierde, þa wende he hine west wið Exanceastres mid ealre þære fierde, buton swiþe gewaldenum dæle easteweardes þæs folces. Þa foron forð oþþe hie comon to Lundenbyrg, 7 þa mid þæm burgwarum 7 þæm fultume þe him westan com, foron east to Beamfleote; Wæs Hæsten þa þær cumen mid his herge, þe ær æt Middeltune sæt. 7 eac se micla here wæs þa þærto cumen, þe ær on Limene muþan sæt æt Apuldre; Hæfde Hæsten ær geworht þæt geweorc æt Beamfleote, 7 wæs þa ut afaren on hergaþ, 7 wæs se micla here æt ham; Þa foron hie to 7 gefliemdon þone here, 7 þæt geweorc abræcon, 7 genamon eal þæt þær binnan wæs, ge on feo. ge on wifum, ge eac on bearnum, ⁊ brohton eall into Lundenbyrig, ⁊ þa scipu eall oðþe tobræcon, oþþe forbærndon, oþþe to Lundenbyrig brohton oþþe to Hrofesceastre. ⁊ Hæstenes wif ⁊ his suna twegen mon brohte to þæm cyninge, ⁊ he hi him eft ageaf, forþæm þe hiora wæs oþer his godsunu, oþer æðeredes ealdormonnes; Hæfdon hi hiora onfangen ær Hæsten to Beamfleote come, ⁊ he him hæfde geseald gislas ⁊ aðas, ⁊ se cyng him eac wel feoh sealde, ⁊ eac swa þa he þone cniht agef ⁊ þæt wif. Ac sona swa hie to B(l)eamfleote comon, ⁊ þæt geweorc (ge)geworht wæs. swa hergode he on his rice þone ilcan ende þe æþered his cumpæder healdan sceolde, ⁊ eft oþre siþe he wæs on hergað gelend on þæt ilce rice þa þa mon his geweorc abræc. Þa se cyning hine þa west wende mid þære fierde wið Exancestres. swa ic ær sæde, ⁊ se here þa burg beseten hæfde; Þa he þærto gefaren wæs, þa eodon hie to hiora scipum. Þa he þa wið þone here þær wæst abisgod wæs, ⁊ þa hergas wæron þa gegaderode begen to Sceobyrig on Eastseaxum, ⁊ þær geweorc worhtun. Foron begen ætgædere up be Temese, ⁊ him com micel eaca to. ægþer ge of Eastenglum, ge of Norþhymbrum. Foron þa up be Temese oþþæt hie gedydon æt Sæferne, þa up be Sæferne. Þa gegaderode æþered ealdormon, ⁊ æþelm ealdorman. ⁊ æþelnoþ ealdorman, ⁊ þa cinges þegnas þe þa æt ham æt þæm geweorcum wæron, of ælcre byrig be eastan Pedredan, ge be westan Sealwuda ge be eastan, ge eac be norþan Temese, ⁊ be westan Sæfern, ge eac sum dæl þæs Norðwealcynnes. Þa hie þa ealle gegaderode wæron, þa offoron hie þone here hindan æt Buttingtune. on Sæferne staþe, ⁊ hine þær utan besæton on ælce healfe, on anum fæstenne. Þa hie ða fela wucena sæton on twa healfe þær e, ⁊ se cyng wæs west on Defnum wiþ þone sciphere, þa wæron hie mid metelieste gewægde, ⁊ hæfdon miclne dæl þara horsa freten. ⁊ þa oþre wæron hungre acwolen. Þa eodon hie ut to ðæm monnum þe

on easthealfe þære e wicodon, ꞁ him wiþ gefuhton, ꞁ þa
Cristnan hæfdon sige; ꞁ þær wearð Ordheh cyninges þegn
ofslægen, ꞁ eac monige oþre cyninges þegnas, ofslægen, ꞁ
se dæl þe þær aweg com wurdon on fleame generede. Þa hie
on Eastseaxe comon to hiora geweorce. ꞁ to hiora scipum.
þa gegaderade sio laf eft of Eastenglum, ꞁ of Norðhymbrum.
micelne here onforan winter. ꞁ befæston hira wif, ꞁ
hira scipu, ꞁ hira feoh on Eastenglum, ꞁ foron anstreces
dæges ꞁ nihtes, þæt hie gedydon on anre westre ceastre
on Wirhealum, seo is Legaceaster gehaten; Þa ne mehte
seo fird hie na hindan offaran, ær hie wæron inne on þæm
geweorce; Besæton þeah þæt geweorc utan sume twegen
dagas, ꞁ genamon ceapes eall þæt þær buton wæs, ꞁ þa
men ofslogon þe hie foran forridan mehton butan geweorce,
ꞁ þæt corn eall forbærndon, ꞁ mid hira horsum fretton on
ælcre efenehðe. ꞁ þæt wæs ymb twelf monað þæs þe hie ær
hider ofer sæ comon.

894 ONd þa sona æfter þæm on ðys gere for se here of Wirheale
in on Norðwealas. forþæm hie ðær sittan ne mehton; þæt
wæs forðy þe hie wæron benumene ægðer ge þæs ceapes,
ge þæs cornes, ðe hie gehergod hæfdon; Þa hie ða eft ut of
Norðwealum wendon mid þære herehyðe þe hie ðær genumen
hæfdon, þa foron hie ofer Norðhymbra lond ꞁ Eastengla,
swa swa seo fird hie geræcan ne mehte, oþþæt hie comon on
Eastseaxna lond easteweard, on an igland þæt is ute on þære
sæ, þæt is Meresig haten. ꞁ þa se here eft hamweard wende.
þe Exanceaster beseten hæfde, þa hergodon hie up on Suð
Seaxum neah Cisseceastre, ꞁ þa burgware hie gefliemdon,
ꞁ hira monig hund ofslogon, ꞁ hira scipu sumu genamon.
Ða þy ylcan gere onforan winter þa Deniscan þe on Meresige
sæton. tugon hira scipu up on Temese, ꞁ þa up on Lygan;
þæt wæs ymb twa ger þæs þe hie hider ofer sæ comon.

895 On þy ylcan gere worhte se foresprecena here geweorc
be Lygan .xx. mila bufan Lundenbyrig. Þa þæs on sumera

foron micel dæl þara burgwara, 7 eac swa oþres folces, þæt
hie gedydon æt þara Deniscana geweorce, 7 þær wurdon
gefliemde, 7 sume feower cyninges þegnas ofslægene.
Þa þæs on hærfeste þa wicode se cyng on neaweste þære
byrig, þa hwile þe hie hira corn gerypon, þæt þa Deniscan
him ne mehton þæs ripes forwiernan. Þa sume dæge rad se
cyng up bi þære eæ, 7 gehawade hwær mon mehte þa ea
forwyrcan, þæt hie ne mehton þa scipu ut brengan. 7 hie
ða swa dydon. worhton ða tu geweorc. on twa healfe þære
eas. Þa hie ða þæt geweorc furþum ongunnen hæfdon, 7
þærto gewicod hæfdon. þa onget se here þæt hie ne mehton
þa scipu ut brengan; Þa forleton hie hie, 7 eodon ofer land
þæt hie gedydon æt Cwatbrycge be Sæfern, 7 þær gewerc
worhton. Þa rad seo fird west æfter þæm herige, 7 þa men
of Lundenbyrig gefetedon þa scipu, 7 þa ealle þe hie alædan
ne mehton tobræcon, 7 þa þe þær stælwyrðe wæron binnan
Lundenbyrig gebrohton; 7 þa Deniscan hæfdon hira wif
befæst innan Eastengle ær hie ut of þæm geweorce foron; Þa
sæton hie þone winter æt Cwatbrycge. Þæt wæs ymb þreo
ger þæs þe hie on Limene muðan comon hider ofer sæ.

896 Ða þæs on sumera on ðysum gere tofor se here, sum on
Eastengle, sum on Norðhymbre, 7 þa þe feohlease wæron
him þær scipu begeton, 7 suð ofer sæ foron to Sigene. Næfde
se here, Godes þonces. Angelcyn ealles forswiðe gebrocod;
Ac hie wæron micle swiþor gebrocede on þæm þrim gearum
mid ceapes cwilde 7 monna, ealles swiþost mid þæm þæt
manige þara selestena cynges þena þe þær on londe wæron
forðferdon on þæm þrim gearum; Þara wæs sum Swiðulf
biscop on Hrofesceastre, 7 Ceolmund ealdormon on Cent, 7
Beorhtulf ealdormon on Eastseaxum, 7 Wulfred ealdormon
on Hamtunscire, 7 Ealhheard biscop æt Dorceceastre, 7
Eadulf cynges þegn on Suðseaxum, 7 Beornulf wicgefera
on Winteceastre, 7 Ecgulf cynges horsþegn, 7 manige eac
him þeh ic ða geðungnestan nemde. Þy ilcan geare drehton þa

hergas on Eastenglum 7 on Norðhymbrum Westseaxna lond swiðe be þæm suðstæðe mid stælhergum, ealra swiþust mid ðæm æscum þe hie fela geara ær timbredon. Þa het ælfred cyng timbran langscipu ongen ða æscas; þa wæron fulneah tu swa lange swa þa oðru. sume hæfdon .lx. ara. sume ma. Þa wæron ægðer ge swiftran ge unwealtran, ge eac hieran þonne þa oðru. næron nawðer ne on Fresisc gescæpene ne on Denisc, bute swa him selfum ðuhte þæt hie nytwyrðoste beon meahten. Þa æt sumum cirre þæs ilcan geares comon þær sex scipu to Wiht, 7 þær micel yfel gedydon, ægðer ge on Defenum ge welhwær be ðæm særiman. Þa het se cyng faran mid nigonum to þara niwena scipa, 7 forforon him þone muðan foran on utermere; Þa foron hie mid þrim scipum ut ongen hie, 7 þreo stodon æt ufeweardum þæm muðan on drygum, wæron þa men uppe on londe of agane, þa gefengon hie þara þreora scipa tu æt ðæm muðan uteweardum, 7 þa men ofslogon, 7 þæt an oðwand; On þæm wæron eac þa men ofslægene buton fifum. Þa comon forðy onweg ðe ðara oþerra scipu asæton, þa wurdon eac swiðe uneðelice aseten. Þreo asæton on ða healfe þæs deopes ðe ða Deniscan scipu aseten wæron, 7 þa oðru eall on oþre healfe, þæt hira ne mehte nan to oðrum. Ac ða þæt wæter wæs ahebbad fela furlanga from þæm scipu. þa eodan ða Deniscan from þæm þrim scipum to þæm oðrum þrim þe on hira healfe beebbade wæron, 7 hie þa þær gefuhton. Þær wearð ofslægen Lucumon cynges gerefa. 7 Wulfheard Friesa. 7 æbbe Friesa, 7 æðelhere Friesa, 7 æðelferð cynges geneat, 7 ealra monna Fresiscra 7 Engliscra .lxii. 7 þara Deniscena .cxx. þa com þæm Deniscum scipum þeh ær flod to, ær þa Cristnan mehten hira ut ascufan, 7 hie forðy ut oðreowon; Þa wæron hie to þæm gesargode. þæt hie ne mehton Suðseaxna lond utan berowan, ac hira þær tu sæ on lond wearp. 7 þa men mon lædde to Winteceastre to þæm cynge, 7 he hie ðær ahon het. 7 þa men comon on Eastengle. þe on þæm anum scipe wæron.

swiðe forwundode. Þy ilcan sumera forwearð nolæs þonne .xx. scipa mid monnum mid ealle. be þam suðriman. Þy ilcan gere forðferde Wulfric cynges horsðegn, se wæs eac Wealhgefera.

897 Her on þysum gere gefor æðelm Wiltunscire ealdormon, nigon nihtum ær middum sumere. 7 her forðferde Heahstan, se wæs on Lundenne biscop.

900 Her gefor ælfred Aþulfing, syx nihtum ær ealra haligra mæssan; Se wæs cyning ofer eall Ongelcyn butan ðæm dæle þe under Dena onwalde wæs, 7 he heold þæt rice. oþrum healfum læs þe .xxx. wintra. 7 þa feng Eadweard his sunu to rice. Þa gerad æðelwald his fædran sunu. þone ham æt Winburnan, 7 æt Tweoxneam butan ðæs cyninges leafe 7 his witena. Þa rad se cyning mid firde þæt he gewicode æt Baddanbyrig wið Winburnan, 7 æðelwald sæt binnan þæm ham mid þæm monnum þe him to gebugon, 7 hæfde ealle þa geatu forworht in to him, 7 sæde þæt he wolde oðer oððe þær libban oððe þær licgan. Þa under þæm þa bestæl he hine on niht on weg, 7 gesohte þone here on Norðhymbrum, 7 se cyng het ridan æfter, 7 þa ne mehte hine mon ofridan; Þa berad mon þæt wif þæt he hæfde ær genumen butan cynges leafe 7 ofer þara biscopa gebod, forðon ðe heo wæs ær to nunnan gehalgod. 7 on þys ilcan gere forðferde æþered. wæs on Defenum ealdormon, feower wucum ær ælfred cyning.

902 Her gefor Aþulf ealdormon Ealhswiðe broðor 7 Uirgilius abbud of Scottum. 7 Grimbald mæssepreost. viii. idus Iulii.

903 Her com æðelwald hider ofer sæ mid þæm flotan þe he mid wæs on East Sexe.

904 Her aspon æðelwald þone here on Eastenglum to unfriðe, þæt hie hergodon ofer Mercna land oð hie comon to Creccagelade, 7 foron þær ofer Temese, 7 namon ægðer ge on Brædene ge ðær ymbutan eall þæt hie gehentan mehton, 7 wendan ða eft hamweard; Þa for Eadweard cyning æfter, swa

he raðost mehte his fird gegadrian, ⁊ oferhergade eall hira land betwuh dicum ⁊ Wusan. eall oð ða fennas norð; Þa he ða eft þonan ut faran wolde, þa het he beodan ofer ealle þa fird þæt hie foron ealle ut ætsomne. Þa ætsæton ða Centiscan þær beæftan ofer his bebod, ⁊ seofon ærendracan he him hæfde to asend. Þa befor se here hie ðær, ⁊ hie ðær gefuhton, ⁊ þær wearð Sigulf ealdormon ofslægen, ⁊ Sigelm ealdormon, ⁊ Eadwold cynges ðegen, ⁊ Cenulf abbod, ⁊ Sigebreht Sigulfes sunu, ⁊ Eadwald Accan sunu, ⁊ monige eac him, þeh ic ða geðungnestan nemde. ⁊ on ðara Deniscena healfe wearð ofslægen Eohric hira cyng, ⁊ æðelwald æðeling ðe hine to þæm unfriðe gespon, ⁊ Byrhtsige Beornoðes sunu æðelinges. ⁊ Ysopa hold, ⁊ Oscytel hold, ⁊ swiðe monige eac him, þe we nu genemnan ne magon; ⁊ þær wæs on gehwæðre hond micel wæl geslægen, ⁊ þara Deniscena þær wearð ma ofslægen, þeh hie wælstowe gewald ahton. ⁊ Ealhswið gefor þy ilcan geare.

905 Her on þys geare gefor ælfred, wæs æt Baðum gerefa. ⁊ on þæm ilcan gere mon fæstnode þone frið æt Yttingaforda, swa swa Eadweard cyng gerædde, ægðer wið Eastengle ge wið Norðhymbre.

908 Her gefor Denulf, se wæs on Winteceastre biscop.

909 Her feng Friðestan to biscopdome on Winteceastre, ⁊ Asser biscop gefor æfter ðæm, se wæs æt Scireburnan biscop. ⁊ þy ilcan gere sende Eadweard cyng firde ægðer ge of Westseaxum ge of Mercum, ⁊ heo gehergade swiðe micel on þæm norðhere, ægðer ge on mannum ge on gehwelces cynnes yrfe, ⁊ manega men ofslogon þara Deniscena. ⁊ þær wæron fif wucan inne.

910 Her bræc se here on Norðhymbrum þone frið, ⁊ forsawon ælc frið þe Eadweard cyng ⁊ his witan him budon. ⁊ hergodon ofer Mercna lond; ⁊ se cyng hæfde gegadrod sum hund scipa. ⁊ wæs þa on Cent, ⁊ þa scipu foran be

suðan east andlang sæ togenes him. Þa wende se here þæt
his fultumes se mæsta dæl wære on þæm scipum, 7 þæt hie
mehten faran unbefohtene þær þær hie wolden. Þa geascade
se cyng þæt þæt hie ut on hergað foron, þa sende he his fird
ægðer ge of Westseaxum ge of Mercum, 7 hie offoron ðone
here hindan, þa he hamweard wæs, 7 him þa wið gefuhton,
7 þone here gefliemdon, 7 his fela þusenda ofslogon, 7 þær
wæs Ecwils cyng ofslægen.

911 Her gefor æðered ealdormon on Mercum; 7 Eadweard
cyng feng to Lundenbyrg 7 to Oxnaforda, 7 to ðæm landum
eallum þe þærto hierdon.

912 Her on þys geare ymb Martines mæssan het Eadweard
cyning atimbran þa norðran burg æt Heorotforda betweox
Memeran 7 Beneficcan 7 Lygean; 7 þa æfter þam þæs
on sumera. betweox gangdagum 7 middum sumera, þa for
Eadweard cyning mid sumum his fultume on Eastseaxe to
Mældune. 7 wicode þær þa hwile þe man þa burg worhte
7 getimbrede æt Witham; 7 him beag god dæl þæs folces
to þe ær under Deniscra manna anwalde wæron, 7 sum his
fultum worhte þa burg þa hwile æt Heorotforda on suþhealfe
Lygean.

913 Her on þys gere rad se here ut ofer Eastron of Hamtune,
7 of Ligeraceastre. 7 bræcon þone friþ. 7 slogon monige
men æt Hocneratune, 7 þær onbutan; 7 þa swiðe raþe æfter
þæm, swa þa oþre ham comon, þa fundon hie oþre flocrade,
þæt rad ut wið Lygtunes, 7 þa wurdon þa landleode his ware,
7 him wiþ gefuhton, 7 gebrohton hie on fullum fleame, 7
ahreddon eall þæt hie genumen hæfdon, 7 eac hira horsa 7
hira wæpna micelne dæl:

914 Her on þysum geare com micel sciphere hider ofer suþan of
Lidwiccum, 7 twegen eorlas mid, Ohtor 7 Hroald, 7 foron
west onbutan þæt hie gedydon innan Sæferne muþan, 7
hergodon on Norþwealas æghwær be þam sæ, þær hie þonne

onhagode; 7 gefengon Cameleac biscop on Ircingafelda, 7 læddon hine mid him to scipum, 7 þa aliesde Eadweard cyning hine eft mid .xl. pundum. Þa æfter þam for se here eall up, 7 wolde faran þa giet on hergaþ wið Ircingafeldes; þa gemetton þa men hie of Hereforda 7 of Gleaweceastre. 7 of þam niehstum burgum, 7 him wið gefuhton, 7 hie gefliemdon; 7 ofslogon þone eorl Hroald 7 þæs oþres eorles broþor Ohteres, 7 micel þæs heres. 7 bedrifon hie on anne pearruc, 7 besæton hie þær utan, oþþe hie him sealdon gislas, þæt hie of Eadweardes cyninges anwalde afaran woldon; 7 se cyng hæfde funden þæt him mon sæt wiþ on suþhealfe Sæfernmuþan, westan from Wealum, east oþ Afene muþan, þæt hie ne dorston þæt land nawer gesecan on þa healfe; Þa bestælon hie hie þeah nihtes upp æt sumum twam cirron, æt oþrum cierre be eastan Wæced, 7 æt oþrum cierre æt Portlocan; Þa slog hie mon æt ægþrum cirre, þæt hira feawa onweg comon, buton þa ane þe þær ut ætswummon to þam scipum, 7 þa sæton hie ute on þam iglande æt Bradan Relice, oþ þone first þe hie wurdon swiþe metelease, 7 monige men hungre acwælon, forþon hie ne meahton nanne mete geræcan; Foran þa þonan to Deomodum, 7 þa ut to Irlande. 7 þis wæs on hærfest; 7 þa æfter þam on þam ilcan gere foran to Martines mæssan, ða for Eadweard cyning to Buccingahamme mid his firde, 7 sæt þær feower wucan, 7 geworhte þa burga buta on ægþere healfe eas ær he þonon fore; 7 þurcytel eorl hine gesohte him to hlaforde, 7 þa holdas ealle, 7 þa ieldstan men ealle mæste ðe to Bedanforda hierdon, 7 eac monige þara þe to Hamtune hierdon.

915 Her on þys gere Eadweard cyng for mid fierde to Bedanforda foran to Martines mæssan, 7 beget þa burg, 7 him cirdon to mæst ealle þa burgware þe hie ær budon, 7 he sæt þær feower wucan, 7 het atimbran þa burg on suþhealfe þære eas ær he þonan fore:

916 Her on þys gere foran to middum sumera for Eadweard

cyning to Mældune, ⁊ getimbrede þa burg ⁊ gestaðolode ær he þonon fore; ⁊ þy ilcan geare for þurcytel eorl ofer sæ on Froncland. mid þam mannum þe him gelæstan woldon. mid Eadweardes cynges friþe ⁊ fultume.

917 Her on þysum gere foran to Eastron Eadweard cyning het gefaran þa burg æt Tofeceastre. ⁊ hie getimbran; ⁊ þa eft æfter þam on þam ilcan geare to gangdagum he het atimbran þa burg æt Wigingamere; Þy ilcan sumera betwix hlafmæssan ⁊ middum sumera se here bræc þone friþ of Hamtune, ⁊ of Ligeraceastre, ⁊ þonan norþan, ⁊ foron to Tofeceastre, ⁊ fuhton on þa burg ealne dæg, ⁊ þohton þæt hie hie sceolden abrecan; Ac hie þeah awerede þæt folc þe þærbinnan wæs oþ him mara fultum to com, ⁊ hie forleton þa þa burg, ⁊ foron aweg; ⁊ þa eft swiðe raþe æfter þam hie foron eft ut mid stælherge nihtes, ⁊ comon on ungearwe men, ⁊ genomon unlytel, ægþer ge on mannum, ge on ierfe. betweox Byrnewuda ⁊ æglesbyrig. Þy ilcan siþe for se here of Huntandune, ⁊ of Eastenglum, ⁊ worhton þæt geweorc æt Tæmeseforda, ⁊ hit budon ⁊ bytledon, ⁊ forleton þæt oþer æt Huntandune, ⁊ þohton þæt hie sceoldon þanon of mid gewinne ⁊ mid unfriðe eft þæs landes mare geræcan; ⁊ foran þæt hie gedydon æt Bedanforda, ⁊ þa foran þa men ut ongean þe þærbinnan wæron, ⁊ him wiþ gefuhton, ⁊ hie gefliemdon, ⁊ hira godne dæl ofslogon. Þa eft æfter þam þa giet gegadorode micel here hine of Eastenglum (⁊ of Eastenglum) ⁊ of Mercnalande, ⁊ foran to þære byrig æt Wigingamere, ⁊ ymbsæton hie utan, ⁊ fuhton lange on dæg on, ⁊ namon þone ceap onbutan; ⁊ þa men aweredon þeah þa burg þe þærbinnan wæron, ⁊ þa forleton hie þa burg ⁊ foron aweg. Þa æfter þam þæs ilcan sumeres gegadorode micel folc hit on Eadweardes cynges anwalde. of þam niehstum burgum, þe hit ða gefaran mehte, ⁊ foron to Tæmeseforda. ⁊ besæton ða burg. ⁊ fuhton ðæron oð hi hie abræcon, ⁊ ofslogon þone cyning, ⁊ Toglos eorl, ⁊

Mannan eorl his sunu, 7 his broþor, 7 ealle þa þe þærbinnan wæron, 7 hie wergan woldon, 7 namon þa oþre 7 eal þæt þærbinnan wæs. Þa æfter þam þæs forhraþe gegadorode micel folc hit on hærfest, ægþer ge of Cent, ge of Suþrigum, ge of Eastseaxum, ge æghwonan of þam nihstum burgum, 7 foron to Colneceastre, 7 ymbsæton þa burg, 7 þæron fuhton oþ hie þa geeodon, 7 þæt folc eall ofslogon, 7 genamon eal þæt þærbinnan wæs, buton þam mannum þe þær oþflugon ofer þone weall. Þa æfter þam þa giet þæs ilcan hærfestes gegadorode micel here hine of Eastenglum. ægþer ge þæs landheres ge þara wicinga þe hie him to fultume aspanen hæfdon, 7 þohton þæt hie sceoldon gewrecan hira teonun, 7 foron to Mældune, 7 ymbsæton þa burg, 7 fuhton þæron, oþ þam burgwarum com mara fultum to utan to helpe, 7 forlet se here þa burg, 7 for fram; 7 þa foron þa men æfter ut of þære byrig, 7 eac þa þe him utan comon to fultume, 7 gefliemdon þone here 7 ofslogon hira monig hund, ægþer ge æscmanna ge oþerra. Þa þæs forhraþe þæs ilcan hærfestes for Eadweard cyning mid Westsexna fierde to Passanhamme, 7 sæt þær þa hwile þe mon worhte þa burg æt Tofeceastre mid stanwealle, 7 him cirde to þurferþ eorl, 7 þa holdas, 7 eal se here þe to Hamtune hierde norþ oþ Weolud, 7 sohton hine him to hlaforde 7 to mundboran; 7 þa se firdstemn for ham, þa for oþer ut, 7 gefor þa burg æt Huntandune, 7 hie gebette 7 geedneowade þær heo ær tobrocen wæs, be Eadweardes cyninges hæse, 7 þæt folc eal þæt þær to lafe wæs þara landleoda beag to Eadwearde cyninge, 7 sohton his friþ 7 his mundbyrde. Þa giet æfter þam þæs ilcan geres foran to Martines mæssan for Eadweard cyning mid Westsexna fierde to Colneceastre, 7 gebette þa burg 7 geedneowade þær heo ær tobrocen wæs, 7 him cirde micel folc to, ægþer ge on Eastenglum, ge on Eastseaxum, þe ær under Dena anwalde wæs; 7 eal se here on Eastenglum him swor annesse, þæt hie eal þæt woldon þæt he wolde, 7 eall þæt friþian woldon þæt se cyng friþian wolde, ægþer ge on sæ, ge on lande; ⁊ se here þe to Grantanbrycge hierde hine geces synderlice him to hlaforde ⁊ to mundboran, ⁊ þæt fæstnodon mid aþum. swa swa he hit þa ared.

918 Her on ðysum gere betweox gangdagum ⁊ middan sumera for Eadweard cyng mid firde to Steanforda. ⁊ het gewyrcan ða burg on suðhealfe ðære eas, ⁊ ðæt folc eal ðe to ðære norþerran byrig hierde. him beah to, ⁊ sohtan hine him to hlaforde. ⁊ þa on þæm setle ðe he þær sæt, þa gefor æþelflæd his swystar æt Tameworþige .xii. nihtum ær middum sumera; ⁊ þa gerad he þa burg æt Tameworþige, ⁊ him cierde to eall se þeodscype on Myrcna lande þe Æþelflæde ær underþeoded wæs; ⁊ þa cyningas on Norþwealum, Howel, ⁊ Cledauc, ⁊ Ieoþwel, ⁊ eall Norþweallcyn hine sohton him to hlaforde. Þa for he þonan to Snotingaham ⁊ gefor þa burg, ⁊ het hie gebetan ⁊ gesettan, ægþer ge mid Engliscum mannum, ge mid Deniscum; ⁊ him cierde eall þæt folc to þe on Mercna lande geseten wæs, ægþer ge Denisc ge Englisce.

919 Her on þysum geare for Eadweard cyning mid fierde onufan hærfest to þelwæle, ⁊ het gewyrcan þa burg, ⁊ gesettan, ⁊ gemannian; ⁊ het oþre fierd eac of Miercna þeode þa hwile þe he þær sæt gefaran Mameceaster on Norþhymbrum, ⁊ hie gebetan ⁊ gemannian. Her forþferde Plegemund arcebisceop.

920 Her on þysum gere foran to middum sumera for Eadweard cyning mid fierde to Snotingaham, ⁊ het gewyrcan þa burg on suþhealfe þære eas, ongean þa oþre, ⁊ þa brycge ofer Treontan betwix þam twam burgum; ⁊ for þa þonan on Peaclond to Badecanwiellon, ⁊ het gewyrcan ane burg þær on neaweste, ⁊ gemannian; ⁊ hine geces þa to fæder ⁊ to hlaforde Scotta cyning ⁊ eall Scotta þeod; ⁊ Rægnald, ⁊ Eadulfes suna, ⁊ ealle þa þe on Norþhymbrum bugeaþ, ægþer ge Englisce, ge Denisce, ge Norþmen, ge oþre; ⁊ eac Stræcledweala cyning, ⁊ ealle Stræcledwealas.

924 Her Eadweard cing forþferde, 7 æþelstan his sunu feng to
rice. 7 Sancte Dunstan wearð akænned. 7 Wulfelm feng to
þan arcebiscoprice on Cantuarebyri.

931 Her mon hadode Byrnstan bisceop to Wintanceastre .iiii.
kalendas IVNII, 7 he heold þridde healf gear bisceopdom.

932 Her forþferde Fryþestan bisceop.

933 Her for Æþelstan cyning in on Scotland, ægþer ge mid
landhere ge mid sciphere, 7 his micel oferhergade; 7
Byrnstan bisceop forþferde on Wintanceastre to Omnium
Sanctorum.

934 Her feng Ælfeah bisceop to bisceopdome.

937 Her æþelstan cyning, ... eorla dryhten,
beorna beahgifa, ... 7 his broþor eac,
Eadmund æþeling, ... ealdorlangne tir
geslogon æt sæcce ... ... sweorda ecgum
ymbe Brunanburh. ... ... Bordweal clufan,
heowan heaþolinde ... ... hamora lafan,
afaran Eadweardes, ... swa him geæþele wæs
from cneomægum, ... þæt hi æt campe oft
wiþ laþra gehwæne ... ... land ealgodon,
hord 7 hamas. ... ... Hettend crungun,
Sceotta leoda ... ... 7 scipflotan
fæge feollan, ... feld dænnede
secgas hwate, ... siðþan sunne up
on morgentid, ... mære tungol,
glad ofer grundas, ... godes condel beorht,
eces drihtnes, ... oð sio æþele gesceaft
sah to setle. ... ... þær læg secg mænig
garum ageted, ... guma norþerna
ofer scild scoten, ... swilce Scittisc eac,
werig, wiges sæd. ... ... Wesseaxe forð
ondlongne dæg ... ... eorodcistum
on last legdun ... ... laþum þeodum,

heowan herefleman ... ... hindan þearle
mecum mylenscearpan. ... ... Myrce ne wyrndon
heeardes hondplegan ... ... hæleþa nanum
þæ þe mid Anlafe ... ... ofer æra gebland
on lides bosme ... ... land gesohtun,
fæge to gefeohte. ... ... Fife lægun
on þam campstede ... ... cyninges giunge,
sweordum aswefede, ... swilce seofene eac
eorlas Anlafes, ... unrim heriges,
flotan 7 Sceotta. ... ... þær geflemed wearð
Norðmanna bregu, ... nede gebeded,
to lides stefne ... ... litle weorode;
cread cnear on flot, ... cyning ut gewat
on fealene flod, ... feorh generede.
Swilce þær eac se froda ... ... mid fleame com
on his cyþþe norð, ... Costontinus,
har hilderinc, ... hreman ne þorfte
mæca gemanan; ... ... he wæs his mæga sceard,
freonda gefylled ... ... on folcstede,
beslagen æt sæcce, ... 7 his sunu forlet
on wælstowe ... ... wundun fergrunden,
giungne æt guðe. ... ... Gelpan ne þorfte
beorn blandenfeax ... ... bilgeslehtes,
eald inwidda, ... ne Anlaf þy ma;
mid heora herelafum ... ... hlehhan ne þorftun
þæt heo beaduweorca ... ... beteran wurdun
on campstede ... ... culbolgehnastes,
garmittinge, ... gumena gemotes,
wæpengewrixles, ... þæs hi on wælfelda
wiþ Eadweardes ... ... afaran plegodan.
Gewitan him þa Norþmen ... ... nægledcnearrum,
dreorig daraða laf, ... on Dinges mere
ofer deop wæter ... ... Difelin secan,
7 eft Iraland, ... æwiscmode.

Swilce þa gebroþer ... ... begen ætsamne,
cyning 7 æþeling, ... cyþþe sohton,
Wesseaxena land, ... wiges hremige.
Letan him behindan ... ... hræw bryttian
saluwigpadan, ... þone sweartan hræfn,
hyrnednebban, ... 7 þane hasewanpadan,
earn æftan hwit, ... æses brucan,
grædigne guðhafoc ... ... 7 þæt græge deor,
wulf on wealde. ... ... Ne wearð wæl mare
on þis eiglande ... ... æfer gieta
folces gefylled ... ... beforan þissum
sweordes ecgum, ... þæs þe us secgað bec,
ealde uðwitan, ... siþþan eastan hider
Engle 7 Seaxe ... ... up becoman,
ofer brad brimu ... ... Brytene sohtan,
wlance wigsmiþas, ... Weealas ofercoman,
eorlas arhwate ... ... eard begeatan.

940 Her Æþelstan cyning forðferde on .vi. kalendas Nouembris
ymbe .xl. wintra butan anre niht þæs þe Ælfred cyning
forþferde, 7 Eadmund æþeling feng to rice 7 he wæs þa
.xviii. wintre. 7 Æþelstan cyning rixade .xiiii. gear 7 .x.
wucan. Þa was Wulfelm arcebiscop on Cantwarebyri.

942 Her Eadmund cyning, ... Engla þeoden,
maga mundbora, ... Myrce geeode,
dyre dædfruma, ... swa Dor scadeþ,
Hwitanwyllesgeat ... ... 7 Humbra ea,
brada brimstream. ... ... Burga fife,
Ligoraceaster ... ... 7 Lindcylene
7 Snotingaham, ... swylce Stanford
eac Deoraby. ... ... Dæne wæran æror
under Norðmannum ... ... nyde gebegde
on hæþenra ... ... hæfteclommum
lange þraga, ... oþ hie alysde eft
for his weorþscipe ... ... wiggendra hleo,

afera Eadweardes, ... Eadmund cyning. Eadmund cyning onfeng Anlafe cyninge æt fulluhte ⁊ þy ylecan geare ymb tela micel fæc he onfeng Rægenolde cyninge æt bisceopes handa. ~~Her Eadmund cing Sancte Dunstane Glæ~~stingeberig behæhte ðær he syððan ærest abbud wearð.

944 Her Eadmund cyning geeode eal Norþhymbra land to him gewealdan ⁊ aflymde ut twegen cyningas, Anlaf Syhtrices sunu ⁊ Rægenald Guðferþes sunu.

945 Her Eadmund cyning oferhergode eal Cumbra land ⁊ hit let to eal Malculme Scotta cyninge on þæt gerad þæt he wære his midwyrhta ægþer ge on sæ ge on lande.

946 Her Eadmund cyning forðferde on Sanctes Agustinus mæssedæge, ⁊ he hæfde rice seofoþe healf gear. ⁊ þa feng Eadred æþeling his broþor to rice ⁊ gerad eal Norþhymbra land him to gewealde, ⁊ Scottas him aþas sealdan, þæt hie woldan eal þæt he wolde.

951 Her forðferde Ælfheah Wintanceastres bisceop on Sancte Gregories mæssedæg.

955 Her forþferde Eadred cining on Sancte Clementes mæssedæg on Frome, ⁊ he rixsade teoþe healf gear, ⁊ feng Eadwig to rice, Eadmundes sunu cinges ⁊ aflæmde Sancte Dunstan ut of lande.

958 Her forðferde Eadwig cyng on kalendas Octobris, ⁊ Eadgar his broðor feng to rice.

959 Her he sænte efter Sancte Dunstane ⁊ gæf him þæt bisceoprice on Wigracæstre ⁊ ðæræfter þæt bisceoprice on Lundene.

961 Her gewat Odo arcebisceop ⁊ Sancte Dunstan feng to arcebisceoprice.

962 Her forðferde ælfgar cinges mæg on Defenum, ⁊ his lic rest on Wiltune. ⁊ Sigferð cyning hine offeoll, ⁊ his lic ligð

æt Wimburnan. ⁊ þa on geare wæs swiðe micel mancwealm, ⁊ se micela manbryne wæs on Lundene, ⁊ Paules mynster forbarn. ⁊ þy ilcan geare wearð eft gestaþelad, On þys ilcan geare for Aþelmod mæssepreost to Rome, ⁊ þær forðferde .xviii. Kalendæ Septembris:

963 Her forðferde Wulfstan diacon on Cilda mæssedæge, ⁊ æfter þon forðferde Gyric mæssepreost: On þys ilcan geare feng Aþelwold abbod to þæm bisceoprice to Wintanceastre. ⁊ hine mon gehalgode IN UIGILIA Sancti Andree. wæs sunnandæg on dæg:

964 Her dræfde Eadgar cyng þa preostas on Ceastre of Ealdanmynstre, ⁊ of Niwanmynstre. ⁊ of Ceortesige. ⁊ of Middeltune. ⁊ sette hy mid munecan. ⁊ he sette æþelgar abbod to Niwanmynstre to abbode. ⁊ Ordbirht to Ceortesige. ⁊ Cyneweard to Middeltune.

971 ~~Her forðferde Eadmund æðeling. ⁊ his lic lið æt Rumesige.~~

973 Her Eadgar wæs, ... Engla waldend, corðre micelre ... ... to cyninge gehalgod on ðære ealdan byrig, ... Acemannesceastre; eac hi igbuend ... ... oðre worde beornas Baðan nemnaþ. ... ... þær wæs blis micel on þam eadgan dæge ... ... eallum geworden, þone niða bearn ... ... nemnað ⁊ cigað Pentecostenes dæg. ... ... þær wæs preosta heap, micel muneca ðreat, ... mine gefrege, gleawra gegaderod. ... ... ⁊ ða agangen wæs tyn hund wintra ... ... geteled rimes fram gebyrdtide ... ... bremes cyninges, leohta hyrdes, ... buton ðær to lafe þa get wæs wintergeteles, ... þæs ðe gewritu secgað, seofon ⁊ twentig; ... ... swa neah wæs sigora frean ðusend aurnen, ... ða þa ðis gelamp. ⁊ him Eadmundes ... ... eafora hæfde

nigon 7 .xx., ... niðweorca heard,
wintra on worulde, ... þa þis geworden wæs,
7 þa on ðam .xxx. wæs ... ... ðeoden gehalgod.

975 Her geendode ... ... eorðan dreamas
Eadgar, Engla cyning, ... ceas him oðer leoht,
wlitig 7 wynsum, ... 7 þis wace forlet,
lif þis læne. ... ... Nemnað leoda bearn,
men on moldan, ... þæne monað gehwær
in ðisse eðeltyrf, ... þa þe ær wæran
on rimcræfte ... ... rihte getogene,
Iulius monoð, ... þæt se geonga gewat
on þone eahteðan dæg ... ... Eadgar of life,
beorna beahgyfa. ... ... 7 feng his bearn syððan
to cynerice, ... cild unweaxen,
eorla ealdor, ... þam wæs Eadweard nama.
7 him tirfæst hæleð ... ... tyn nihtum ær
of Brytene gewat, ... bisceop se goda,
þurh gecyndne cræft, ... ðam wæs Cyneweard nama.
Ða wæs on Myrceon, ... mine gefræge,
wide 7 welhwær ... ... waldendes lof
afylled on foldan. ... ... Fela wearð todræfed
gleawra godes ðeowa; ... ... þæt wæs gnornung micel
þam þe on breostum wæg ... ... byrnende lufan
metodes on mode. ... ... þa wæs mærða fruma
to swiðe forsewen, ... sigora waldend,
rodera rædend, ... þa man his riht tobræc.
7 þa wearð eac adræfed ... ... deormod hæleð,
Oslac, of earde ... ... ofer yða gewealc,
ofer ganotes bæð, ... gamolfeax hæleð,
wis 7 wordsnotor, ... ofer wætera geðring,
ofer hwæles eðel, ... hama bereafod.
7 þa wearð ætywed ... ... uppe on roderum
steorra on staðole, ... þone stiðferhþe,
hæleð higegleawe, ... hatað wide

cometa be naman, ... cræftgleawe men,
wise soðboran. ... ... Wæs geond werðeode
waldendes wracu ... ... wide gefrege,
hungor ofer hrusan; ... ... þæt eft heofona weard
gebette, brego engla, ... geaf eft blisse gehwæm
egbuendra ... ... þurh eorðan westm.

978 Her wearð Eadweard cyning ofslegen. On þis ylcan feng
æðelred æðeling his broðor to rice.

983 Her forðferde ælfhere ealdorman.

984 Her forðferde se wellwillenda bisceop Aðelwold, 7 seo
halgung þæs æfterfilgendan bisceopes ælfheages, se ðe
oðran naman wæs geciged Godwine. wæs .xiiii. kalendæ
Nouembris 7 he gesæt þone bisceopstol an þara twegra
apostola dæge Simonis 7 Iudæ. on Wintanceastre.

988 Hoc anno obiit sanctus Dunstanus archiepiscopus.

993 Her on ðissum geare com Unlaf mid þrim 7 hund
nigentigon scipum to Stane, 7 forhergedon þæt onytan, 7
for ða ðanon to Sandwic, 7 swa ðanon to Gipeswic, 7 þæt
eall ofereode, 7 swa to Mældune; 7 him ðær com togeanes
Byrhtnoð ealdorman mid his fyrde, 7 him wið gefeaht. 7 hy
þone ealdorman þær ofslogon, 7 wælstowe geweald ahtan.
7 him man nam syððan frið wið, 7 hine nam se cing syððan
to bisceopes handa. ðurh Sirices lare Cantware bisceopes, 7
ælfeages Wincæstre biscop.

994 Her forðferde Sigeric arcebisceop. 7 feng ælfric Wiltunscire
bisceop to ðam arcebisceoprice.

1001 Her on þysum geare wæs micel unfrið on Angelcynnes
londe þurh sciphere, 7 welgehwær hergedon 7 bær<n>don,
swa þæt hy upp asetton on ænne sið þæt hy coman to
æþelingadene. 7 þa com þær togeanes Hamtunscir, 7 him
wið gefuhton. 7 ðær wearð æþelweard cinges heahgerefa
ofslegen. 7 Leofric æt Hwitciricean, 7 Leofwine cinges
heahgerefa, 7 Wulfhere bisceopes ðegn, 7 Godwine æt

Worðige, ælfsiges bisceopes sunu. ⁊ ealra manna an ⁊ hund eahtatig. ⁊ þær wearð þara Denescra micle ma ofslegenra. þeah ðe hie wælstowe geweald ahtan. ⁊ foran ða þanon west oþ þæt hy coman to Defenan, ⁊ him þær togeanes com Pallig mid þan scipan ðe he gegaderian mihte, forþam þe he asceacen wæs fram æðelrede cyncge ofer ealle ða getrywða ðe he him geseald hæfde, ⁊ eac se cyng him wel gegifod hæfde on hamon, ⁊ on golde ⁊ seolfre. ⁊ forbærndon Tegntun, ⁊ eac fela oðra godra hama þe we genemnan ne cunnan, ⁊ heom man syððan þær frið wið nam. ⁊ hy foran þa þanon to Exan muðan, swa þæt hy asettan him upp on ænne sið oð hy coman to Peonho, ⁊ þær wæs Kola ðæs cyninges heahgerefa, ⁊ Eadsige þæs cynincges gerefa togeanes him mid ðære fyrde ðe hy gegaderian mihtan, ⁊ hy ðær aflymede wurdon, ⁊ ðær wearð fela ofslegenra, ⁊ ða Denescean ahtan wælstowe geweald; ⁊ ðæs on mergen forbærndon þone ham æt Peonho, ⁊ æt Glistune, ⁊ eac fela godra hama þe we genemnan na cunnan, ⁊ foran ða eft east ongean oð hy coman to Wiht; ⁊ þæs on mergen forbærndon ðone ham æt Wealtham. ⁊ oðra cotlifa fela. ⁊ hiom man raþe þæs wið þingode. ⁊ hy namon frið.

1005 Her ælfricus arcebiscop forðferde.

1006 Her mann halgode ælfehg to arcebiscope.

1017 Her Cnut wearð ge coran to kinge.

1031 Her com Cnut ~~agean to Engla lande.~~ Sona swa he becom to Engla lande. he Her com Cnut agean to Engla lande. Sona swa he becom to Engla lande. he geaf into Cristes cyrican on Cantwarebyri þa hæfenan on Sandwic. ⁊ ealla þa gerihta þe þarof arisaþ of æiðre healfe ðare hæfene. swa þæt loc whenne þæt flod byþ ealra hehst ⁊ ealra fullost beo an scip flotigende swa neh þan lande swa hit nyxt mæge. ⁊ þar beo an mann stande on þan scipe ⁊ habbe ane taper æx on his handa afwyrpe up swa feorr on þæt land of swiðre healfe swa he swiþost mæge. Swa feorr begað þa munekas Cristes cyrican þa gerihta þe þarof cumað. Ne nan mann þarof nanes es þingeon þa ða heora ofer bates þæt eall of þam ber 7 of eaþcumað uð.

1036 Cnut obiit.

1038 Hic obiit Æþelnor archebiscop.

1040 Her Eadsige arcebiscop for to Rome. 7 Harold cing (king) forðferde:

1042 Her forðferde Harðacnut king.

1043 Her wæs Eaduuard gehalgod to kinge.

1050 Her forðferde Eadsige arcebiscop. 7 Rodbert. feng. to. arcebiscoprice.

1053 Her Goduuine eorl forðferde.

1066 Her forðferde Eaduuard king. 7 Harold eorl feng to ðam rice 7 heold hit .xl. wucena. 7 ænne dæg. 7 her com Willelm 7 gewann ængla land. 7 her on ðison geare barn Cristes cyrice. 7 her atiwede cometa .xiii. kalendæ MAI.

1070 Her Landfranc se þe wæs abbod an Kadum com to ængla lande, se efter feawum dagum wearð arcebiscop on Kantwareberig. He wæs gehaded .iiii. kalendæ Septembris, on his agenum biscopsetle fram eahte biscopum his underðioddum; ða oþre ðe þær næron þurh ærendrakan 7 þurh gewrite atiwdon hwi hi ðær beon ne mihton. On þam geare THOMAS se wæs gecoran bisc<o>p to Eferwic com to Cantwareberig þæt man hine ðær gehadede efter þan ealdan gewunan. Ða ða Landfranc crafede fæstnunge his gehersumnesse mid aðswerunge. þa forsoc he. 7 sæde þæt he hit nahte to donne. Þa gewraðede hine se arcebiscop Landfranc. 7 bebead þam biscopan ðe þar cumene wæran be ðas arcebiscop Landfrances hæse þa serfise to donde. 7 eallan þan munecan, þæt hi scoldan hi unscrydan. 7 hi be his hæse swa didan. Swa Thomas to þam timan agean ferde buton bletsunga. Þa sona æfter þysan belamp þæt se arcebiscop LANDFRANC ferde to Rome 7 Thomas forð mid. Þa þa hi þyder comon 7 umbe oþer þing gesprecon hæfdon umbe þæt hi sprecan woldon. þa angan Thomas his spæce hu he com to Cantuuarebyri, 7 hu se arcebiscop axode hyrsumnesse mid aþswerunge at him. 7 he hit forsoc. Þa agann se arcebiscop Landfranc atywian mid openum gesceade. þæt he mid rihte crafede þas þa he crafede 7 mid strangan cwydan þæt ylce gefæstnode toforan þam papan Alexandre. 7 toforan eallan þam concilium þe þar gegadered was. 7 swa ham foran. Æfter þysan com Thomas to Cantwarebyri 7 eal þæt se arcebiscop at him crafede. eadmedlice gefylde. 7 syþþan þa bletsungan underfeng.

MORE FROM THE SAME SERIES

Most books from the 'Military History from Original Sources' series are edited and endorsed by Emmy Award winning film maker and military historian Bob Carruthers, producer of Discovery Channel's Line of Fire and Weapons of War and BBC's Both Sides of the Line. Long experience and strong editorial control gives the military history enthusiast the ability to buy with confidence. The series advisor is David McWhinnie, producer of the acclaimed Battlefield series for Discovery Channel. David and Bob have co-produced books and films with a wide variety of the UK's leading historians including Professor John Erickson and Dr David Chandler.
Where possible the books draw on rare primary sources to give the military enthusiast new insights into a fascinating subject.

The English Civil Wars

The Zulu Wars

Into Battle with Napoleon 1812

Waterloo 1815

The Anglo-Saxon Chronicle

Medieval Warfare

Renaissance Warfare

1914-1918

Sea Battles in the Age of Sail

Sun Tzu - The Art of War

Recollections of the Great War in the Air

Soldier of the Empire

For more information visit www.pen-and-sword.co.uk

Tracing Your Family History?

Read *Your Family HISTORY*

ESSENTIAL ADVICE FROM THE EXPERTS

FREE COPY!

Your Family History is the only magazine that is put together by expert genealogists. Our editorial team, led by Dr Nick Barratt, is passionate about family history, and our networks of specialists are here to give essential advice, helping readers to find their ancestors and solve those difficult questions.

In each issue we feature a **Beginner's Guide** covering the basics for those just getting started, a **How To** … section to help you to dig deeper into your family tree and the opportunity to **Ask The Experts** about your tricky research problems. We also include a **Spotlight** on a different county each month and a **What's On** guide to the best family history courses and events, plus much more.

Receive a free copy of *Your Family History* magazine and gain essential advice and all the latest news. To request a free copy of a recent back issue, simply e-mail your name and address to marketing@your-familyhistory.com or call 01226 734302*.

Your Family History is in all good newsagents and also available on subscription for six or twelve issues. For more details on how to take out a subscription, call 01778 392013 or visit **www.your-familyhistory.co.uk**.

Alternatively read issue 31 online completely free using this QR code

*Free copy is restricted to one per household and available while stocks last.

www.your-familyhistory.com